COGNITION

An Epistemological Inquiry

. . . the soul is all things, but in a certain sense; for things are either sensible or intelligible, and in a certain sense, *knowledge* is the objects *known* while sensation is the sensible objects.

--Aristotle,

De Anima, 3.8.431b21-23; Apostle trans.

COGNITION

An Epistemological Inquiry

JOSEPH OWENS, C.Ss.R.

Pontifical Institute of Mediaeval Studies, Toronto

CENTER FOR THOMISTIC STUDIES
University of St. Thomas
Houston, Texas 77006

Copyright © 1992 by
The Center for Thomistic Studies

Library of Congress Cataloging-in-Publication Data

Owens, Joseph.
      Cognition : an epistemological inquiry / Joseph Owens.
         p.   cm.
      ISBN 0-268-00791-8
      1. Knowledge, Theory of.   2. Cognition.   3. Aristotle.
   4. Thomas, Aquinas, Saint, 1225?-1274.   I. Title.
   BD161.094   1992
   121--dc20
                                                    92-70254
                                                      CIP

Manufactured in the United States of America

Contents

Foreword

The following coverage of epistemological problems was initiated by an invitation from Donald A. Gallagher in 1965. Originally it was meant for a series he was then editing for the Bruce Publishing Company. Dr. Gallagher had requested that my narrowly metaphysical treatment of knowledge in *An Elementary Christian Metaphysics* (Milwaukee, 1963), pp. 211-308, be expanded into a fullfledged epistemology for printing in a separate volume. In that more conventional approach to the subject matter, fuller attention was to be given to the whole range of interest that had been customary for epistemology during the past hundred or so years.

The requested manuscript was completed and submitted by the agreed date. But already the situation for books of this type was changing drastically. The Bruce Publishing Company had by that time passed into other hands. The new proprietors, after over a year of seesaw deliberations and conclusions, finally (1970) decided that the rapidly declining market for books of Scholastic orientation did not warrant publication for the work.

More recently, however, some colleagues acquainted with the manuscript have suggested that it still might have utility for the teaching of philosophy. Be that as it may, there are in the fascinating history of western thought a number of insights basic for a philosophic understanding of knowledge, and especially for making sense of today's generally accepted pluralism for philosophy itself. Some of these astonishingly important insights have long since been forgotten. At least, they are given no emphasis at present in the pursuit of study. To bring these crucial tenets once more to the attention of philosophical readers seems to be ample justification for a revised and updated version of work done some twenty-five years ago, especially now when the postmodern announcements of epistemology's unmourned demise have proven decidedly premature. With that motivation may I express my gratitude to the Center for Thomistic Studies at Houston for the offer to publish this volume, and to professors Armand Maurer and Ronald Tacelli for corrections and improvements in the typescript.

Joseph Owens

COGNITION

An Epistemological Inquiry

PART ONE . . . . SENSE COGNITION

CHAPTER I

The Problem of Cognition

Cognition. Can anyone fail to recognize spontaneously what cognition is? We see, hear, taste, smell, imagine, judge, believe and reason. These activities, we are well aware, keep taking place within us. They purport to bring us into contact with things other than ourselves. They make those things come to be for the moment inside our cognition. Likewise they allow us to examine our own tendencies and purposes and doings.

Considerations of this kind are, in fact, obvious. They require no proof. But they do give rise to troublesome questions. What is meant by being "brought into contact" with other things? What kind of contact is involved? How do things come to exist in our awareness, or to be in our minds? And how can we understand the order that our different kinds of awareness, namely sensation, imagination and intellection, have to one another in building up our global and indefinitely extending edifice of thought?

Questions like these inevitably prompt a philosophical inquiry into our cognition precisely insofar as it is cognition. This is the investigation that has come to be called epistemology. It is now widely acknowledged to be a special branch of philosophy. That need not be surprising in an age that has developed philosophies of language, of technology, of sport, of the unconscious, and of other such varied topics. Why should there not be likewise a philosophy of the conscious, of knowing, of cognition? If there is, "epistemology" proves an apt designation for it, and the problems it faces as well as the inquiry into its procedures may be conveniently termed epistemological in character. One need only keep in mind that here the notion "epistemological" is taken to bear on all types of knowing, whether sensation, imagination or intellection.

Epistemology. The term "epistemology" is coined from two Greek words. Etymologically it denotes an "account" (*logos*) of--with the overtones of a treatise on--"knowledge" (*episteme*). It was never an ancient Greek expression. It dates, in fact, from only the mid-nineteenth century. But it has become among other titles an accepted designation for the study of human cognition as such.[1] As used in recent times it extends its coverage to both knowledge in the strictest sense and knowledge in the wider range that includes sense perception and imagination. One may *know* advanced calculus, but one also may *know* that the weather is cold or that the ghost appeared to Hamlet in Shakespeare's play. The word covers all three types.

In the understanding of the term "epistemology," then, you have to keep in mind that it bears upon knowledge in this very wide sense. It does not restrict the theme to narrowly intellectual knowledge.[2] But in spite of that remote possibility of misleading, "epistemology" remains by far the most readily understood and convenient and serviceable title in English for the inquiry into cognition precisely under the aspect of cognition.

Subject Matter. Epistemology may accordingly be described as the study of human cognition in its characteristic features as cognition. In consequence it is not concerned specifically with any of the objects of the other sciences or branches of philosophy. It does not focus upon plants or stars or anything else in what is regarded as the world of nature. The directly observable objects constitute the themes of botany, of astronomy, of the philosophy of nature, and of similar disciplines. They are dealt with specifically in their own sciences without need for attention to the nature of the cognition by which they are known. The botanist or the astronomer does not first ask what cognition means. Rather, he is not distracted in the least by scruples that he should first examine what cognition is before trusting it to give him information about the plants or the stars. He takes cognition for granted, and goes about his business of studying what it directly presents to his consideration.

Cognitive Reflexion. In contrast, our cognition itself is not known directly. We are of course aware that we are knowing, and with effort may focus upon the cognition in itself reflexively, insofar as it does "bend back" upon itself in knowing something else. Through reflexion, understood in this almost literal sense, cognition becomes a special object for philosophical study. In a word, it is always aware of itself in its awareness of something else, and in reflexion can inquire into its own nature and procedures. This is a matter of internal observation as we examine our cognitive experience. The cognition does in fact become actually known to us, through reflexion, as a special object of investigation.

Epistemological reflexion, however, is different from psychological focuses upon the introspectively observed *processes* of cognitive and appetitive life. Cognition as such does not consist in a process. Precisely as cognition its entire essence is present in each of its occurrences. In any act of seeing you have seen, in any act of knowing you have known.[3] The processes thereby involved are the subject matter of psychology on the empirical level, and of the philosophy of nature on another level. Nor does epistemology aim at setting up the correct forms and patterns of reasoning. That is the occupation of logic. Through study of the cognitive and reasoning *processes*, psychology and logic have, like botany and astronomy and other such sciences, been able to establish themselves satisfactorily apart from any special philosophical study of cognition in its characteristic features just as cognition. They became fully constituted sciences in their own right without experiencing any essential need for a prior philosophical study of cognition *qua* cognition. Systematic reflexion on cognition just in itself would seem to be a study on which they have no necessary dependence.

In the epistemological inquiry, moreover, both the act of knowing and the object known have the same name. Here both act and object are called awareness or cognition, thereby showing the essentially reflective character of the study. "Awareness" in its English origin, is a basic and acceptable term for denoting generically both the activities with which epistemology is concerned, and the further reflexion upon them. "Cognition" is an equivalent of Latin origin. Together the two terms provide serviceable nomenclature for the inquiry. Their meaning is grasped easily enough through an inductive survey of the activities they denote.[4]

✳✳✳✳✳✳✳✳✳✳✳✳✳

Historical Background. But why did epistemology emerge so late in the history of western philosophy? The reason seems straightforward enough. Thinkers before the time of René Descartes (1596-1650) showed no tendency to regard cognition as a distinct subject matter for a philosophical discipline. True, philosophers throughout those long centuries were well aware of the problems involved in human cognition. They had felt the clash between the ordinary estimates of appearance and the close examination of the reality. From the time of Zeno of Elea (5th century B.C.) on, they were alert to the tricks human reasoning and language could play in the sequences of rational discourse. They had no hesitation in setting up a special science, logic, to study the forms of thinking. They recognized another science, grammar, for dealing with the verbal expression of thought. Through Socrates (470-399 B.C.) and Plato (429-347 B.C.) and Aristotle (384-322 B.C.) they were profoundly cognizant of problems occasioned by the singular and the universal, the many and the one. These problems, however, were treated in the course of overall investigations into the reality of the world. Plato, for instance, had faced questions of that type while developing his doctrine of the Ideas and the participation of Ideas by sensible occurrences. Aristotle had met them in the context of his study of matter and form, potentiality and actuality. Aristotle and Plotinus (204-270 A.D.), moreover, had probed with especially surprising depth into the problems of the identity and difference in knower and thing known. Yet for these Greek thinkers the issues remained immersed in the general topics now called metaphysical. They were dealt with in the procedure of general inquiries about being and soul. They were not brought together as the subject matter of a special science.

Other Greek philosophical currents took an eminently practical turn. Stoics, Epicureans, Cynics and Skeptics tended to look upon knowledge as a means for attaining happiness or contentment, contentment that was found essentially in something other than knowledge itself. They centered their interest more on what knowledge effects, than on questions about what it is. Except in logic, accordingly, they had little occasion to probe the nature of human cognition for its own sake.[5]

In the middle ages the problems left by the Greeks remained under close scrutiny. Some questions, for instance the status of the universals and the cognitional identity of knower and the thing known, were investigated in considerably greater depth.[6] But this was regarded as done in metaphysics and in natural philosophy. There was as yet no inkling that these problems might suggest for their treatment a special science over and above the traditionally recognized branches of knowledge.

Cartesian Starting Point. With Descartes, however, the orientation of western philosophical inquiry charged in a quite radical fashion. Beginning with his Discourse on Method (1637) his extremely influential writings proposed a new method for correct reasoning and for seeking the truth in the sciences. Basically mathematical in character, the Cartesian method discredited sensible entities as a starting point for philosophical reasoning. A mathematician can ground his reasoning on an abstract sphere, without having to bother about the question whether a perfect sphere is anywhere found in perceptible reality. In this freedom from the uncertainties of sensible cognition Descartes envisaged the only real certitude attainable by men:

> . . . among all those who till now have sought truth
> in the sciences, there have been only the
> mathematicians who have been able to find any

demonstrations, that is, any reasons certain and evident.[7]

Nevertheless the new method was not offered as a path easy to enter. In actual fact, people have become accustomed to base their reasoning on sensible things and on traditional views long before they are introduced to philosophy. These habits become deeply ingrained:

Since we have been born infants, and before reaching the full use of reason have made varying judgments about sensible things, we are turned away from the cognition of truth by many prejudices; and from these it seems we can be freed only if once in our life we undertake of set purpose to doubt about all the things in which we find even the least suspicion of uncertainty.[8]

This Cartesian doubt required a thoroughgoing mental asceticism to rid the mind of its accustomed way of thinking, a way that had grown upon it unwittingly since childhood.[9] But need the doubt mean continued skepticism? That was anything but the author's intention. The Cartesian doubt was intended rather to make the mind realize that while it can doubt about all sensible things it absolutely cannot doubt about its own existence and its nature as pure thought: "I think, therefore I am."[10] The reason given was that this idea is clear and distinct. By the same token, accordingly, the mind cannot doubt about any other evident ideas and principles that it finds within itself.

In this way the mind and its ideas, considered apart from anything sensible, became the starting point for the Cartesian reasoning. But an unforeseen difficulty arose. If you start from mind alone, how can you ever get outside it and reach the sensible world? Various answers were suggested in the immediately following years. None proved satisfactory.[11] Finally, David Hume (1711-1776) showed convincingly where this way of thought leads. In Hume's development of its implications there was no room for any "idea of self"[12] to justify the assertion of a thinking subject for the Cartesian *cognito*. From one's own self the same reasoning was then extended to all other persons:

> I may venture to affirm of the rest of mankind,
> that they are nothing but a bundle or collection of
> different perceptions, which succeed each other
> with an inconceivable rapidity, and are in a
> perpetual flux and movement.[13]

Causal connection of objects was explained in Hume by
"Custom or Habit" that "makes us expect, for the future, a
similar train of events with those which have appeared in the
past."[14]

Kantian Revolution. Even before the Cartesian way of
thinking had come to the end of its natural course in Hume,
its implication of a still more revolutionary setting for
human thought had begun to emerge. The mind itself required
study in priority to its objects. John Locke (1632-1704) had
already urged a new approach:

> . . . it came into my Thoughts, that we took a wrong
> course; and that, before we set ourselves upon
> Enquiries of that Nature, it was necessary to
> examine our own Abilities, and see what Objects
> our understandings were, or were not, fitted to deal
> with.[15]

The complete change in direction became fully conscious of
itself in Kant (1724-1804). Taking the lead given by Hume's
tenet that the notion of causality was imposed upon the
objects by the knower, the German philosopher extended this
viewpoint to all the universal and necessary aspects found in
experience:

> Hitherto it has been assumed that all our
> knowledge must conform to objects. . . . We must
> therefore make trial whether we may not have
> more success in the tasks of metaphysics, if we
> suppose that objects must conform to our
> knowledge.[16]

This Kant likened to the revolution in   astronomical

knowledge that had been effected by Copernicus:

> Failing of satisfactory progress in explaining the
> movements of the heavenly bodies on the
> supposition that they all revolved round the
> spectator, he tried whether he might not have
> better success if he made the spectator to revolve
> and the stars to remain at rest. A similar
> experiment can be tried in metaphysics, . . . I
> assume that the objects, or what is the same thing,
> that the *experience* in which alone, as given
> objects, they can be known, conform to the
> concepts.[17]

The Copernican revolution in philosophical procedure
meant, accordingly, that the starting point had to be sought in
the nature or structure of human thinking. In this respect it
was a reversal of the procedure followed in western
philosophy up to the time of Descartes. Philosophers, as well
as the non-philosophical public,[18] had made *things* the
starting point of their reasoning. Only in knowing things
other than themselves did they consider that they were
conscious of their own thinking processes. Aristotle (384-322
B.C.) had expressed this tenet succinctly as though it had been
regarded as a matter of common observation and acceptance
in his day:

> "But evidently knowledge and perception and
> opinion and understanding have always
> something else as their object, and themselves
> only by the way."[19]

In this historical perspective, however, does the image of a
"Corpernican revolution" correctly describe the new trend?
The Ptolemaic astronomy had placed man at the center of the
universe. The Copernican advance taught man to regard
himself as revolving around a sun. Man was no longer the
center. His was a subsidiary planet. The epistemological
revolution, on the contrary, made man's thought the central
point. In pre-Cartesian philosophical procedures, as well as

for the non-philosophical thinker, things other than thought had been the center around which human thinking functioned. Things had been primary as objects. Thought, as their mental expression, had been secondary. Now, on the contrary, a human activity becomes the hub around which all else revolves.[20]

But no matter from what vantage point one views the situation, the stage was set for nineteenth century idealisms that aimed to develop thought systematically just in itself, for phenomenologies that probed the vivid appearances of things, and for realisms that sought to preserve an external world in spite of the new starting points located interiorly in one's own thinking. All this could hardly help but focus attention on human cognition itself. The result was a special discipline devoted to a study of the cognition just as cognition. Epistemology was born.

★★★★★★★★★★★★

Initial Issues. Though laborious, the detailed historical survey just undertaken is indispensable as a requisite for an intelligent approach to epistemology as found today. In clear fact, the need for a special philosophical discipline called epistemology went unrecognized through many long centuries of western thought. Epistemology would seem to have arisen because of new trends in modern times that were meant to improve drastically on earlier methods. This consideration prompts some queries that need to be asked at the beginning of the inquiry and kept continually in mind throughout its progress.

Why, for instance, did not epistemology emerge much sooner as a definite and self-contained philosophical discipline? Is the reason to be found in the difficulty of focusing upon cognition as an object for philosophical investigation? Cognition, as already remarked, is something very obvious. Taken globally, it could not go unnoticed. But, as has also been noted, it is not directly observable. It is not something that you can look out at and see, like plants and stars. It does not lie directly before your gaze. It has to be somehow detached from the things upon which it bears and which specify it, if it is to be set up as the subject matter of a distinct discipline.

Further, cognition as an activity is not something external that may be observed in common by all and sundry, in the way actions like walking or house-building may be observed. It seems rather to be something very private. You alone are immediately aware of your own knowing and thinking, as others alone are of theirs. How then can cognition be given the public character required in an object for common study? How can it be exteriorized in a way that will allow it to serve as the subject matter of a truly philosophical investigation? As a branch of philosophy it cannot be left in the status of a merely private meditation, either your own or that of someone else.

From another angle, could the late appearance of epistemology in the history of western thought be attributed to a supereminent role claimed for it? Like nuclear physics or geopolitics might it not have required the cultivation of many much more readily accessible procedures before it itself could be approached? Was the modern interest in epistemology a sign that at last mankind had come of age? Did it indicate that people had finally reached the intellectual maturity in which they can probe and control the sources of their knowledge, and thereby render themselves masters of their own fate? In a word, does genuinely philosophic or scientific knowledge of things require that you first know what knowledge itself is? From this viewpoint epistemology would be basic for all truly philosophical knowledge. It would, however, need preceding journeys to it through various other disciplines, apprentice-journeys that would not be really philosophical in character. This would explain its late arrival on the scene, while still leaving its role basic for philosophical understanding.

Yet in that perspective one might ask how sciences and other philosophic disciplines had reached their admirable heights without benefit of epistemology. Must one say that an understanding of the nature of knowledge is of no service whatever to the individual arts and sciences, quite as Aristotle (*E N*, 1.6.1097a1-13) could not see in the Platonic Ideas any help for the particular sciences, professions and crafts?   Even if epistemology is not demanded as their foundation, might it not be a help to them in elucidating their various methods of procedure and their relations with other disciplines?   Might not acquaintance with the nature of the cognition by which the objects are known provide feedback through which greater penetration into the clearer understanding of the subject matter could be attained?   Even though history shows that the past development of these disciplines did not require epistemology, might there not be question of its serviceability to them in the present and future?

These three initial issues, namely the public status of human cognition, the question of epistemology's basic role for all other human knowledge, and prospect of its serviceability for the progress of the other disciplines, come to the fore in the wake of the above historical survey.   Each of these issues calls for examination in particular and in greater detail before one proceeds to the central and hard core epistemological problems.   For the moment there can be no attempt to solve their difficulties.   The effort in the present chapter has to restrict itself to setting out in greater length the important considerations involved in these basic issues.   The chapter is concerned only with the problem side of the undertaking.   It bears entirely upon the problematic that makes the approach to epistemology differ from what has been encountered in facing the traditional philosophic disciplines.

Public Status. No person besides yourself has any natural means of looking directly into your own sensing or imagining or thinking.   Nor have you any natural capacity for looking into anybody else's cognition.   To become an object for discussion and dialogue the cognition obviously has to be externalized in some way.   This is done through language, spoken or written.   The language is external in regard to the speakers and writers.   Where the same language is used and understood, the content of one's internal cognition and thought can be conveyed to others.   It can be discussed in common and evaluated.   It can be preserved for wider and future circulation through printing and recording.   In these ways it becomes a public object.

But is there no deeper basis for its public character? Till the time of Descartes philosophers did not doubt, even methodically, that the external world is known directly in human cognition and that it is the same real world for all men and women. It was regarded as something common for all percipients. It provided an identical global object for everyone's perceiving and thinking. To that extent what humans thought and said had a common, public basis. A real world, something outside cognition and thought, served as the common measure to which everybody's cognition was meant to conform in basic outlines. A public character was thereby furnished, no matter how private the act of cognition. Such had been the traditional attitude.

This conception met with serious difficulties in the Cartesian critique. Since then it has been widely discarded among philosophers as naïve realism. Nevertheless the question needs to be approached today with an open mind. One has to ask if we are facing an artificially induced problem. Without the attitude brought about through the Cartesian asceticism would anybody seriously doubt about the world's extramental existence? Would the errors encountered in everyday life and in the sciences lead one to require a science of knowledge itself, instead of recourse to each particular discipline to correct the mistakes in its own field? Do the problems actually reveal a distinct object for a science of knowledge? Or, on the contrary, does cognition itself require explanation in terms of externally existing things? The latter alternative faces great philosophical difficulties, but so does the former one. Neither may be dismissed offhand. Only after careful consideration of the evidence on both sides is one in a position to give a genuinely philosophical answer. Yet the presence of the difficulties serves to emphasize the fact that public status of cognition as a distinct object for a branch of philosophy is not something immediately evident.

Other explanations for the public character of thought and discourse have in fact been offered. For Plato the eternally existent Ideas made common knowledge and continuous discourse possible. For Plotinus each intelligible object implicitly contained all the rest, somewhat as for Leibniz all the monads could be seen in each individual monad if the power of observation were sufficiently strong. For Augustine the divine illumination, in which all knowable objects were exhibited, was present to every knower.[21] For Malebranche and Berkeley things were seen in God. These explanations have not proven satisfactory and can hardly expect any general acceptance today. But they reinforce the stand that cognition cannot easily be isolated from its object as a distinct theme for consideration.

How, then, may cognition as a common object be in some way detached from its content and viewed just in itself as the subject matter of a philosophical study? You are of course conscious of your own activity when sensing or imagining or thinking. You are aware that the activity is a different thing from the tree you are seeing or the heat you are feeling or imagining, or the dinosaur about which you are thinking. But if you try to describe the sensing or imagining or thinking apart from the object sensed or imagined or known, you find it difficult to characterize just in itself. It remains the cognition of a color or leprechaun or geometrical figure. You are aware that it is different from those objects, but you cannot describe the cognition clearly without bringing them in. The problem of viewing any cognition apart from its object makes itself keenly felt. But the fact that you and others are alert to a glaring difference between the content and the cognition should serve as a guarantee that somehow a way may be found to present cognition as a public object for philosophical consideration. For the moment, however, this must remain a problem to be approached with an open mind.

The problem itself, though, is sufficiently clearcut. It is whether you can legitimately ask what cognition is, as you can ask what glaciers are, or what viruses are, or what syllogisms are. With glaciers and viruses and syllogisms there is in each case a distinct object held before the mind's gaze for consideration. There is something that can at least mentally be viewed apart from other observable objects. But cognition seems to become manifest only in terms of the object it attains. It is indeed observable, but only reflexively in terms of something else. There is real difficulty in seeing how it can have public status as an object apart from the individual in which it takes place.

Basic Role. In the not so distant past the stand had been taken that epistemology is the gateway through which genuinely philosophical procedure has to be entered.[22] From that angle it was regarded as the philosophical basis upon which all other disciplines rest. This is no longer a widespread view. Yet it poses the problem whether you can really know anything else if you do not know philosophically what knowledge itself is. If you do not understand the nature of human cognition, how and to what extent can you put confidence in what it makes you aware of in other things? But on the opposite side of the ledger there is the experience of the past in which people have gone about knowing things and developing particular sciences successfully without a preceding study of what cognition itself is.

On the one hand, it seems simple enough to ask: "How can one be sure of one's knowledge about anything in particular, if one does not first know what knowledge itself is?" On the other hand, the difficulty just discussed about isolating cognition as a distinct object for consideration should make one hesitate before giving cognition epistemological priority as an object for study. If it actually turns out to be knowable only in terms of its object, the order would be to investigate the objects first, in the ways done in traditional philosophy. The issue in this is whether epistemology is the most fundamental of the philosophical disciplines. If so, it should be the first branch to be studied in a philosophy course. Or is epistemology rather just one branch alongside others in the philosophical panorama? If that is the case, it can be assigned some other position in the curriculum according to the order of the different types of subject matter.

Both these alternatives call for unprejudiced consideration. Again, it is a question of keeping an open mind till the evidence has been painstakingly examined.

Serviceability. If epistemology should turn out to be the most fundamental of the philosophical disciplines and the entrance to truly philosophical mastery of the others, no doubt need arises about its utility and its pre-eminent position in the philosophical spectrum. But even if it proves to be merely one discipline alongside others, there still may be important services it can render. Aside from the prospect that cognition like any other scientific object may have enough attractiveness in its own right to warrant philosophical study on account of its intrinsic worth, there is the question of the subsidiary aids it may provide for work in the other disciplines. One may legitimately ask if these possible services are sufficient just by themselves to merit a place for the laborious pursuit of epistemology in the academic curriculum.

For instance, can the problem of existence as a synthesizing actuality be elucidated in metaphysics by a consideration of the way existence is expressed through the composition in judgment and proposition? The way existence is expressed in a judgment seems to offer the best means of understanding it. Likewise the proper understanding of ethics as dependent upon moral habituation and nevertheless as cognitive in its nature requires explanation by the difference between practical knowledge and theoretical knowledge. Epistemological considerations are crucial here. Also the question whether Eddington's two tables, the solid one upon which he was writing and the "mostly empty space" one he knew as a scientist, are really two or just one and the same table, has to be answered on the epistemological plane.[23] Problems like these are numerous enough and can be met only by an incursion into the philosophy of cognition.

Further, a cogently elaborated demonstration of the existence of God or of the indestructibility of the spiritual soul can be abruptly dismissed by alleging that the categories of human reason are meant to apply only within the realm of sensible experience, and that any use of them to reach the transcendental is vacuous. Or, statements that cannot be verified in sensible experience may be disregarded, on the ground that they are neither true nor false but meaningless. In a word, the feet may be cut from under assertions in other sciences because of epistemological tenets. Quite understandably such rebuttals are immune to any defense, and their difficulties to any medication, outside the philosophy of cognition.

Finally, there is the problem of understanding pluralism in philosophy. Different philosophies will argue cogently from their own starting points and come to widely different and reciprocally opposed conclusions. There are no flaws in their reasoning. The one cannot be refuted by the other. How is this possible? An understanding of the radical plurality in philosophies is of prime importance in today's multicultural world. But it can be attained only in epistemology. History of philosophy can set out the multitudinous variety of philosophies that our cultures have known, and can study philosophically the differences and the resemblances and the kinds of interdependence that these philosophies exhibit. But in order to evaluate them, and to explain why they differ so radically, epistemological study is required. It should provide a final critique of philosophical activity itself.

Like the two previous issues of public status and basic role for epistemology, that of its serviceability from the above angles can for the moment be presented only in tentative and problematic fashion. These initial issues need to be kept in mind for the orientation of the study. But one's attitude towards answers to the problems they involve should remain scrupulously open till the relevant data have been carefully probed. Upon the serviceability will depend to a certain extent the answer to the question whether epistemology results from an inborn urge of the mind to understand cognition *qua* cognition, or whether the discipline is pursued mainly because of an artificial stimulus given by the Cartesian doubt.

★★★★★★★★★★★★

Subsequent Issues. Besides the initial questions regarding the approach to epistemology, and the main hard core investigation of cognition in itself, the aspects of the truth and certainty that one seeks to attain through knowledge will require detailed examination. The ways in which this truth and certainty may be achieved, along with the criteria by which they may be recognized, will call for investigation. These matters quite obviously come under the scope of epistemology.

The quest for truth and certainty, however, is carried out in highly developed fashion through the sciences and the philosophical disciplines. A summary inquiry into the nature and reciprocal relations of these branches of knowledge will therefore be necessary to round out the whole epistemological enterprise.

In broad lines, then, the field of epistemology, after the initial approaches, will be human cognition considered just as it is in itself. The investigation will bear upon what that cognition is *qua* cognition, and upon its truth and certainty as well as upon its organized development through the sciences and through the various types and branches of philosophy that have arisen in the course of the long development of western culture.

Previous Knowledge. You come to the study of epistemology after primary and secondary education. You bring to it a mentality trained in logic and in the methods of other sciences, steeled in the ways of general scientific procedure, and schooled through long experience to attend to every road sign. All this knowledge or skill is yours to apply to the present undertaking. Is there any reason for not using it to its full extent in providing aids for the study of cognition itself? Can the fact that knowledge itself is under scrutiny disqualify your own actual knowledge on the ground that none of it can be presumed reliable until cognition in general has been proven to be so in its basic features? An attitude of this kind would obviously be suicidal to the epistemological enterprise. Rather, a solid basis for all knowledge is to be sought.

Yet can you hope to get back to an absolutely primitive act of cognition that would intuit what cognition itself is? One might well doubt whether an attempt to dig down to a chronologically first act of cognition could hope for any success. As a psychological process it would hardly seem feasible, given the difficulties if not the impossibility of recalling one's earliest cognition. Even if a chronologically first could be reached, there would still be doubt whether it would be an intuition of what the nature of cognition is. It might not be any more informative on the present question than the cognition we currently experience. Graduate students have been heard to say as they looked admiringly on a newborn child: "If only the baby could talk and tell us what it was first aware of before prejudices set in, the epistemological problem would be solved!" But what reason is there for expecting any other report than that of simultaneous awareness of both object and act? The baby would be aware of bassinet or bottle, and at the same aware that he or she was seeing or touching or knowing it, without any recognition of which was epistemologically prior. The same problem would remain, and the same means would have to be used to solve it.

The prospect, then, is not that of getting back to a psychologically first, and proceeding to build upon it. Epistemology is not the construction of a system for directing thought, in the fashion of logic. Rather, it is the examination of an object already present, in an effort to understand its nature. Here cognition itself is the topic for the inquiry, while it is also the examiner. On that account the charge of circularity might arise, with the reliability of cognition resting on cognition's own reliability. But with the ground in things other than cognition, why may not cognition bring to bear upon itself all the skills and techniques it would use for the examination of other objects? It manifestly reflects upon itself, and it appears *prima facie* to have the power to use its acquired abilities upon itself as object just as readily as upon other things. It should accordingly be investigated by means of all the relevant particular knowledge it possesses. In this way it holds out the prospect that its nature may somehow be reached by reasoning, just as in the case of other things whose natures are not immediately evident. In the discovery of what its nature is, the reasons why it may be trusted and the way it makes mistakes can be expected to emerge, together with criteria for the reliability. Premature conclusions in this regard should not be permitted. Rather, patience has to be sternly exercised in investigating cognition as a reflexively known object, and in letting its very nature explain how and why it is trustworthy and how it can go wrong.

Quite as one may enjoy an excellently functioning digestion without any physiological knowledge of what is involved, so one may let one's cognition go about its work without having prior epistemological expertise in regard to its nature.[24] The possibility that its trustworthiness may be based upon something other than itself need not be dismissed offhand. If its reliability is shown to rest upon something outside itself, the charge of circularity fades from the picture. The important attitude is to keep a genuinely open mind in watching one's cognition run its course as it investigates itself, and to be patient in waiting for it to reveal its own nature, regardless of more or less currently accepted views. In epistemology, as with philosophy in general, authority is the weakest of arguments. That is an old and commonly accepted principle. But until the nature of philosophy has been probed, one may tentatively acquiesce in it on the authority of general acceptance. One's own thinking is what counts, here as in any philosophical inquiry. Whether others agree or not is a secondary consideration.

Vocabulary. Since epistemology will deal with such commonly discussion topics as sight, hearing, colors, sounds, thinking, knowing and reasoning, it will presumably make copious use of terms taken from ordinary language. It will be obliged to respect the exigencies demanded by the meanings of these words in their accepted use, with normal attention paid to the overtones accompanying them. Yet, like any other scientific or philosophical procedure, epistemology may be expected to sharpen the terms into exact technical significations when occasion requires. The technical meanings are often imperative in order to preserve unity of thought and to avoid ambiguity or obscurity in the course of reasoning processes.

In spite of that inevitable rigidity, however, secondary or extended meanings of the terms in ordinary language need not always be avoided for the sake of precisely technical discourse. Words like "see" and "look," for instance, may unhesitatingly be used for intellectual apprehension instead of remaining limited just to sensory vision. One may readily speak of "seeing the point," or "taking a look at the cogency with which conclusions follow from premises." "Grasp" and "attain" may similarly be used for knowing. Technical as a philosophical inquiry about cognition must be in its use of terms, it has no obligation to practice even with epistemic words the austerities of an artificial language. Likewise a currently employed term such as "observe" may be freely applied to reflexive cognition in epistemology, quite as it is used for introspection in psychology.

Finally, there can be no question of renouncing abstraction or abstractive terms, even for the moment, on the plea that their objects do not come under perception and therefore are not basic. No matter how strictly perception bears on the individual, to investigate and to speak of it you have to use abstract terms. Abstraction is a built-in technique of human thought. That is something one "observes," in the sense just noted. It has therefore to be used from the start. Later it can be explained in the course of the epistemological investigation.

Procedure. What emerges decisively from these preliminary considerations is the importance of locating the appropriate starting point for epistemology. Is the starting point something that has its existence only in the activity of the percipient or knower, for instance in sensations or ideas? Or is it something that has real existence outside the cognitive agent, such as the things in the sensible universe? Moreover, if it exists both in human cognition and in the real world, in which of the two does it have epistemological priority? Here one should be very precise. If the starting point is something really existent in the sensible world, the empirical formula that cognition begins in sensation needs careful understanding. Is the starting point a human activity or product, as in the empiricism of Locke or Hume or Condillac? Or should it be regarded and characterized rather as the externally existent sensible things?

That, then, will be the question for the next chapter of the present study, for the way the starting point is understood will determine the whole course of the inquiry. This does not at all mean that epistemologies based on other starting points may be neglected. In the pluralistic conception of philosophy as widely accepted today, the mutual help of deeply varying procedures is gladly acknowledged. For instance, the Kantian construction of experience can be of help in explaining how purely spiritual beings may be conceived by the human mind under the categories of space and time. God in Michelangelo's Sistine Chapel fresco is portrayed in bodily form, and the activities of God and angels are described by the Scriptures in temporal sequence. It is always permissible to learn from an adversary, even--one might say especially--in philosophy, in accord with the Latin proverb *fas est ab hoste doceri*. This pluralism is a phenomenon that will require careful assessment at the end of the whole study.

Résumé. Epistemology means the study of cognition from the viewpoint of cognition itself. Historically it is a late arrival in the philosophical world. It stems remotely from the Cartesian attempt to make thought the starting point of philosophy, and proximately from the nineteenth century confrontations of Realisms with Idealisms. Its opening problem is to discover whether cognition actually can be made a distinct subject matter for philosophical study. The difficulty is that cognition is not directly describable in itself, but only in terms of existence and an object. This situation opens possibilities that the object through which cognition is delineated and studied may be something that exists independently of the cognitive activity, and something common or public. If that turns out to be the case, it will allow cognition to be observed and examined in the public way requisite for a scientific or philosophical investigation. But careful scrutiny will first be necessary in order to see if in fact this is the actual situation, and if the independent object does in truth dominate the cognitive act in a way that will make manifest what cognition itself is.

If cognition shows itself to be in the above fashion a topic susceptible of philosophic inquiry, it prompts the further overall question whether epistemology thereby becomes the most basic of philosophical disciplines. But if it is not the most fundamental type of knowledge, a third question arises, namely, what auxiliary services can it render? If none, then one might ask whether it is a spontaneously arising discipline or an artificially stimulated enterprise. Upon these general issues follow subsequent problems about the truth and certainty of human cognition and about the ways in which knowledge can attain its best development scientifically and philosophically. Finally, the pluralistic nature of philosophy will call for investigation.

In the approach to these problems, an entirely open mind is always required. Commitment to predetermined frameworks of philosophizing can hardly help but narrow one's vision. The Argus-eyed ability to keep seeing in a hundred directions at the same time is imperative if the proper clues are to be discovered and followed through. In every case the decision has to rest ultimately upon what one observes, and not upon presuppositions accepted uncritically from currently entrenched philosophical positions. On the other hand, all previously acquired knowledge and training should be regarded as at one's disposal for the investigation. There is no ground for banning any of them on a pretext that they presuppose cognition itself. Since in epistemology cognition is observing its own self in action, it should be allowed to function in the full bloom of the development it already has at the stage in which the epistemological inquiry begins. If human cognition itself shows, as a matter of observation and analysis, that something other than itself is epistemologically prior to it, it should be allowed to present its own case in this regard. The charge that there is circularity in looking to it to establish its own reliability has to be faced. But the genuinely philosophical mind should remain fully open to the account cognition itself gives of its own nature and activity.

Notes to Chapter 1

1. The title "epistemology" found acceptance through James Frederick Ferrier's use of it in *Institutes of Metaphysic* (Edinburgh and London, 1854). "Theory of Knowledge" (e.g., Woozley, Chisholm, Hamlyn), in conformity with the German *Erkenntnistheorie* or *Erkenntnislehre*, also became well established. *Gnoseologia* (see *Enciclopedia Filosofica*, s.v.) has been about equally popular in Italian, but its English rendition "gnosiology" (see *Oxford English Dictionary*, s.v.) has not met with any notable success. "Ideology" was used in the wake of some Italian writing, e.g., Rosmini, *Nuovo Saggio* (Rome, 1830)--see English translation of the fifth edition, *The Origin of Ideas* (London, 1883-1886), III, 352 (no. 1463). But "ideology," coined in 1798 by Destutt de Tracy against a background in Locke and Condillac, soon became appropriated to social and political philosophy. Yet it served as the title for the subdivision of logic that studied the origin of ideas, as may be seen in a Neoscholastic manual widely used in the last half of the nineteenth century--Gaetano Sanseverino, *Elementa philosophiae christianae*, 2d ed. (Naples, 1873), I, 442. Longer lasting in Neoscholastic circles, against the background of Kant's use of the word *Kritik*, was the title *Critica*--e.g., *Logicae Pars Critica* (Tongiorgi), *Critica* (Gény), or in French, *Critique de la connaissance*--(Tonquédec). An English translation "Critics," in line with "Physics" or "Metaphysics," was attempted by A. J. McNicholl, "Epistemology and Metaphysics," *Angelicum*, 38 (1961), 206-212. *Criteriologia* (San Severino) and *Critériologie* (Mercier) have been used to express the notion of the study as the search for criteria of truth and certitude against Skeptical attacks. *Ontologie du connaître* (Yves Simon) and "Metaphysics of Knowledge" (G. B. Phelan, *Proceedings of the American Catholic Philosophical Association*, 21 [1946], 110-111), as well as Leslie Stevenson's *Metaphysics of Experience* (Oxford, 1982), are titles that present the study of knowledge as a branch or aspect of metaphysics. *The Philosophy of Knowledge* (Kenneth T. Gallagher) is a title that is neutral in regard to metaphysical character for epistemology. A Neoscholastic tendency to regard it as the higher part of logic (e.g.,

Francis Varvello, *Major Logic*, trans. Arthur D. Fearon [San Francisco, 1933]), survived into the fourth decade of the present century. Finally, "noetics" is commonly used as a designation for the study, though not as a title for books dealing with it.

Sometimes one of the titles has been used for the whole study, and others for its parts. E.g., For René Jeannière, *Criteriologia* (Paris, 1912), 3, epistemology was the whole, criteriology a part. For McNicholl (206), on the other hand, "critics" was the whole enterprise, while criteriology and epistemology were its parts.

2. The notion "sense knowledge" (*episteme aisthetike*) goes back to Aristotle's *Nicomachean Ethics*, 7.5.1147b15-17. The phrase is common enough today. But for Plato (*Tht.*, 210AB) neither perception nor opinion could be knowledge. See also Harold Arthur Prichard, *Knowledge and Perception* (Oxford, 1950), 213.

3. The *processes* in which cognition takes place are studied on the experimental level by psychology, and on the philosophical level by the Aristotelian philosophy of nature. The cognition itself, however, does not consist in a process: "For every motion is incomplete, as in losing weight, learning, walking, and building. . . . On the other hand, the same thing has seen and is seeing at the same time, and likewise it is thinking and has thought." Aristotle, *Metaph.*, 9.6.1048b28-34; trans. H. G. Apostle. In regard to sensations, see S. Munsat, "Could Sensations be Processes?" *Mind*, N.S. 78 (1969), 247-251, especially 250. Aristotle's meaning is clear enough. While the something seen is *always* present in the act of seeing, the something built (e.g., a house) is not present till the process of building has been completed. But the thing *has been* seen from the very start of the act of seeing.

4. The all-embracing range of the term "cognition" in its philosophic sense is brought out by the *O.E.D.* (s.v.) in defining it as "the action or faculty of knowing taken in its widest sense." Similarly, "awareness" cannot be explained any more clearly than by cognizance of something. In consequence one is thrown back to indicating instances for both these terms. On "noticing, realizing, perceiving and apprehending" as some instances that may be

reasonably accepted, see Rodney Julian Hirst, *The Problems of Perception* (London & New York, 1959) 224.

5. A short sketch of the history of ancient and medieval views on cognition may be found in David Walter Hamlyn, *Sensation and Perception* (London & New York, 1961), 5-54. The Aristotelian tradition has always maintained the essential worth of perception and knowledge just in themselves, aside from any use to which they may be put, as outlined by Aristotle in Metaph., 1.1-2,980a21-983a11. But the opposite view is as prevalent today as it was in antiquity, especially in pragmatic and Marxist traditions. Even aside from these traditions a writer can today lay down as a starting point that anticipates no opposition the tenet that knowledge is of its nature a means for something else: "The primary and pervasive significance of knowledge lies in its guidance of action: knowing is for the sake of doing"--Clarence Irving Lewis, *An Analysis of Knowledge and Valuation* (La Salle, Ill., 1962), 3. This view of cognition as essentially something meant for activity other than itself can hardly help but deeply affect one's understanding of its nature.

6. On the status of the universals, see for instance Thomas Aquinas, *On Being and Essence*, trans. Armand Maurer, 2nd ed. (Toronto: Pontifical Institute of Mediaeval Studies, 1986), 45-50, and other medieval discussions of the relations between the universal and the common nature. For texts, see J. Owens, "Common Nature: A Point of Comparison Between Thomistic and Scotistic Metaphysics," *Mediaeval Studies*, 19 (1957), 1-14, and "Thomistic Common Nature and Platonic Idea," ibid., 21 (1959), 211-223, and, on the explanation of cognition in terms of existence, "Aquinas on Cognition as Existence," *Proceedings of the American Catholic Philosophical Association*, 48 (1974), 74-85. Cf.: "For knowledge does not mean something flowing from the knower to a thing known, as happens in physical actions. It means, rather, the existence of the thing known in the knower." Aquinas, *De ver.*, 2.5, ad 15m; trans. Robert W. Mulligan, Truth (Chicago, 1952), I. 91.

7. Descartes, *Discours de la Méthode*, Seconde partie (AT, VI, 19.20-240. On the general Cartesian setting for the more outstanding epistemological problems, see Etienne Gilson, *The*

Unity of Philosophical Experience, cc. 5-6; reprint, (Westminster, MD, 1982), 125-220. On its lesser appeal now, see Hirst, 18. The situation has been aptly described as ". . . Descartes is a mathematician, first last and always, a mathematician extending the professional mark of his calling to knowledge as a whole." Marjorie Grene, *The Knower and the Known* (London, 1966), 65. On the way Descartes could appear as an atomist, see Daniel Garber, "Descartes, the Aristotelians, and the Revolution that Did not Happen in 1637," *The Monist,* 71 (1988), 482.

8. Descartes, *Principia philosophiae,* 1.1 (AT VII, 5.5-11; IX2, 25).

9. In spiritual asceticism the method of meditation to rid the soul of attachment to worldly things and ways of thinking was stressed by the Jesuits, under whom Descartes had made his studies. Parallel on the speculative place is the method in Descartes' *Meditations on First Philosophy.*

10. Descartes, *Discours,* Quatrième partie (AT VI, 32.19; 33.17); *Principia,* 1.7 (AT VIII, 7.8; IX^2, 27).

11. On the details, see Gilson, *The Unity of Philosophical Experience,* cc. 7-8, (1982), 176-220, and for their bearing on later epistemological problems, Prichard, 69-199.

12. Hume, *A Treatise of Human Nature,* 1.4.6; ed. Peter H. Nidditch (Oxford, 1978), 252. Malebrance, *Recherche de la vérité,* 3.2.7.4, ed. Geneviève Rodis-Lewis (Paris, 1962) I, 451, had shown that people have no clear and distinct idea of the soul, but only a more obscure consciousness (*conscience*) or interior sentiment of it. See also 3.2.1.1; I 415. Likewise Locke had emphasized that the mind has no clear idea of substance or substantial form--*An Essay Concerning Human Understanding,* 2.23.1-9; ed. Peter H. Nidditch (Oxford, 1975), 295-301. From this it was but a step for Hume to draw the inference that the Cartesian method could not establish an idea of the self. In the present century the *cogito* has been revived in the context of a phenomenological method--see Edmund Husserl, *Cartesian Meditations,* trans. Dorion Cairns (The Hague, 1970), 1-6. But outside that context it is not hard to accept the judgment that "the '*Cogito*' at

least is a blind alley"--Peter Geach, *Mental Acts* (London, 1957) 121.

13. Hume, *Treatise*, 1.4.6; 252.

14. Hume, *An Enquiry Concerning Human Understanding*, 5.1.36; ed. Peter H. Nidditch (Oxford, 1975) 43-44.

15. Locke, *Essay*, Epistle to the Reader; ed. Nidditch, 7.21-25.

16. Kant, *KRV*, B xvi; trans. Norman Kemp Smith, *Immanuel Kant's Critique of Pure Reason* (London, 1950), 22.

17. *KRV* B xvi-xvii; trans. N. K. Smith, 22.

18. Husserl, "Ideen zu einer reinen Phänomenologie und phänomenologischen Philosophie," Jahrbuch für Philosophie und phänomenologische Forschung, 1 (1913), 187, speaks of "nätürlich eingestellte Menschen." The English translation reads: ". . . starting as men in our natural setting the real object is the thing out there." *Ideas*, trans. W. R. Boyce Gibson (London & New York, 1931), 264.

19. *Metaph.*, 12.9.1074b35-36; Ross trans. Cf. Aquinas, *De ver.*, 10.8c.

20. Cf.: "To most critics, the endeavor to make the known world turn on the constitution of the knowing mind, seems like a return to an ultra-Ptolemaic system. . . . That the consequence was Ptolemaic rather than Copernican is not to be wondered at." John Dewey, *The Quest for Certainty* (New York, 1929), 287. "For Kant, as for Descartes, the problem springs not so much from the contradiction between two accounts as from the fact that there can be *only one narrator*, the human reason. How can one single teller infallibly recount two contradictory stories?" Louis Marie Régis, *Epistemology*, trans. Imelda Choquette Byrne (New York, 1959), 38. The answer is to be sought in the pluralistic nature of philosophy, with the one external world as the standard for assessing all procedures. Cf. infra, Epilogue, n. 9.

21. "For he is taught not by my words, but by the realities

themselves made manifest to him by God revealing them to his inner self." Augustine, *The Teacher* (*De Magistro*), 12.40; trans. Joseph M. Collerman (Westminster, MD, 1964), 179. Cf. "Hence, 'that which was made' was already 'life in Him,' and not any kind of life, but that life which was 'the light of men,' the light certainly of rational minds . . ." Augustine, *The Trinity*, 4.1.3; trans. Stephen McKenna (Washington, DC, 1963), 132-133. In the above text from *De Magistro*, ed. G. Weigel, *CSEL* 77.6.4 (1961), 49, 3-4, the Latin is more vivid in speaking of "things" and with overtones of their being "spread out" interiorly as they are made known in the mind.

22. E.G.: "At the threshold of philosophy, then, the mind must first examine knowledge itself, as it first appears to consciousness, . . ." Fernand Van Steenberghen, *Epistemology*, trans. Martin J. Flynn (New York, 1949) 12. Van Steenberghen (10) regards philosophical studies made before epistemology as merely an apprentice trip taken "just for the ride" through the terrain of philosophy. Today, in view of the tremendous development of the sciences without a study of epistemology as their basis, there is difficulty in seeing how anyone could look upon epistemology as the philosophical foundation of the other disciplines. Yet that view seems clearly enough implied in describing it as a procedure that "heads through an understanding of all understanding to a basic understanding of all that can be understood"--Bernard J. F. Lonergan, *Insight* (New York, 1957), xxviii. With "insight into insight" (xxvii), "*you will possess a fixed base, an invariant pattern, opening upon all further developments of understanding*" (xxviii). The unacknowledged hurdle confronting this conception is the question whether knowledge actually does appear to consciousness in a way that could from the epistemological viewpoint properly be called "first." Against the long accepted Cartesian background the possibility of this query seems to have gone unsuspected. On the model of material presence, in which no other finite thing can be more present to an object than that thing itself, the notion that in the cognitional order nothing can be more present to cognition than the cognition itself has been accepted without scrutiny. The baneful conclusion that "true philosophical work . . . must therefore necessarily begin with a critical reflection upon knowledge" (Van Steenberghen, 10) follows logically from this unwarranted premise.

23. Arthur Stanley Eddington, *The Nature of the Physical World* (Cambridge, 1928) ix-xi. The fact is that the table known through the senses provides the data for the scientist's reasoning to its own atomic constitution. Sensibly perceived dimensions, qualities and activities ground his explanation of the one identical thing.

24. On this reflection, see Désiré Mercier, *Critériologie générale*, 7th ed. (Louvain, 1918), 399.

CHAPTER 2

The Primacy of the External

Outside World. When you reflect upon your own cognition as a whole, you will notice at once that it bears in overwhelming extent on things that are presented as really other than itself, and other than you. For the people to whom you talk and with whom you live, the streets on which you walk, the house in which you stay, the desk on which you write, the food and beverage on your table, all have the *prima facie* standing of real persons or real things, existent there in themselves. They do not exhibit the status of creatures of your cognition, as do things in fantasies and pipe dreams. As long as you stay sane you cannot shake the basic certainty that you share a real world with other real beings, a world that does not depend upon your thought for its existence.

The ancient Greek Skeptics, while doubting about everything taught by philosophers, did not doubt that they lived in the real external world.[1] Descartes, in introducing his methodical difficulties, was careful to shield himself from the ridiculous in that regard. He remarked that nobody had any real doubt about the existence of material things.[2] Locke would not have any discussion with a person who claimed to doubt the reality of things exterior to one's own cognition.[3] Hume, when depressed by his speculations about non-substantial selves and appearances, turned to a real world of dinner with his friends, and backgammon afterwards, to bring him back to even keel.[4] All these philosophers realized full well that the external world existed in itself, and that the people and things in it were existents aside from any human cognition of them.

But in the Cartesian epoch the starting points for philosophy became located in objects other than external things. The philosophers were thereby forced to seek ways of *proving* that the people and the things really existed in an outside world, since they no longer regarded anything external as an immediate object of awareness. The question was not one of real doubt about the world's external existence, but rather of the way to justify philosophically the unavoidable and unshakable certainty that the world and its people exist outside one's own personal cognition. It follows that if external things themselves are not the starting points for philosophical thinking, they will have to be reasoned to from objects inside the mind. Accordingly ideas for Descartes and Malebranche, and sensations for Locke, Hume and Condillac, became the basic objects of human cognition.[5] With the starting points viewed in this way as interior to the knower or percipient, the world in which other people lived and in which material things existed could be regarded as external or outside. The first problem, then, is to discern what is actually the basic object upon which your cognition directly bears, whether upon externally existing things or upon internally present ideas and sensations. Upon that foundation the subsequent epistemology will depend.

Basic Object. The above considerations suggest an exacting scrutiny of the basic object encountered by human cognition. Is it primarily something inside or outside cognition itself? Spontaneously your cognition is aware of itself as sensing or imagining or knowing other things. The other things are stones, trees, houses, stars, animals, human beings, and so on indefinitely. But your cognition does not offer its own self as an object directly known in the way the other things are grasped. It does not present itself as an object seen apart from them, in the way a tree is something apart from a stone. Awareness of its own self is accordingly dependent on the awareness of something else. It presupposes the other object. It does not show itself to be the basic object upon which all other cognition rests. Human cognition does not exhibit epistemological priority to the thing on which it bears.

This factual bearing of human cognition upon an object other than itself was stressed by Aristotle. For him it posed a difficulty confronting his inference that immaterial substance is knowledge of itself alone--a "knowing of knowing."[6] The Aristotelian conception lasted through the middle ages. In modern times it has been quite commonly neglected, despite some rare mention of an inherent bearing of thought upon something other than itself.[7] Yet nobody has been able to show in refutation of it that an examination of the facts just in themselves yields any other conclusion. The data gathered by a scrutiny of one's cognition as it is presented to a reflexive gaze point decidedly to a direct awareness of things other than the cognition itself, namely of things like houses and people that can exist in themselves and not just in one's cognition of them. There is no immediate evidence of any direct awareness of itself.

Of course, to show that human cognition is by its nature an awareness of something else does not immediately indicate that the "something else" must exist outside the cognitive activity. Unicorns, utopias, six-dimensional entities and the like do not exist outside one's imagination and intellection. Moreover, our direct acts of awareness may themselves become the objects of a new act of reflexive cognition, while remaining something other than that new act. Our cognition presents these sensations and thoughts as objects existing only in its own activity, with sharp contrast to the way houses and friends exist in an outside world. For the moment, however, our scrutiny is directed to the latter type of objects, things that exist in themselves. They are the objects upon which our everyday awareness predominantly bears. Consideration of the purely imaginary or the mathematical or the reflexive types can be left for later study. At the present stage of the inquiry one need merely note that the built-in otherness of the object of human cognition leaves open the possibility of external otherness for an outstanding number of the things of which we are ordinarily aware in daily life. No reason against the possibility is immediately apparent.

Moreover, the things considered to be external are presented in our cognition as directly and immediately perceived. You see the instrument panel in front of you. You hear the purring motor. You feel the levers as you shift gears or signal. You have no awareness that you are reasoning to or inferring any of these objects. Spontaneously you accept them as playing a basic role in your cognition. Awareness of them insofar as they are things and existents is not derived from the awareness of anything else. As far as the immediate data make manifest, each functions as a cognitionally basic object.

A philosophically induced difficulty, however, does arise. Whatever is beyond thought, this objection runs, is by that very description shown to be unthinkable.[8] In order to be thought of at all, it has to be already in some way in our mind, or in our awareness. If it is outside our awareness, then, we cannot be immediately cognizant of it. We can at best infer it from something of which we are immediately aware. Consequently, the objection maintains, no external thing can be truly basic to our cognition.

Distance. This objection may be intensified by the distance factor. It has been expressed vividly by Malebranche:

> I think everybody agrees that we do not perceive through themselves the objects that are outside us. We see the sun, the stars, and an infinity of objects outside us; and it is not likely that the soul goes out of the body and takes, so to speak, a walk around the skies to contemplate all those objects there. It therefore does not see them through themselves; and the immediate object of our mind, when for example it sees the sun, is not the sun but something that is intimately united to our soul. It is something that I call an *idea*."[9]

The objection, however, will hold equally for things close to us and even in immediate contact with us, as with things touched. The reason alleged is the same, namely that the things are outside our cognitive activity. According to this all-pervasive objection, what we are first and basically aware of has to be something within our own cognition regardless of what the spontaneous data report. For Malebranche, as for Descartes before him, the philosophical starting point lay in human ideas. For subsequent philosophers, such as Locke, Hume and Condillac, it became located in sensations.[10] With these latter the sensible origin did not mean origin in sensible things as it had meant for Aristotle and Aquinas, but origin in sensations as cognitive activities. The objection throughout was that the very notion of cognition required its basic object to be inside itself. The conclusion drawn was that no external thing could function in that basic fashion.

This objection calls for most careful consideration on its own merits. It has also been bolstered with accounts of the errors and illusions that occur continually in regard to external reality. Each of these aberrations is to be taken seriously and given explanation by the sciences appropriate to the subject matter, such as physics and psychology. But the objection in itself is philosophical. It requires a philosophical answer. The nature of cognition itself is what needs to be examined. Is it in fact an activity that cannot have an external thing as its immediate object? Or is it an activity that is of its general nature open to both the internal and the external for its basic objects? Though it does not produce anything external, as do activities like building and engendering, can it nevertheless attain something distant from it as an object of which it is immediately aware? If so, how is this done?

These are not easy questions to answer. They call for exacting investigation and study. But the effort, painstaking and time-consuming though it may be, is necessary for successfully answering the charge that one is naïve in thinking that our cognition bears directly on outside things, as it spontaneously presents itself to be doing. Possible even greater naïveté rests in the belief that to see the sun and the moon really means seeing images or ideas that are inside one's own cognitive activity. An idea, like a photo, is really other than the thing it portrays.

Cognitional Presence. There need be no doubt whatever that anything you are aware of is in your cognition. Otherwise you would not be aware of it. But need the presence within your cognitive activity be understood in a way that would preclude the object's real presence in a world outside your cognition? Certainly simultaneous double presence in any material way would be contradictory. A liter of milk cannot at the same time be both inside and outside the plastic container in which it was bought. That type of presence and of being would restrict a thing to the one place at any given time. That way, however, is not what is meant in cognitional presence. The huge hospital building that covers a city block cannot be present within your cognition under the extent of those material dimensions. Yet it is the hospital that you see and know. There must be a way other than material presence for it to be inside your acts of awareness.

There is of course no question here of a picture in drastically reduced size, in the way all the pages of a large book are reproduced on a single microfiche. The print would still be outside your cognition. The thing directly seen would be the small film lying in front of you, and not the pages of the original book. Where an externally existent hospital is being seen, the hospital itself, and not just a picture of it, is inside your cognition. Otherwise not the externally existent hospital would be seen, but only an image of it. Even when it is later recalled in memory, it is the external hospital itself, and not merely an image of it, that is being remembered.

Being in the mind or in sensation, then, is a way of being that is different from material presence. Material presence could never account for cognition. Water may be in a jug, but it is not known or sensed by the jug. The jug holds the water, and in that way has the water within itself. But it does not feel or know the water. The water is in it, but not in the manner required by cognition. Rather, cognition gets inside the thing perceived or known, penetrates it, permeates it, absorbs it to the full extent of the aspect under which the awareness is taken place, whether the aspect is color, sound, extension, substance or being. To that extent the percipient or knower is, in the actuality of cognition, thoroughly identical with the thing sensed or known. This can be expressed by saying that the one *is* the other in the actuality of the awareness. It is not a question of having, for you do not have a house when you see one or think of one. You have the image and the concept of the house, and through them you are aware of the house. But in saying that you have the house itself in your memory or in your mind you do not mean to say that you possess it. What happens is that for the moment the house has its existence within your cognition in an altogether new way in which you may be said to *be* it cognitionally. That is what is meant by its cognitional presence within your sensation or imagination or thought. It is not like photography or recording.

Cognition, then, has to be explained in terms of existence. The house exists in itself, but also exists in the awareness of the one perceiving it or knowing it. The two kinds of existence are obviously different from each other. For convenience, the existence of the house in itself may be called *real* existence. Its existence in somebody's awareness may be called intentional or *cognitional* existence.[11] A house may lose its real existence through fire or demolition, yet keep on existing in the memories of those who lived in it. It acquires new cognitional existence every time anyone starts to think about it. Aristotle repeatedly pointed out that being has various meanings.[12] This is an instance of that doctrine. Through cognitional being, the soul, as Aristotle observed, is potentially all things.[13] In being them cognitionally, the percipient or knower is one and the same with them in the actuality of the awareness and is for that reason necessarily aware of himself in knowing them. He is one with them in that actuality, so much so that to be aware of the thing is to be aware of himself in a way that can make the cognition and himself the objects of subsequent consideration.

This traditional explanation of cognition as a way of existence is strange at first to those who approach it from a background of modern or postmodern philosophy. But it fits normally into an Aristotelian or Scholastic setting. Adjustment to it may take much careful thought and persevering attention. It is essential, however, for a philosophical understanding of cognition. The effort and time required for grasping it will accordingly be amply repaid. The twofold existence--real and cognitional--that a sensible thing can have explains how the same thing exists in the real world outside cognition and is simultaneously present within one's awareness through thoroughgoing

cognitional identity with the percipient or knower. The fact
that a thing perceived or known has to be inside cognition,
then, does not at all militate against its real existence in itself
outside the cognitive activity.   The thing itself remains
exactly the same thing.

Cognitional Identity.   But how is the thoroughgoing
cognitional identity of percipient and thing perceived, or
knower and thing known, brought about? What makes the
one *be* the other? Obviously an efficient cause is required to
bring a thing into cognitional existence quite as an efficient
cause is necessary for bringing it into real existence.   The
activity of the carpenter and other workmen make the house
come to exist in the real world.   The activities of one's
cognitive faculties make it come to be in one's awareness. But
there is a crucial difference. The activities of the workmen
produce a house that was not there before.   The cognitive
activities, in perceiving and knowing something that exists in
the outside world, attain something that is already there in
real existence. They do not produce it. In fact, the existent
external thing in being seen or heard is quite evidently
exercising efficient causality upon the percipient through the
light or sound waves it emits. For real activity, it has to be
already existent in itself.

To explain the distant causality one has to draw copiously
upon knowledge acquired in other sciences and other
branches of philosophy, as noted in the preceding chapter.
The activities of light and sound waves, as well as the
transmission of odors, are studied in physics.   The
stimulation of the nerves and cortex are investigated in
physiology and psychology. The philosophical aspects of the
efficient causality are probed in the philosophy of nature and
in metaphysics. The philosophy of nature examines how a
sensible composite is produced by the activity of an efficient
cause that brings a given matter into a new form, as the
workmen for instance bring the bricks, glass, wood and
mortar into the form of a house. Metaphysics shows how the
new form is the cause of the thing's existing, of its being a unit,
and of its being what it is.[14]   The causality that the form
exercises is of course causality in its own order, namely

formal causality. The form itself requires an efficient cause to work it into the matter. But once brought into the matter it itself is the cause, as form, that makes the matter and the composite exist and be what they actually are. The form is in this way the cause of being.

When the workmen, however, bring the materials into the form of the house as known from the blueprints, they produce a third thing. The third thing is the composite, the house. The materials were one thing, the design thought out by the architect was another thing, and the house, made up of both, is the third thing. In contrast, awareness of the house does not consist in the production of a new house. It is the same house, but now attained in cognitional activity. Otherwise you would not be aware of that house but of a new product that is something different. What is known is not a third thing, a composite made up of the knower and the thing known.[15] There remain just the two, the knower and the known. But each has acquired the one new cognitional existence, in which they are one and the same.

Efficient causality in the world of nature, on the other hand, produces a composite that is a new individual. The new individual may be specifically the same, as are offspring in regard to parents. It may be the same in design, as houses constructed from the same blueprint, or tables from the same sketch. But as regards individuality, products are always different from their efficient causes. Things perceived or known, though, remain not only specifically but also individually the same both in their real and in their cognitional existence. The tree outside your window is the same individual tree that is seen when you look at it. The individual with whom you are talking is the same person that exists in your awareness at the time. While the efficient causality in procreation makes the child be of the same species as the parents, the efficient causality in perceiving or knowing the child makes the percipient or knower be, not another individual just specifically the same as the child, but that individual child itself in cognitional existence. The form into which the percipient or knower is brought by the efficient causality is the same individual form that actuates the child in real life. It is not just specifically the same, as is human form in child and parents. It is individually the same form, actuating both child and percipient in two different ways of existing. It makes the percipient *be* the individual object that exists in reality.

But how is the percipient working into the form of thing perceived? The efficient causality is twofold.[16] It is exercised by both the percipient and the thing known. You are immediately aware of your own seeing and hearing and feeling and tasting and smelling. It is you who are performing these actions, even though you are the subject into whom the forms have been worked. But the things perceived are also acting, and acting upon you. In physics you study how the distant things act upon your sense organs through light and sound waves, and proportionately in regard to the other types of sensation. An outer galaxy may still be acting upon the eye of an astronomer through light waves that left it well over a million years ago. Just as in speaking into a telephone you are able to act upon the hearing of a person in faraway cities like Berlin or Buenos Aires, so in general distant things are able to bring a percipient into their forms through faraway efficient causality. They cause a physical effect, in exciting the organs and nerves. They also bring about a cognitional effect, in making you see, hear, smell or feel them. The physical effects are examined in physics and neurophysiology. The analysis in terms of form and subject and cognitional existence pertains to the philosophy of nature and to metaphysics. General acquaintance with the findings of those disciplines is accordingly necessary at even this introductory stage of the epistemological inquiry. The point they establish is that distance offers no obstacle to the cognition of a tree in front of your window, or to the cognition of an outer galaxy. The same thing can still be brought to exist in all its individuality within your awareness. It can exist there cognitionally in thoroughgoing identity with the percipient. The combined efficient causality of percipient and thing perceived has made the percipient be the individual thing not in the way physical causality makes matter be a third thing, but in a much closer union that that of matter with form. In it the form of the thing perceived becomes the form of the percipient in the actuality of cognition. From this viewpoint there is reception of form into form instead of form into matter. The result is that the one and the same form makes the sensible particular thing exist both in the real world and in the percipient. The adage that form is the cause of being extends to both kinds of existence. It makes the same individual thing exist both outside and within the percipient's awareness. There is no question of having to look for a "bridge" from the one to the other. The two are identical in the actuality of the cognition. For this it does not matter epistemologically whether the identity is brought about in the sense organ or in the brain or in the intermediary reciprocal nerve activity. All that is required is that the distant thing act efficiently upon the *percipient*, bringing the percipient into the object's own form.

Immaterial Reception. Although both in perception and in material production a form is received through the activity of an efficient cause, the manner of its reception is quite different in the two cases. From what has just been seen, reception of form as studied in the philosophy of nature meant the changing of some matter from one form to another. The result was the production of a third thing. In contrast, Aristotle had described perception as meaning the reception of form "without the matter."[17] This did not imply that either the matter of the percipient or the matter of the thing perceived was somehow eliminated. Both percipient and thing remained corporeal beings. The Greek commentators on Aristotle gradually came to explain the phrase as referring to the manner of reception.[18] It meant that in perception the form of the thing is received "immaterially," in the sense of a reception different in kind from that which modifies or changes matter. Here the form is received in a manner that avoids alteration of anything in the natures of either the recipient or the thing perceived. It brings each into a new cognitional existence in which they are one and the same, but without change in the natures of either.[19] It makes them exist not only together, but as one. It makes the one be the other cognitionally, with the percipient performing the act of cognition and alone having the awareness.

From this viewpoint, then, the reception of the form in

cognition is not material reception. Rather than being received *qua* cognitional into any matter, it is united with the form of the recipient in giving the one and the same cognitional existence to both percipient and thing in the actuality of the cognition. That is the way it may be regarded as a reception of form into form, in contrast to the reception of form into matter as known in the philosophy of nature. There is of course a concomitant material reception of the modifications taking place in sense organs, nerves and brain. There is also the production of images and concepts, which are accidental entities in the category of quality.[20] These all are means by which or in which the cognition takes place. They are produced through an internal activity with its form given by the distant cause that is acting efficiently upon the percipient. There is neither more nor less mystery here than in the pictures of the the Olympics in Europe that are at once brought into existence on the television screens in America. But the percipient, besides having the physical potentiality to receive the images in material fashion on the retina of his eyes, has also the cognitional potentiality to receive their forms immaterially and thereby to become what the retinal images represent. What the televiewer is aware of is the game being played in Europe. The game is what exists in his cognition.

Everywhere there is mystery in the imparting of existence, that is, in the bringing of something new into being. We can know *that* the existence is being given, but we do not know *what* existence is. We can know by a long process of reasoning in general metaphysics that existence is a nature in God, a nature infinite in every perfection. Because as a nature existence is infinite, it cannot be understood as a nature by a finite mind. So, while there is mystery for us in the imparting of cognitional existence, the mystery is no greater than in the imparting of real existence through generation or alteration. Philosophy completes its task in this regard by showing why the human mind cannot get inside the nature of existence and explain fully how existence is given. But it can relate effect to cause, and in this way show *that* the existence has been imparted by an efficient cause.[21] In the present case both the physical and the cognitional potentialities of the percipient are actuated concomitantly by the activity of the remote efficient cause, namely the game that is being played thousands of miles away. We know the facts. But our knowledge does not get inside the nature of the existence to see how the newly imparted being makes matter in procreation become human, or the percipient in cognition become the thing perceived.

The knowledge we have, however, is sufficient to show that the notion of immateriality in cognition arises from the way the form of a thing is received in perception. No change or alteration is caused in the thing by the cognitional reception. Both percipient and thing perceived remain material beings. They do not become immaterial themselves through the act of perceiving. The cow you see in the field remains a material object when it comes to exist immaterially in your cognition. There is no such thing as an immaterial cow, either outside or inside the mind. Its nature requires it to be material, and the perception of it does not change its nature. Nor do you yourself become an immaterial agent when you are reflexively aware of your own self in the act of perceiving the cow. The designation "immaterial" in regard to cognition arises from the way the form is received in perception. It does not require that either agent or object be without matter.

Nevertheless it is correct to say in Scholastic terminology that immateriality is the root of cognition, that the grades of cognition vary according to the degrees of immateriality, and that in this way the nature of cognition lies in immateriality.[22] Reception of form results in possession of form, and where the reception is immaterial the possession of it is correspondingly immaterial. If the immaterial possession of the form is what makes the agent cognitive, a form that exists in itself apart from matter will by that very fact be determined to know itself. But separate form does possess itself in that immaterial fashion. It possesses itself just as truly as a human percipient acquires the forms of other things. A separate form is therefore substantially the knowledge of itself. Aristotle could describe a separate substance as "a knowing of knowing."[23] A human soul is potentially the knowledge of itself, even though by its nature it requires material images in which to actualize that knowledge. An angelic form actualizes its knowledge of itself without the aid of such images. Finally, in God there is no passive potentiality whatever, and therefore no possibility of possessing a form materially, even in the potential way in which a creature is a subject for its own activity.[24] In this perspective the divine cognition is the highest degree of immateriality.

These are questions for general metaphysics rather than for epistemology. A glance at them, however, is necessary for understanding what immateriality means when used to describe cognition. It does not mean that a cognitive being is necessarily a spiritual agent, as the term "spiritual" is used today.[25] Lower animals can be cognitive, through sensation, without being spiritual. The application of the notion "immaterial" to their perceptive activity falls into focus only after the various grades of cognition have been surveyed, and after origin of the term's use in this regard has been traced to Aristotle's phraseology for describing the manner in which a cognitive form is received in perception. The immateriality of cognition refers basically to the way in which sensible forms are received in cognition, and from that fundamental instance the notion is extended to intellection and to our conception of the way cognition takes place in spiritual beings.

Epistemological Priority. The thoroughgoing union of percipient and thing perceived still leaves open the question whether either has any priority over the other in our awareness. This is an issue of utmost importance for epistemology. Both percipient and thing perceived are known simultaneously, since the one is the other in the cognitional actuality. By the same token both are known immediately, for they are attained in an existence in which the one is the other. But does either of them have a prior role epistemologically? The fact is that observable things other than our cognitive activities, things such as stones, trees, animals and human bodies, are directly present to our awareness while the cognitive activity and oneself as agent are perceived only reflexively in the awareness of something else. This would indicate a definite epistemological priority for those other objects. It is upon them that perception originally focuses.

As already seen, the nature of cognition as such does not require that its object be other than itself. In divine and angelic cognition there is direct self-awareness, quite as Aristotle gave his separate substances direct cognition of themselves in explicit contrast to the human manner of knowing. Further, the fact that human cognition is always of something else and only concomitantly of itself does not necessarily mean that the object directly known exists in a real world outside cognition. Phoenixes and banshees have never so existed, even though they are direct objects of imagination. The problem has to be examined, therefore, from the viewpoints both of the nature and of the existence of the objects directly present to our awareness.

As regards the nature of the objects we directly perceive or know, the answer is clear enough. All the things of which we have immediate and direct awareness are objects extended in length, breadth and thickness. They are sensible things. Even our direct perception of our own selves is that of a body seen and felt. Our bodies are here what we immediately and directly perceive. Search the immediate objects of our awareness as we will, we find only sensible things.[26] We may reason to inextended points, to spiritual souls or to immaterial substances, but we are not immediately aware of any of them. Every immediate object of our awareness, even oneself as immediately known, is sensible in its nature.

The natures of these sensible things directly known are obviously different from the cognitive nature of the percipient. Stones, trees and animals exhibit specifically different kinds of activity, thereby indicating different natures. Even one's own body, as perceived directly through sight and touch, is not directly known as cognitive. One's body is directly known only as extended in three dimensions and as solid and as living. As cognitive it is known only through reflexion upon its own cognitive activity. This is amply sufficient to show that non-human sensible things, besides manifesting their differences in specific type from each other, are also different in type from the cognitive nature of which one is conscious in reflexion.[27] Whether the sensible things are seen or felt like houses, or just imagined like unicorns, they are attained as objects different in nature from the cognitive activity of the percipient. This is too obvious to call for further amplification.

More crucial is the question of the existence exercised by those direct objects of our cognition. We know *what* they are through a simple apprehension that is expressed interiorly by a concept and exteriorly by a word, for instance cat or milk or saucer. By a complex intellectual act that may be called judgment we know *that* they exist and *that* they have this or that predicate. By judgment we know that the cat exists there in front of us, that it is black and that it is sipping the milk. The judgment is expressed interiorly by a proposition and exteriorly in a sentence. The object it precisely attains is the being of a thing, either in the sense that the thing exists or that it is what is predicated. It shows both that the cat exists and that it is black. While what a thing is is known through simple apprehension, either direct or reflexive, its being, whether real or cognitional, is known concomitantly through judgment. Being and nature are always concomitant in anything known or perceived, for without being of some kind the thing just would not be there to function as the object of a cognitive act. Correspondingly every simple apprehension of a nature is accompanied by a judgment of existence, whether real or cognitional.

Moreover, quite as in simple apprehension natures are recognized to be of different kinds, such as inanimate, plant, animal or human, each distinct from the other, so in judgment cognitional and real existence are seen to differ sharply from each other. Judgment distinguishes between the two kinds of existence just as clearly as simple apprehension does between saucer and cat. There can of course be illusions. These have to be examined carefully and explained through physics and neurophysiology and psychology, in order to discover how the mix-up occurred. In dreams and nightmares, things that do not exist at all externally may appear as vividly existing as things in the real world. But on the instant of awakening, when they are contrasted with what is seen as really existing, the great difference between the two kinds of existing becomes crystal clear. Cognitional existence, after all, is a genuine existence. When it alone is perceived, as in dreams, it appears frankly as existence, without distinction or contrast. When contrasted with real existence, however, the enormous cleavage between the two kinds is fully apparent.[28] The contrast can be made in the waking state, but not in sleep or in some states of intoxication.

The existence perceived through the external senses, such as sight, hearing, touch and so on, is always real. Imagination is aware of the cognitional existence of its constructs. Senses and imagination always attain nature and being in the one act. The intellect is not only aware of both, but is able to consider each as a separate object. In this way it can examine them and discuss them. A thorough examination of what our mind perceives and knows will then show that our whole cognition is based upon sensible things existent in themselves. The content of all things existent in our imagination will be found taken from what had already been perceived in really existent things. Wings and horse, for instance, already seen in the real world, are united in the imagination to form the object "Pegasus." This means that really existent sensible things are epistemologically prior to all else in our cognition. We perceive them directly. Only in function of them are we aware reflexively of our cognitive activity and of ourselves as cognitive. We are one and the same with them in the actuality of cognition, but the original focus is upon them, and not upon the cognition. They come first, from the viewpoint of what is known. All other perception or knowledge is in one way or another built upon them. From the viewpoint of efficient causality, our own action is required to bring about the cognition. In that respect our own nature and real activity, as well as the efficient causality of the sensible things upon our cognitive organs, are prior to the cognition. But from the standpoint of awareness as such the really existent sensible things are first. The epistemological priority is theirs.

From the epistemological viewpoint, then, we do not go through our own awareness to reach external sensible things. Rather, on account of their thoroughgoing union with us in cognitional being we are immediately aware of our own cognition, not directly, but reflexively. We do not infer that we know. Accordingly our cognition originates not in sensations or ideas, but in really existent sensible things, external things that we have become through the immaterial reception of their forms. Their forms make us the things themselves in cognitional existence, and in consequence really existent sensible things function as the basis of our cognition. Their real external existence is too basic in our cognition to admit, let alone require, proof. That is what is meant by the epistemological primacy of the external. It justifies philosophically our spontaneous and unshakable acceptance of the real world as something really external to our cognition.

Nature of Cognition. As should be apparent from the foregoing considerations, cognition means a new existence in which the natures of both the knower and the thing known remain unchanged. No third thing is brought into being through the cognition *qua* cognition. Cognition is explained in terms of existence, not of natures. Does this mean that cognition has no nature? Hardly, for an existence without a determining nature is subsistent existence, namely God. Consequently there is little hesitation in speaking of the nature of cognition.[29] Cognition, of course, is always specified by its object. Each of its acts is the cognition of a stone, a tree, a square root, or whatever else. But it is also specified by the agent. Cognition is human, brute, angelic, divine, according to the agent. These are different kinds of cognition. They are types of it that are distinct in nature. Further, cognition in the same agent can differ in kind. Sensation is different specifically from intellection. Sight, hearing, smell, taste, and so on, are different kinds of sensation. Simple apprehension, judgment and reasoning are different types of intellection. There are ample indications that cognition has somehow a nature of its own, even though unlike production it does not change the nature of the object upon which it bears. Nor, *qua* cognition, does it change the nature of the agent that is performing the act. The object remains a stone, the agent a man. They change only in existence.

What then is the nature of cognition? First of all, it is an activity. It belongs consequently to the category of action.[30] That is its basic nature. The substance from which the action flows will further specify it as human, brute or angelic. The formal aspect under which its object is attained gives it still more distinctive specification. If the aspect in the thing is color, the cognition is specified as sight. If it is sound, the cognition is hearing. If essence is the specifying object, the cognition is simple apprehension. If existence is the actuality attained, the cognition is judgment. All these designations refer to what the cognition is. It is sight, taste, judgment, and so on. Cognition quite definitely has a nature.

Unlike talking, walking, skiing, or house-building, however, cognition *qua* cognition does not consist in a process. *Qua* cognition it is something complete in its first instant.[31] In the first instant of the cognition the object is already perceived or known. In this respect the new cognitional existence is imparted instantaneously, comparable to the way new existence is brought about in substantial change. The change from hydrogen and oxygen to water is instantaneous. It is not like alteration, growth or locomotion, in which the process is gradual and continuous. When cognition is regarded as an action, then, it is not being categorized as a process by which a goal is gradually reached, as when a house is being built or a distant destination is being approached. In human cognition the accompanying physical changes in organs, nerves and brain are processes. But the cognition itself, *qua* cognition, is not. It is being rather than becoming. When in cognition the percipient is said to become and to be the thing perceived, the becoming can refer to the accompanying physical process or to the instantaneous change from a non-existence to an existence in the cognitional order. But as an actuality the cognition is complete in the first instant. It is not an imperfect actuality, as is motion. The cognition means the existence of the perceived thing in the percipient, rather than any process by which it comes to be there. Through the cognitive activity the agent has become and is the thing perceived or known, but the cognition *qua* cognition consists in the existence in which the one is the other in the immaterial fashion proper to awareness. It is an existence located in that activity.

With these considerations in mind, one may say that in nature cognition is an activity by which a percipient or knower is something else immaterially. The activity is further specified by the substance from which it proceeds, insofar as it is human, brute or angelic cognition, and by the aspects in its object that distinguish it as sight, hearing, imagination, memory, judgment and so on. It is a nature that falls into the category of action, action on the part of the knower. But the external thing has already acted efficiently upon the percipient, imparting its own form in the immaterial way in which the nature of the cognitive agent is not at all intruded into the thing perceived. From this viewpoint the percipient is entirely passive.

Things perceived and known can therefore be investigated by the other sciences and philosophical disciplines prior to and independently of any epistemological study of our cognitive activities. In fact, the natures of those things and their existence, whether real or cognitional, provide the criteria by which human cognition of them is to be judged. Here it is not a question of cognition trying to justify itself. Human cognition is never its own absolutely primary object. It is always of something else, and has to seek the knowledge of its own nature in what the "something else" makes manifest about it. Thus the external things, in what they are and in the ways they exist really and immaterially, present the basis upon which the aspects of reliability in our cognition are to be gauged. In general, nothing in the line of nature is added to the natures of things in their cognitional existence, nor are their natures changed in any way through this new existence. In the particular, mix-ups keep occurring in point of actual fact. It is in the things themselves that the explanations for both the general condition and the particular aberrations are to be sought. No circularity occurs.[32]

The complicated nature of human cognition, spread out as it is through sensation, imagination, simple apprehension, judgment and reasoning, shows possibility, for many vagaries. A detailed study of its content and structure is accordingly required. In its wide panorama of sensation and thought it offers a fascinating topic for inquiry, and at the same time promises a ready defense against charges that our cognition is somehow basically unreliable. The ensuing chapters will pursue an inquiry of this type.

Résumé. Spontaneously we are aware of an external world in which we live and work. But the reliability of this naturally unshakable acceptance of externally existing things has been challenged artificially by certain philosophical trends, with support from the frequent occurrence of factual errors and illusions. A close examination of the nature of our cognition, conducted with the help of findings from various sciences and philosophical disciplines, shows however that things existing in themselves outside our cognition have epistemological priority. We are one with them through the immaterial reception of their forms, which makes us be in immaterial fashion the external things as they are actuated by real existence. In this thoroughgoing cognitional union the external existents are the objects directly perceived and known. They are the basis upon which we become aware of all else, including ourselves and our cognition. Their external existence therefore neither admits nor requires proof, and as external existents they serve as the ground upon which all our philosophical conclusions rest, without exception and independently of epistemological guarantee.

For this reason the other sciences and philosophical disciplines are fully justified in proceeding directly with the investigation of whatever constitutes their object. Use of their findings for an epistemological inquiry is therefore completely legitimate. In a word, far from serving as the spacious atrium through which genuine philosophy is entered, epistemology is among the last sections to be reached in an orderly tour of the edifice. By its very nature it has to call upon much knowledge that has been attained in the sciences and in other philosophical disciplines. And by its nature as *human* cognition it shows why the myth of an obligatory direct bearing upon ideas, sensations, or sense data different from real existents, may today be exorcized from an acceptable philosophic procedure. Our cognition of external things, which we find naturally unshakable insofar as they

Notes to Chapter 2

1. Their attitude was reported as "We confess to human weaknesses; for we recognize that it is day and that we are alive, and many other apparent facts in life; but with regard to the things about which our opponents argue so positively, claiming to have definitely apprehended them, we suspend our judgment because they are not certain, and confine knowledge to our impressions." Diogenes Laertius, *Lives of Eminent Philosophers*, 9.103; trans. R. D. Hicks, II, 513-515. On Skepticism as a way of thinking, see Barry Stroud, *The Significance of Philosophical Skepticism* (Oxford, 1984). On the outstanding topics in the area, see the essays in *The Skeptical Tradition*, ed. Myles Burnyeat (Berkeley and Los Angeles, 1983).

2. "Although no one is not sufficiently convinced that materials things exist, nevertheless since this was called into doubt by us a short time ago, and numbered among the prejudices of our early age, it is now necessary that we investigate the reasons by which it may be known with certitude." Descartes, *Principia*, 2.1; AT VIII, 40.5-9 (IX^2, 63).

3. "For I ask anyone, Whether he be not invincibly conscious to himself of a different Perception, when he looks on the Sun by day, and thinks on it by night; when he actually tastes Wormwood, or smells a Rose, or only thinks on that Savour, or Odour?" Locke, *An Essay Concerning Human Understanding*, 4.2.14; ed. Peter H. Nidditch, 537.15-19. "For I think no body can, in earnest, be so sceptical, as to be uncertain of the Existence of those Things which he sees and feels. At least, he that can doubt so far, (whatever he may have with his own Thoughts) will never have any Controversie with me; since he can never be sure I say any thing contrary to his Opinion." Ibid., 4.11.3; 631.20-25.

4. Hume, *A Treatise of Human Nature*, 1.4.7; ed. Peter H. Nidditch (Oxford, 1978), 269.

5. On sensations as ideas, see "the ideas which we call sensations"--Etienne Bonot de Condillac, *An Essay on the Origin of Human Knowledge*, trans. Thomas Nugent (London, 1756; reprint,

New York, 1974), 19.

6. Aristotle, *Metaphysics*, 11.9.1074b34-35. Shortly before (11.6.1071b20-22), Aristotle had reasoned to forms without any matter. He then (1075a3-5) concluded that in things without matter the knowing is one with the thing known, in contrast to the kind of cognition of which we are conscious in ourselves. Cf. Aristotle, *De anima*, 3.6.430b24-26.

7. "It lies in the nature of all knowledge to be directed not towards itself but towards its object." Nicolai Hartmann, *New Ways of Ontology*, trans. Reinhard C. Kuhn (Chicago, 1953), 16. Cf. John E. Smith, "Hartmann's New Ontology," *Review of Metaphysics*, 7 (1954), 583-601.

8. On this topic, see Etienne Gilson, *Le réalisme méthodique* (Paris: 1936), 83; 87-90. There is a legitimate sense for the Parmenidean axiom that the object of thought coincides with what exists. Consequently one may say that "anything beyond thought is unthinkable because the object of thought is *everything which exists*"--Fernand Van Steenberghen, *Epistemology*, trans. Martin J. Flynn (New York, 1949), 187. The present point is that human thought cannot know itself except in terms of sensible things existent in themselves outside thought. It means that the human mind cannot have itself as the object of its thought except "in and through the thought of that which is other than itself"--Aimé Forest, *La structure metaphysique du concret selon saint Thomas d'Aquin* (Paris, 1931), 275.

9. Nicholas Malebranche, *Recherche de la vérite*, 3.2.1.1; ed. Geneviève Rodis-Lewis (Paris, 1963), I, 413-414. On the ambiguities here in "through themselves" (*par eux-mêmes*) and "presence," see Ralph Withington Church, *A Study in the Philosophy of Malebranche* (Port Washington, NY, reprint, 1970) 143-169. For English translation of the *Recherche*, see *The Search after Truth*, trans. Thomas M. Lennon and Paul J. Oldcamp (Columbus, OH, 1980).

10. Locke speaks in quite the same way as Malebranche regarding the location of the mind's first object in ideas: "For since the Things,

the Mind contemplates, are none of them, because it self, present to the Understanding, 'tis necessary that something else, as a Sign or Representation of the thing it considers, should be present to it; And these are *Ideas*." *Essay*, 4.21.4; ed. Nidditch, 720.29-721.3. But from the start he had regarded the basic ideas as received through sensation: ". . . those simple *Ideas*, which from Sensation or Reflection it hath received." *Essay*, 2.10.2; 149.21-22. For Condillac, see supra, n. 5.

11. The term "intentional" in the sense of "cognitional" goes back to the medieval Latin translations of Avicenna. In them *intentio* translated a frequently occurring Arabic word that means "Idea." If "intentional" is understood merely as denoting something that pertains to a concept or notion or sensation, there need not be any serious objection against it. But already in Aquinas (e.g., *Summa theologiae*, 1.79.10.ad 1m; 1-2.12.1c; *De veritate*, 21.3.ad 5m) it had taken on its etymological implications of "tending towards" its object. On this topic see H. D. Simonin, "La notion d'"intentio' dans l'oeuvre de S. Thomas d'Aquin," *Revue des sciences philosophiques et théologiques*, 19 (1930), 445-463. As known to modern philosophy through Brentano, Husserl and Sartre, intentionality explains cognition through tendency of notion towards object, retaining the Cartesian starting point in ideas.

12. Aristotle, *Metaph.*, 4.2.1003a33-b15; 5.7.1017a7-b9; 7.1.1028a10-31. On the explanation of the variations in meaning through "focal reference," see G. E. L. Owen, "Logic and Metaphysics in some Earlier Works of Aristotle," in "Aristotle and Plato in the Mid-Fourth Century," ed. Ingemar During and G. E. L. Owen (Göteborg: *Studia Graeca et Latina Gothogurgensia*, 1960), 163-190.

13. Aristotle, *De an.*, 3.8.431b21-28. Aristotle (b28-29) did not wish to speak of the thing being in the soul, because, in the Presocratic background that he had in mind (1.5.410a10-11), the reception of the thing would have been material. Instead he preferred to say that the form of the thing is in the mind, and serves as the instrument by which the cognition is brought about (3.8.432a1-3). In the Middle Ages, against the background of the distinctions between a thing and its existence, the thing could readily be said to

have existence in the mind, in contradistinction to its existence in reality. So, for Aquinas "cognition does not mean an outflow of the knower upon the thing known, but means rather the existence of the known thing in the knower" (*De ver.*, 2.5.ad 15m). On the theme that the cognitional union in existence is the greatest of all unions, see Joseph Gredt, "De unione omnium maxima inter subiectum cognoscens et obiectum cognitum," *Xenia thomistica*, ed Sadoc Szabó (Rome, 1925), I, 303-318. In the framework of this existential understanding of cognition the Aristotelian tenet that the soul is potentially all things finds expression in Aquinas as ". . . something is known by a knower insofar as the known is in some way in the knower. And in this way it is possible for the perfection of the whole universe to exist in one thing." *De ver.*, 2.2c. The explanation is through existence in the cognitive agent.

14. See Aristotle, *Metaph.*, 7.17.1041a10-b28; 8.2.1043a2-26.

15. A composite of matter and form, such as soul and the matter it informs, is referred to by Aquinas as "third"--*De an.*, 2.1.412a9. They are but the one existent (b6-9), yet in their union the parts remain really distinct from each other. In contrast, the cognitional union was described by Averroes, *In III De an.*, 5, 506-508; ed. F. Stuart Crawford (Cambridge, Mass., 1953), 404, in terms of two things joined together without constituting a third: "quod enim componitur ex eis non est aliquod tertium aliud ab eis sicut est de aliis compositis ex materia et forma." The notion does not seem to have been exploited by Averroes, who was speaking of intellection only, nor by Aquinas, though it was taken up by Cajetan and became incorporated into Thomistic tradition.

16. Augustine used the metaphor of engendering to describe this twofold causality: "For knowledge is born from both, from the one who knows and the object that is known." *De trinitate*, 9.12.18; ed. W. J. Mountain (Turnhout, 1968) 309-30-31. Trans. Stephen McKenna.

17. Aristotle, *De an.*, 2.12.424a17-b16. In contrast, Aristotle (a32-b3) describes plants as receiving the forms of heat and cold "with the matter." They are warmed or cooled, but do not feel heat or cold.

18. For the texts, see Alexander of Aphrodisias, *De anima*, 60.3-62.4; Themistius, *De an.*, 77.34-78.10; Philoponus, *De an.*, 437.30-438.13; Simplicius, *De an.*, 166.3-34; Sophonias, *De an.*, 102.20-104.13.

19. If being known made any change in the nature of the thing known, there would be no way of finding out what that nature in the thing itself exactly is. This would mean "you cannot ever get your product standing apart from its process"--Francis H. Bradley, *Appearance and Reality*, 9th impr. (Oxford, 1930), 23. Against that stand, cf.: "I could no longer believe that knowing makes any difference to what is known:--Bertrand Russell, in *Contemporary British Philosophy*, ed. J. H. Miurhead (London & New York, 1924), I, 360. The notion was expressed by Aquinas in saying that cognition does not mean an outflow of the knower upon the thing known. See text supra, n. 13.

20. In late Scholasticism the images and concepts were known as *species expressae*. See John of St. Thomas, *Ars Logica*, 2.22.2; ed. B. Reiser (Turin, 1930), I, 702a44-b18. In contrast, the term *species impressa* was used for the form received through the action of the sensible thing or of the agent intellect. Cf. infra, c. 4, n. 18.

21. This reasoning is based upon the accidental and prior status of the existence we immediately know in things, in relation to their essence. The problematic is discussed in my article "The Causal Proposition: Principle or Conclusion? *The Modern Schoolman*, 32 (1954-1955), 159-171; 257-270; 323-339. On Hume's attitude, see ibid., 171, n. 35.

22. See Aquinas, *De ver.*, 2.2c. "Immateriality," in this meaning, is not restricted to purely spiritual things, since it applies to the cognition of the senses. The application of it to cognition is based upon the way form is received in cognition, a way different from the physical modification of matter, and meaning reception of form into form. On the medieval use of "spiritual being" in sensation, see infra, n. 25.

23. Aristotle, *Metaph.*, 12.9.1074b34-35. Cf. supra, n. 6.

24. See Aquinas, *De ver.*, 2.2c. All other things have their primary existence in the divine intellect (Aquinas, *Quodlibeta*, 8.1c). Accordingly no new action or any reception of a form is required for the divine cognition of other things.

25. The application of the Latin phrase *esse spirituale* to sense and sense medium was already established in Albertus Magnus. See Lawrence Dewan, "St. Albert, the Sensibles, and Spiritual Being," in *Albertus Magnus, Commemorative Essays 1980*, ed. James A. Weisheipl (Toronto, 1980), 291-320. In Albert's *De anima*, "the source of spiritual being, in general, is identified as form *qua* form" (319). This concept of "spiritual" fits neatly enough into the notion of immaterial reception as the reception of form by form. On its use in Averroes, see Dewan, 319, n. 55. It is employed without hesitation by Aquinas, e.g. "color habet duplex esse, unum naturale in re sensibli, aliud spirituale in sensu"--*Sentencia libri De an.*, 2.26.100-101; ed. Leonine, XLV[1], 179a (Aristotle, 425b22).

26. It was claimed by Descartes (*Discours*, 4.34: AT VI, 37.9-14; 561) that the ideas of God and the soul have never been in the senses, and that therefore the senses cannot be the origin of all our intellectual knowledge. This claim cannot stand up against careful scrutiny. Close examination shows that our idea of a spiritual soul is that of the substantial form taken from material things with the denial of essential dependence upon matter for operation and existence, while our idea of God is formed from the notion of being that is taken from sensible things, but with the denial of any dependent or accidental character. See survey, infra, chapter 3, nn. 26-29.

27. The essential natures of material things become known to us through their attributes, as Aristotle (*De an.*, 1.1.402b16-403a2) pointed out. Likewise: "Even in the case of sensible things we do not know their essential differences; we indicate them through the accidental differences that flow from their essential differences, as we refer to a cause through its effect. In this way 'biped' is given as the difference of man." Aquinas, *De ente*, 5.76-81; trans. Maurer (1968), 63. Similarly Locke (*Essay*, 3.3.18; ed. Nidditch, 418-419) showed that the real essences of material things remain unknown to

us. Nevertheless the natures are sufficiently indicated in their attributes and activities to allow definite distinction of one from the other, for instance water from gold.

28. Locke (see supra, n. 3) characterized the perception of this difference as invincible. Wilder Penfield, *The Mystery of the Mind* (Princeton, NJ, 1975), 55-56, noted how there is no confusion in a patient between an artificially stimulated "flashback" from the past and what is known in his contemporary consciousness, even though both streams are simultaneously present to him. The patient realizes that the events in the "flashback" had their real existence in the past. On "flashbacks" see ibid, 21-27. Vividness, however, cannot be advanced as the criterion for distinguishing real from cognitional existence, for nightmares can be most vivid.

29. E.g., "in eis natura cognitionis invenitur"--Aquinas, *De ver.*, 2.2.165; ed. Leonine, XXII, 44. On the specification of acts and faculties by their objects, see Aristotle, *De an.*, 2.4.415a14.22.

30. On action as a category, see Aristotle, *Categories*, 9.11b1-7. The *Summa totius logicae*, a treatise falsely attributed to Aquinas, denied (6.2; in *S. Thomas Opusc. Om.*, ed. P. Mandonnet [Paris, 1927], V, 55) that immanent action is directly in the category of the action; in later Thomistic tradition immanent action such as cognition came to be placed in the category of quality. There is no ground for this in Aquinas himself. As far as the present point is concerned, the fact that cognition is placed in a category, whether action or quality, is sufficient to show that it has a nature.

31. See supra, c. 1, n. 3. There is no process that could change the nature of the object, as noted above, n. 19.

32. The comment of Gilson, *The Unity of Philosophical Experience* (New York, 1937) ". . . it became apparent that, like Caesar's wife, the existence of the world should be above suspicion," is accordingly not to be understood as opposed to philosophical explanation of the way external things get into human cognition. The epistemological priority of the external things has first to be established, and then the causality that brings them into existence

CHAPTER 3

Cognitional Content

Descriptive Survey. As the preceding chapter has shown, human cognition bears directly upon things other than itself. It makes us directly aware of things really existent in themselves and not merely in our cognition. Prominent are things extended in the three dimensions of length, breadth and thickness, things like sticks and stones and plants and animals and human beings. These are seen or touched or otherwise attained in sensation. They may therefore be readily termed sensible objects. But we can also think about objects that are other than directly observed sensible things, for instance about the square root of two, about two-dimensional surfaces and six-dimensional products, or about the spiritual soul, God, angels, freedom. Are we aware of any of these objects immediately in themselves? Or do we derive all these other notions from concrete sensible things? The general panorama of the mind's cognitional content needs to be surveyed descriptively to determine whether or not it offers any source other than sensation for our knowledge of these non-sensible objects.

If the results of the inquiry show that sensible things offer the means for reasoning to these further objects, and that all we actually know can be accounted for through what is grasped in sense perception, obviously no other source will be required to explain our natural knowledge. But to establish that tenet, the manifold variety in the objects of sense perception needs to be carefully examined, in order to see what the various facets of those objects are, and how these facets are related to one another in ways that ground knowledge of things beyond themselves. This is a task for epistemological reflexion on the mind's own content. It does not at all mean that the epistemological procedure is even for a moment being cut off from its basis in external sensible things. It is not setting up any new or alternative starting point. The sensible things have their real existence in themselves outside the mind. They remain the same things in the cognitional existence they acquire in one's perception. But what they are, is seen first in real existence. Awareness of their content stays based on that original real status. This means that *what* they are in reality can continue to be examined in the content of our cognition. Further, since percipient and things perceived are identical in the actuality of the cognition, the percipient *qua* percipient as well as the cognition itself will be amenable to description in terms of what they are thus grasping as objects. A survey of our sensations and imaginings and thoughts from this viewpoint of their content should show how the internal world of our cognition is built up, how its different features are distinguished from one another, how these can lead to things beyond the sensible realm, and how errors can creep in during the process of going from one aspect to others.

When you turn your reflexive gaze upon your own cognition, then, of what are you globally aware? Are you not aware of yourself and your own cognitive activity, and of a present world in which you are actually living? Do you not find spread out before your reflexive gaze a complicated series of events and situations that stretch back through at least nearly two decades of family, school, and social life? Does not this awareness involve an accumulated store of knowledge and skills gained through years of study in the humanities and sciences, and of training in arts and crafts? Is it not also accompanied by aspirations and hopes and plans that extend into the future?

You can go over all these items in detail. As in any other scientific matter, you will wish to know what is primitive and what is derivative. In learning to spell you had to become acquainted with the alphabet out of which the words are formed. In geometry you first studied the lines and figures on which the rest of the science is built. In logic you acquired the basic principles of the system you are following. So, in investigating your own cognition, may you not in like fashion commence by sorting out what is basic and elementary, and then examine how the rest of the structure is erected upon these foundations?[1]

The global descriptive survey of all that appears when one reflects on the totality of one's awareness may be called a phenomenology of cognition.[2] Like "epistemology," the word "phenomenology" is of Greek derivation. It means an account or study of the *phainomena*, that is, of whatever may happen to appear. Expressed in this way in the plural, the phenomena will include the details and outlines observed when one sets one's gaze deliberately on some field of investigation. The term signifies a descriptive report on the whole panorama.

In sorting out what is basic, however, one's spontaneous and habituated interpretations of the panorama will have to be carefully isolated and incisively examined. From this viewpoint even the phenomenology will include a preliminary critique of the way the details in the panorama actually appear, in contrast to the ways in which they come to be interpreted. In this manner what is truly basic will be critically distinguished from added interpretation. The spontaneous interpretation will then appear as a further phenomenon that presents itself to one's reflexive gaze. For instance, what is actually being seen may be only the shiny asphalt road ahead. But at the moment it may be spontaneously interpreted as a pool of water. Interpretation can add to what is being sensed. In this case it adds the perception of water that in fact is not being seen. The immediate interpretation of what we see or hear, then, is an added phenomenon that calls for examination. It can add something extra to what is actually being seen, felt or heard.

Perception. Will any one type of cognition straightway appear basic? Even at first glance does not the awareness of objects like tables, chairs, beds, houses, food, marbles, trees, animals and people seem somehow to have that role? Objects like these were the earliest encountered in childhood, if you can trust your memories. They were the first kind with which you dealt in everyday life. They were what you counted and measured in learning mathematics. They are the things that were catalogued, described, or experimented with as you began the natural sciences. Objects like stones and fossils are what yield the record of prehistoric days to the geologist and the paleontologist. Visible and audible instruments are the means for acquiring knowledge of the interior of the atom or of the outer expanse of galaxies and radio stars. Newspapers, books, tapes, and radio and television sets, are required in order to communicate and store the extensive, always increasing information. Tangible computers have to be used for its modern processing. In every case, at least at first sight, objects like these appear basic for any other type of cognition. Without them, no other type seems even viable. Without them, in fact, nothing else comes into view in the panorama that presents itself to one's reflexive gaze. Even the more sophisticated notions of distinct objects for the separate senses, such as a "color patch" for sight, or a "prement patch" for touch, are presented, as the metaphor "patch" shows, in terms of a fully rounded out object like those just listed. The color is always presented as the color of some thing, even though the thing be only a patch. In all these cases, *things* colored or tangible or otherwise grasped through sensation appear to be basic in our cognition.

If the term "sensation" may for the moment be reserved for the type of cognition by which you originally become aware of the things just noted, in contradistinction from imagining them or remembering them, it will serve as a convenient and acceptable designation for the kind of awareness that at first sight seems to be basic. You know from psychology what sight and hearing and touch and the other senses are. The prima facie indications that the type of cognition they give is truly basic, will of course need careful critique. But the initial step, understandably enough, has to be an overall descriptive account of the way sensation functions in making us aware of the things on which it bears.

Since cognitive acts are specified by their objects, so by

things other than themselves, the description has to be given in terms of what the actions formally bear upon. Once the primitive objects have been isolated and examined and tabulated in the appropriate order, epistemological explanations can be sought and conclusions drawn. Only after that is one able to give a satisfactory answer to the question of what human perception itself is. A sufficiently extensive and clearsighted phenomenology of what is basic in the percepts[3] is a preliminary requisite for the desired epistemological understanding.

The Percept. How do you go about the phenomenology? To it you bring your some twenty years or more of conscious life. Drawing upon your training as an investigator in other fields, then, what outlines can you discern in the global content of your awareness?

First, you look for describable characteristics. Upon close examination, do you not find that the things just listed as instances of what is perceived are all spatially extended in length, breadth and thickness? Moreover, does not each have at least one further characteristic like color, temperature, hardness, sound, odor or taste? For convenience, anything that exhibits three-dimensional size and at least one qualitative trait of the kind just mentioned may well be called an object of sensation. The three-dimensional size or quality is common to them all. Every sensible quality, such as color or hardness, is found spread out in both space and time. That quantitative aspect goes with each of them. But what allows them to be grasped by the different special senses is a qualitative aspect such as temperature, sound, odor, taste, and the like. An immediately noticeable feature in perceiving objects is in consequence their sensible character. If the term "percept" may be used technically in the epistemological setting to denote any object of perception, it will always refer to something that has been attained in virtue of at least one sensible quality. It may be "enriched" or "transformed" by additions from past experience or memories. But these additions will be found to come from previous acts of sensing. You claim to be "seeing" your neighbor Jones dozing on his veranda across the street, when all you are strictly seeing are the figure and colors and posture of a body. The rest you add from previous experience. It all belongs to the percept at the moment. But only color, size, shape and disposition of parts are literally "seen." The name, the distance, the neighborly relations are all added.

How, then, is sensing to be described? Epistemologically an account is required in terms of the object grasped. From this viewpoint sensing is the cognition of something extended under one quality of the kind listed above. The percipient becomes and is cognitionally the thing characterized at the moment by that quality. You see something colored, you feel something hard. But is the percept ever of something just colored and nothing else? Is it not always of a stick or a stone or a plant or an animal that is characterized by numerous other features and determinations? It is of something definitely located in a space and with a name or designation familiar to the percipient. All those aspects and precisions go together in the spatially extended things that are the objects of our perception. They are all present in the percept. But the sensible qualities, primary and secondary, are the original aspects under which the whole is grasped. The quantity is common, the quality is particular.

Examining the content of our cognition, then, we do not find anything in it that is perceived just as something colored. Rather, it is perceived as colored along with numerous other aspects and determinations that make up the whole picture of the stone, the plant, the animal or the person. In that perspective it is convenient to distinguish sensation from perception on the ground that any sensation attains the object under one specific sensible quality, such as color or heat. The rest of the perception is added from memory or customary experience, or is being simultaneously grasped through another sense. In practice the vocabulary here is flexible, with "sensation" and "perception" quite commonly used interchangeably. Yet for close epistemological scrutiny some verbal means has to be used to distinguish what a particular sense attains from what is globally perceived. The percept is never in practice a unitarily simple object.

In this way specification in terms of the objects precisely attained enables perception to be distinguished partially from the less general activity of sensation, while the necessary relation between the two is safeguarded. It also establishes an independent and characteristic starting point for the philosophical treatment in epistemology, different from the mere acceptation of the commonly recognized division of the five senses and the further findings of experimental psychology. It thereby grounds an epistemological probe into the credentials of the percept as basic among the objects of human awareness.

Origin of Knowledge. If the percept's entire content comes originally through sensation, the provenance of all human cognition from sensible things will be indicated. Is the content of universally applied notions, such as "man" and "animal," merely the content of the individuals so grouped? Do the universals, and the mathematical roots and powers, and our conceptions of supersensible beings such as God and angels, require any other source?

If you thoroughly scrutinize the content of your awareness you will most likely find no other origin for them, in the relevant sense of an objective origin. Notions like "man" or "animal" seem clearly to originate in sensible objects, as do the most intricate mathematical and scientific formulae. Do you not find, moreover, that you have to represent any non-sensible thing in a sensible image? Try to focus on an angel or a spiritual soul, or on Aristotelian primary matter or substantial form. In every case you will find you are representing the object as something sensible, no matter how much you deny that any of these four items is in itself a sensible object. Does not this suggest, in preliminary fashion, that as objects of human cognition they are all derived in some way from sensible awareness? At least two notable philosophic traditions, empiricism and Aristotelianism, have been throughout the centuries insistent that all human cognition begins on the sensible level, and they have cogently stated the arguments for this stand.[4] Your own experience will in all probability coincide with their finding. Unless it manages to discover contrary evidence, it should allow you to proceed without much trouble to the conclusion that the sensible order provides the only objective origin of human cognition.

True, some outstanding thinkers have claimed a different origin for knowledge of common characteristics and a priori principles, and of the human soul and of God.[5] Others have advanced various theories of extrasensory perception.[6] Others have reported the attainment of incommunicable knowledge through mystical experiences.

As far as the cognition of all these witnesses has been communicated, however, it does not seem to differ from the kind based on sensation. As given in the reports, its content can be explained satisfactorily in terms of cognition derived from sensible experience. Where it claims to have something that cannot be grasped by anybody thinking in sensible images, it would seem to be restricting drastically its public character. Without commonly shared sensible representations it would be an incommunicable type of cognition. It would not allow for ordinary scientific treatment and consideration. This kind of cognition would not come under the object of a science. Accordingly it will not be a concern of epistemology. What you can do in your own case, against this varied background, is to examine carefully your own cognition and see if it contains any kind that is not based upon sensation. In view of centuries of investigation and experience in the two above-mentioned philosophic traditions, the presumption is that the answer will turn out to be entirely negative.

If you do find that in fact all your cognition appears to originate in sensible things, you still encounter a further question. How can a sensible quality be regarded as something ultimate? Is it really something simple in itself, after the fashion of logical atomism? Our percept, for instance of a table or a chair or a mat or a cat, is always of something complex, something able to be "enriched" or "transformed" by what is attained through other sensations. But does not the object of each sensation show a corresponding complexity? Is the immediate object of any of the basic sensations ever an entirely simple object? Does not the most finely honed object of a sensation present itself as something that has color or heat or hardness? Is there not a duality here, with the thing somehow different from what it has? In a word, is there ever a sensible object that is just a color or a sound or an odor?

Substance. That question, because so basic, is crucial for epistemology. What, then, is exactly the object of a sensation? In the perspective of experimental psychology, you learn that what is immediately attained in one's sensation lies in the end product of the interaction between stimulus and sensory apparatus.[7]   That process is very complicated and is   still not   too   well   understood   psychologically   and neurophysiologically. But whatever the sensed object seems to be from those viewpoints, must it not obviously be regarded as "something"? It is something of which you are aware through the sensation. No matter how jejunely you may describe it as a color patch or a prement patch, it is undoubtedly something. Try as hard as you wish to shake that estimate of it as "something." You will find that you do not succeed. As long as you are seeing or hearing or touching, you find that you are seeing or hearing or touching "something." The aspect of "something" is found necessarily involved in it. The object of any sensation, no matter how closely it is pared down, always appears as something.

What does the notion "something" involve? It seems to be the most obvious and widest notion possible. Yet it is too vague to be satisfying. It prompts the further inquiry about *what* this "something" is. That query is answered by finding that the "something" is gold or silver or a tree or an animal or a human being, and so on. You can ask further how large it is, how bright it is, where it is, how it is related to other things, and similar questions. But these subsequent queries presume that you are regarding it as something already there in its own right in order to be capable of possessing the further characteristics.

A traditional vocabulary that goes back to Aristotle (*Categories*, 2-9.1a20-11b14) is at hand to designate the two different types of answer. When you say that something is a metal or a plant or an animal, you are stating what its substance is. When you answer the other questions, you are giving its accidents. But the notion of accident is never independent of the notion of substance. Aristotle (*Metaphysics*, 7.1.1028a25-29) pointed out incisively that the notion of substance always appears in the definition of an accident. The accident is the size or the color or some other characteristic *of the substance* in which it inheres. The substance is in this way the primary answer to the question what the thing is, while the accidents are secondary instances of the answer in focal reference to the primary instance. Aristotle spelled this out in detail in the same chapter of the *Metaphysics* (b1-2) by showing that the questions regarding the thing's accidents are questions about what the thing is in secondary ways, *what* its size is or *what* its qualities are. The accidents all involve substance focally, and have to be represented in terms of that substantial feature when they are made the subject of a question. They cannot even be thought of alone, or understood as something there just in themselves. What is primarily there, no matter what the accident may be, is the substance. A "something" always has a substance as its basis.

In regard to the problem at present under consideration, this will mean that what is sensed is never just a color, a sound, or a surface. The sensation is always of the thing that is colored, sounding, or extended. Ordinary speech is correct in the phrasing that we see the stones, the flowers, the animals. Strictly speaking we do not see the color, but rather the colored thing. It is a cloth patch that we see, and not at all a color just in itself. The other mode of speech, current from the times of Locke and Hume, in which substance has been dispensed with the qualities represented as there in themselves, is merely an attempt to turn all the accidents into substances. The ultimate result was Hume's phenomenalism that left the objects of our cognition without any rationally knowable causal connection with one another.[8] It means a logical atomism in which both substances and accidents have equal status as terms.[9] It is in solidarity with Descartes' clear and distinct ideas in which the content of each idea is precisely cut off from the content of the others. In fact, it may be shown that to his own contemporaries Descartes could quite readily be viewed as an atomist.[10] The inherent order of the objects of our cognition to one another through Aristotelian focal reference, and the intrinsic involvement of one notion in another as with the notion of substance is that of accident, was entirely set aside.

There is not question, then, of first sensing colors and sounds and surfaces, the reasoning from them to a substance beneath them. The substance itself is primarily grasped in the initial act of awareness. What you primarily sense is a corporeal substance, namely a body, that has the appropriate qualities for being sensed. These bodies sensed in the real world are all individual things. They are really apart from each other. Yet they exhibit order not only in regard to their accidents but also in regard to one another within their own category of substance. They are not individuals in the rout of a Humean flux, even though it may require a bit of thought to perceive the order. Aristotle (*Post. Analytics*, 2.19.100a3-b3) in fact uses the rout simile to show how with the aid of memory and experience the individuals are gradually lined up to make an ordered soldierly stand, and the the process is continued till the highest universals are reached. In the later Porphyrian tree this process was represented in explicit fashion in the grouping of all individual human beings together in the one specific notion of mankind, then extending this further to all sentient beings under the common aspect of animals, then still further to the even more generic aspects of living things and bodies. Along with the accidents these substances were all brought through focal meaning under the one supreme classification as beings.

In this way the whole content of one's cognitional panorama manifests profound unity and order, in spite of the fact that everything in the real world is individual. Again unity is obtained at the expense of clear and distinct ideas, for the specific and generic objects contain indistinctly everything that is under them. Nothing in their content goes outside the sensible realm, however, for the content that is grasped indistinctly in the universal is the same content that is perceived distinctly in the individual.

So far we have been considering only two of the accidents in sensible things, namely quantity and quality. But to realize how complex the inborn constitution of the things originally perceived is, a quick look at the other accidents is necessary. It will serve as a prophylactic against the tendency to seek absolutely simple objects that would function as building blocks for the structure of our cognition. In fact, the primitive objects are highly concrete. Anything sensible, for instance, has parts that are nearer or further or equidistant from one another. In qualities it may exhibit degrees as warmer or colder, harder or softer, louder or fainter. In these and many other ways the accidental feature of relation is manifest.[11] Sensation does not articulate the relations. It does not present them as distinct objects, but only as they are globally involved in the object as a whole. Insofar as it attains them, the object appears larger or smaller, warmer or colder, than others with which it is associated at the moment. Many of these relations have real influence. Through relations of distance that emerge from their extended nature, the objects confronting our vision appear located in a definite place. That place is called where they are. Since they are observed to be in motion, with its successive parts, and as beginning to exist and ceasing to exist, they are interpreted as present in a definite time. That is called when they exist.[12] Further, what is cognized as a unified individual thing may be observed with different dispositions of its parts, as when a man sits or kneels or stands. Any of these dispositions may be called a posture. As a category, posture in human beings, and disposition of parts in non-human things, is an elaboration of the category *where* the various parts of the same things are, namely where the parts are when viewed in relation to one another. Likewise, in subsequent elaboration, things are cognized as in a certain state, on account of special relations with surrounding objects or persons. There is the state of being clothed or armed, married or unemployed. Also you are aware of yourself as acting when you do something, and as undergoing the discomfort inflicted upon you by inclement weather or by the actions of others. One could keep on with more intricate elaborations and combinations of these basic objects of awareness, thereby adding to the list. For practical purposes, however, these traditionally acknowledged Aristotelian categories seem amply sufficient from the epistemological viewpoint. The designations "substance" and "accidents," though avoided by many current writers, are difficult to replace satisfactorily. But they are recognized as currently acceptable English terms.[13] There need be little hesitation, therefore, in making use of them.

Further, motion and change are apparent in the objects of perception. Change in the category of substance occurs when water becomes hydrogen and oxygen, or when a living thing is engendered or dies. Change in the category *where* is observed as a thing moves from one place to another. Change in the category of quantity is seen as things grow or increase or diminish in size, and in the category of quality as they become warmer or cooler, softer or harder, or undergo other kinds of alteration. Again, changes and movements do not present themselves to sensation as things in themselves, but as occurrences in other things. The complexity of the apparently unitary sensible things that constitute the basis of all we observe, namely of things like metals or plants or animals, is thereby emphasized still more strongly. However, though their status is clearly accidental, the changes were not classed as a special category in the tradition of Aristotelian logic. They were called "postpredicaments," in the sense that they had been treated in Aristotle's *Categories* (14.15a13-b17; cf. 10.11b15-16) *after* the ten supreme genera, and were found in more than one of them, including substance.

Things. But does the distinction of categories into substance and accidents add any significant precision to the commonly used designation "thing"? "Thing" is meant to indicate in the widest possible way what an object is. It is a notion that has been used all along for any object of our awareness. With the categories the answer to the question what something is, is spread throughout them all, but always in focal meaning, with substance as the primary instance. You ask what a tree is. The widest definite answer is that it is a substance. You ask what "red" is. The widest generic answer is that it is a quality. You ask what motherhood is. The corresponding answer is that it is a relation. In this way the distinction into categories adds a very significant precision to the answer given the question "what." Their use marks out the notably different ways in which an object of cognition can be a thing.

Yet the notion "thing" does not function as a higher generic aspect over and above all the categories in a univocal manner. It is a notion that is found in its full innate meaning in substance only. That is why substance is its primary instance. In all other instances it is present through focal reference to substance. Its unity as a single notion is that of focal meaning.[14] How this situation comes about may be seen perhaps at its best in the way the notion "thing" is usually understood in common parlance. The perceived world is usually regarded as a multitude of things each distinct from the others. If you are asked to identify some of those things, you would have no hesitation in pointing out individual stones or plants or trees. You would call each of them a thing without the least hesitation. The individual tree is surely a thing that is planted, that grows, that is round and colored, and that occupies a definite place in a definite time. That is the way it is with all individual substances. Each is a thing in the full sense of the term. Each presents the complete meaning that the term is intended to convey.

But you can say the same of each of its accidents? You do not feel some hesitation in saying that the tree's nearness to the fence is a thing? Would you say at once that its size is a thing, or that its color or flexibility is a thing, or that its destruction when it is being cut down is a thing? Would you call its growth a thing? There is certainly no lack of individuality in each of these accidents. Each is individuated insofar as it pertains to one individual substance only. Each is individually distinct from the corresponding accidents in other trees. Each substance appears as having its own size, space, coloring, place and duration. Yet in spite of this evident individuality you tend to recoil at naming any of these accidents a thing, unless you are willing to add further qualification. Individuality alone is not enough to set the accident straightway up as a thing in the common use of the notion. The accident is rather the color of the thing, the size of the thing, the relation the thing has to its surroundings. There would seem to be but the one thing there, namely the silver, the tree, or the animal. When you say that somebody's laziness is a bad thing, you feel that you are merely using a roundabout way for saying that it is bad for that person to be lazy. Correspondingly, when you call a color or a taste or an odor a thing, you might like to explain to yourself that the thing thereby involved is really the substance that has the color or taste or odor.

"Thing," then, taken in its ordinarily accepted meaning, would seem to find its complete sense in the individual substance only. There appears to be hardly any doubt that the notion in its full meaning is to be looked for in the individual substance. At least that seems to be implied in one's hesitation at using the term for accidents, without appropriate clarification. But what this does establish solidly is that there need be no hesitation whatever in calling individual substances "things" in answer to the query about *what* they are in the widest possible sense.

Does this mean, though, that an accident is really not a thing? Surely each of the accidents seems to be something, and to this extent a "thing." The color is obviously something, the size is something, the growth of the tree is something, and so on. Yet none of these is something just in itself. It is in each case a modification of something else. May it be called "a thing," even though it is not a thing in itself? Can a modification of something else be legitimately regarded as a thing?

One may well hesitate to give an exclusive type of answer. An accident is not just nothing. It is something. From that viewpoint, it seems to have a right to the title of thing. Yet because the notion of a thing, without qualification, seems to be understood ordinarily as something in itself like a cat or a mat, the term fits rather awkwardly. The accident does not appear that way. Running or kneeling or squareness or paternity would hardly be given as obvious instances of "things." Nevertheless you say that jogging is a good thing, marriage is a good thing. Accidents are in fact, though in weaker ways, called things.

"Thing," accordingly, expresses a feature that appears in a gradation of meanings. Basically and without further qualification it means something there in itself. It signifies first and foremost a substance. But each accident, implying as it does the substance of which it is a modification, may be regarded as a thing in a secondary way. A color, a quantity, an action may in this sense be regarded as a thing. With relation, time, and place, the claim becomes more tenuous. Yet in implying a substance, each is something, a thing. "Thing" has therefore different but related senses, all of which bear ultimately on substance in one way or another. This phenomenon of a notion remaining the same notion while varying in meaning is a phenomenon that runs through a surprising number of our important philosophical concepts. It was highlighted by Aristotle, and has to be kept constantly in mind when dealing with metaphysical and ethical topics.[15]

Natures, Essences. Closer inquiry into *what* things are is made in terms of their nature or essence.[16] Continuing to express what the thing is, the successively narrowing generic natures descend to that of the ultimate species. In the category of substance, for instance, the individual man Socrates is a body, a living thing, an animal and finally a man, as one comes down the Porphyrian tree. Corresponding descent can be made in the other categories. In consequence both the substantial and the accidental natures in a thing answer in increasingly sharper outlines the question what a thing is, in accord with the focal grading to which the notion of "what" is subject.

There is crucial difference, however, in the cognitional penetration allowed by the various natures in a thing. In the category of quantity the nature can be discerned in terms of its ultimate constitution. The nature of the number five is to consist of five units, the nature of a triangle is to be of three sides on a plane surface. Artifacts such as automobiles, and moral entities such as acts of bravery or justice, are constituted by human endeavor and are known from the inside by the human mind. Accidental combinations and occurrences, such as an oil spill or an avalanche, can be explained in terms of their components. But natural substances are not open to corresponding penetration in their own proper category. You cannot know from the inside what constitutes the specific nature of a dog or a cat or a lion, or of silver or gold or oxygen.[17] For scientific inquiry into their constitution you have to proceed from their accidents, and explain these and the substance itself in the quantitative terms of measurements and pointer readings. In this way in the natural and life sciences the things are catalogued and explained materially as composites, in common, of molecules, atoms, and fundamental particles. Formally, each is explained through its chemical constitution, and in living things through the deoxyribonucleic acids (DNA), in which they are differentiated specifically from one another. Somewhat correspondingly in natural philosophy generic explanation of bodies and change is given in terms of matter as the common element and form as the differentiating factor. But this type of explanation does not descend to the specific level. As John Locke pointed out trenchantly, we do not know the real essences of natural things, though we do have that kind of knowledge in regard to the ideas with which mathematics and moral philosophy deal.[18]

The two terms "nature" and "essence" denote the same object. The only nuance is that "nature" tends to refer to it as the principle of activity and distinction, while "essence" is meant to relate it to existence.

Existence. Thing, nature and essence all answer the question what an object is. But the most thorough search of what the things immediately confronting our cognition are, will not tell us whether they exist or not. We can know what the Loch Ness monster is without knowing whether or not it exists in reality. To know that it exists we have to look and see, or else reason to its existence in order to account for things we do see existing. But no amount of reasoning from *what* anything is will tell us *that* it exists. We have to see it directly existing in reality, or be aware of it reflexively as existing in our cognition. *What* a thing is, and *that* it exists would seem therefore to be the most basic division in the objects that meet our cognitive gaze. Existence, moreover, manifests the absolutely fundamental principle that a thing cannot be and not be at the same time in the same respects, and in this way carries with it the notion of necessity. Hence arose the Scholastic adage that the three aspects immediately striking our cognition are thing, existence and necessity.[19] In them, thing and existence are basically distinct.

Does this mean, though, that existence cannot be regarded as a thing? In none of the objects that directly confront our cognition can it be looked upon as a secondary instance of a "*what*," in the way predicamental accidents appear. But from immediately known instances of it, one can reason to its primary instance in God where it subsists and therefore is a nature, an essence, a *what*.[20] In the things of which we are immediately aware, on the contrary, the nature and the existence are different from each other. Every sensed object appears as necessarily both a thing and an existent combined. That is why epistemologically the basic object of our awareness is "a being" or an "existent" (Latin *ens*). "Essence" and "existence" are as separate notions only later derivatives.[21] Sensation obviously does not articulate either of these characteristics, any more than it articulates the difference between substance and accidents. It does not present them apart, in the way for instance it presents blue apart from red, or one portion of a surface apart from another portion. Rather, they are originally cognized as interpenetrating features of what appears holistically as the one global thing. Each stone, tree or horse appears as a distinct three-dimensional existent. This raises the question how perception is able to distinguish things as separate existents in their status of sensible solids.

Interpretation. The retinal pattern stimulating the visual organism does not seem to give much immediate awareness of the third dimension, nor do the tactual stimuli.[22] Depth and distance, in any sharply determined fashion, require a long process of learning. Through complicated coordination of different sensations and with the help of kinesthetic feeling in the visual organs, one has from infancy on become habituated to projecting the comparatively flat object of sight into the familiar and livable world.[23] Normally this process occurs spontaneously in one's natural development. Only the correction of errors, for instance that a stick is bent where it enters the water, that the moon seen at the horizon is really level with it, and that all the stars in the same constellation are about equidistant from earth, alert one to the interpretative element in the perception of the three-dimensional world.

Further, what is presented immediately in a single panorama is interpreted as many separate things. Where various groupings of qualities and movements and changes are found in consistent union, their subjects are cognized as stones and trees and dogs and houses and planets and men. Appearing as existent and substantial, and distinguished from each other on the basis of recognizable qualities and quantities, these groupings are regarded as each an individual thing. Still more surprisingly, one has become habituated to project into each of them an activity analogous to the activity of which one is aware in oneself as one thinks and acts in the course of daily life.[24]

As you reflect upon your own cognitive activity, you are moreover aware of it not only as an activity, but as being performed by yourself. You are immediately conscious of yourself as an agent. But have you any such immediate awareness of activity on the part of anything else? Do you not rather see effects that seem to proceed from your own activity, and then compare these with corresponding changes in apparently similar relation to the various groupings that you have interpreted as separate things? Do you not accordingly attribute the changes to analogous activity on their part?[25] You cognize them as agents also. Moreover, as you force yourself to keep on with the difficult study, you are aware of undergoing the influence of your own strong will. In experiences of this kind, the category of passivity or undergoing is immediately apparent to you, and you similarly project it into anything else that appears correlative to an agent. In this way metals and minerals and plants and animals and artifacts are isolated in the role of individual units existing and functioning each in itself, and undergoing change through being acted upon by other agents.

Most important of all, you are aware of changes that regularly follow upon your own thinking and deciding, for instance physical effects, social activity, business dealings, and planned undertakings of other sorts. You are likewise aware of quite similar changes regularly associated with many constant groupings of phenomena that you cognize as people. By analogy you interpret these other changes as proceeding from conscious agents corresponding to the self of which you are immediately aware in your own activity. You likewise observe the physical grouping that is always present when you are thinking, and cognize it as your own body. But you are also aware of that body in a much more pertinent way, through sensations of warmth and cold, pain and pleasure, and through innumerable kinesthetic feelings. In these ways, through spontaneous interpretation, the world of men and women is now perceived. Oneself and other human selves are interpreted as separate agents and participants in its life.

Through the categories an originally single and practically flat panorama has from days preceding one's memories been habitually interpreted as the three-dimensional universe of active beings, with time serving, on the basis of change, as a fourth dimension. If these individual things are regarded as the objects of enriched perception, they obviously contain additions to what is immediately sensed. The notion of perception accordingly adds something to the notion of immediate sensation.   It   adds   the   interpretation spontaneously made of the object of sense activity. The interpretation becomes another phenomenon that appears before one's reflexive gaze in the scrutinizing of one's own cognition. But it is a phenomenon that is subsequent to sensation and that does not add any radically new content. It is merely an habituated reading, into a present object, of content already given in previous sensations. But whether sensed or perceived, the object grasped is always something existent, substantial, extended and sensibly qualified in at least one way. There is no experience of anything that is just color or sound and nothing else. A sense datum, in the meaning of something immediately attained in sensation, is never just a quality. It is a substantial existent that has the quality. Throughout the whole of our spontaneously interpreted universe, we find no object that is not attained originally through sense experience. Even in the percept of the really non-existent pool of water on the road ahead, the basic cognition was the sight of the shiny asphalt. A shiny thing, in the sense of a substance, was indeed seen. But the substance was mistakenly interpreted to be water, through resemblance to the perception of a shiny surface in other circumstances.

Other Objects. Further, the deeply differentiated content of perceived objects allows openings to others that are not strictly perceived. Quantity, for instance, can be taken as the accident of a corporeal substance, with the specific differentiae of animate, sentient and rational left out of consideration. When it is so taken in abstraction from qualitative and further determinations, the quantity of a sensible thing exhibits all the possibilities required for the development of the pure mathematical sciences. Isolated in this way as an object just in itself, it is no longer confined to the three dimensions of the sensible world. It can proceed indefinitely with the square, cubic and further roots of numbers, even though it may be a square root, say of two, that cannot be envisaged as a sensible thing. It can treat objects of just one dimension, lines, or of just two dimensions, surfaces. It can deal with geometrical solids of three dimensions without regard to their sensible conditions. For instance, it can have a sphere touch a surface at only one unextended point, and can take the solids as infinitely divisible into ever smaller and smaller parts. It can go on to fifth, sixth and further dimensions without limitation.

The origin of mathematical objects, accordingly, need not be sought outside the sensible world. The tradition of the Platonic Academy required a separate order of objects, existent in themselves and outside any sensible things, as the basis for mathematical reasoning.[26] But the presence of quantity both continuous and discrete in observed sensible things, and the mind's exercised ability to consider that quantity in detachment from specific substantial differentiae and sensible qualities, are together amply sufficient for providing the objects of the pure mathematic sciences. No origin for them outside the sensible realm need be sought. The constitution of the sensible thing, that presents the thing's quantity as an accident different from its substance, allows the mathematical abstraction to take place.

The situation in regard to metaphysics corresponds proportionally. The aspect of a being, that is, the aspect of an existent thing, can be taken just itself and made an object of study without regard to generic and specific and accidental determinations. Substance is in consequence seen as something that does not necessarily require material and quantitative determinations. The notion of immaterial substance, such as in an angel, is in this way derived from sensible things. The aspect of existing can likewise be regarded as a substance in itself, apart from anything else that it would be actuating and in which it would be inherent. In that way the philosophical notion of God, namely subsistent existence, is derived from the sensible existents experienced in the visible world. All other metaphysical notions can be accounted for in similar fashion as derived from sensible things.

Further, universals exhibit no nature that cannot be found in sensible things or derived from them. The intelligible content of the universal is the same as that of the individual thing. The universal is just the individual content known in a wider way. That is why Aristotle could claim that a Platonic Idea merely added one more instance to what was already attained in the particulars.[27] The whole content has its origin in sensible objects.

Also the principles for the philosophy of nature are derived from sensible things. It is true, as noted above, that the Aristotelian primary matter is not something that can be observed by the senses. In itself it has no distinguishing or

perceptible traits.   But it is knowable on the analogy of
sensible materials. Just as wood is changed into a table by the
acquisition of an artificial form, so it is changed into ashes
by the substitution of a different natural form. Change of its
nature means that some kind of matter passes from one form
to another. For the change from the form of wood to the form
of ashes there has to be some underlying matter. But here the
matter is in the category of substance, and form in the
category of substance is the most basic of all formal
determinations. In consequence the matter in the category of
substance has of itself no formal determination whatever. In
itself it is not perceptible, but its notion is derived in this
analogous way from perceptible matter.[28] Knowledge of it
needs no other origin than observed sensible things.
Correspondingly the notion of form that is used in natural
philosophy is known in contrast to primary matter, on the
analogy with the way the artificial form of table or house is
related to the observable materials out of which each is made.

Likewise the notion of immaterial reception of form, used
to account for cognition in Aristotle's *De anima* and in the
natural philosophy that stems from it, is derived from the
sensible realm.[29] Change in the world of nature takes place
through the material reception of form. It is the reception of
form into matter.   In contrast, the cognitional reception
means the reception of form into form, as noted above (c. 2,
nn. 17-19). The notions used in this explanation, namely
matter, form, and reception, are in that way derived from
what is seen in observable change.

Finally, the notion of freedom, and of the obligations and
duties and rights and laws that follow upon it in the moral
order, needs no other objective origin than sensible
experience. You are internally aware of yourself as a sentient
agent. You do things, you take part in athletics, in social life,
in community undertakings. You know what it means to be
forced to do something, to be pushed backward by the wind, to
be swept around by a current in the water, to have to yield to
the pressure of increasing resistance. You know that in your
ordinary way of acting you are not forced to do things in that
manner. In contrast you form the notion of acting freely,

with all the moral consequences it entails. On the intellectual plane a positive explanation of freedom will be sought, and will be replete with difficulties. But the negatively geared acceptation of the fact is had through the internal experience of the sensible composite agent. It need not have any other objective origin than the sensible experience, though it will point the way to a spiritual dimension in the agent that is exercising free action.

Errors. But if the distinctions between the various facets presented by sensible things allow them to be the origin of all other notions in the content of our cognition, by the same token they make possible the occurrence of error on a surprisingly large scale. Mistakes in distance and arrangement, eidetic images and after-images, mirages, illusions, hallucinations, mescaline phenomena, bring about combinations of the facets in ways that conflict with what is actually present in the sensible world.[30] They are numerous enough to suggest the claim that error predominates in our everyday life.[31]

After having noted the difference between the substantial and the accidental in the world of sense experience, one should not have too much trouble in seeing how these mix-ups occur. The reflexion of light rays from the smooth shiny surface seen on the road ahead is associated spontaneously with one's past experience of seeing pools of water. Since the specific natures of the substances are not immediately knowable to us, the accidental aspects in this case are wrongly attributed to water instead of to asphalt. In the same vein, people who resemble each other very closely can easily be mistaken one for the other. At a side show you can watch for five minutes the stiff movements and wooden gestures of a robot-like figure without even getting the suspicion that it might be a human, until at the end of the performance the rigid face relaxes into a cordial human smile and delights in the applause.

Likewise the conditions of the media between sense object and sense organ can occasion differences in the way the object is presented. Colors may appear different as the light varies, as in Chesterton's description in his poem *Lepanto*:

> Stiff flags straining in the night-blasts cold,
> In the gloom black-purple, in the glint old
> gold.

Different refractions, likewise, may bring about different percepts. A person may decide it is time to stop driving when he or she begins to see things where they are not, and not see things where they are. Always something is being seen. But the percept that is built upon the basic sensation is regulated by the conditions of the media and becomes spontaneously interlarded with distance and depth and with numerous associations from one's memory. Physical and psychological research explains how this takes place, and provides the means for getting back to what was originally sensed and for discerning it from what has been added to it in the percept.

More difficult, undoubtedly, are the instances in which there is nothing basic in the real world to correspond actually to the percept. There was nothing outside the mind in actual existence to correspond to Macbeth's dagger. Dreams place us in situations that are not actually existent. Artificial stimulation of nerves may seem to locate the patient in another room and have him listening to the music being played there. Cases like these call for serious consideration. Each has to be evaluated on its own merits and decided accordingly. One's memory is stored with images. These can be associated and reassociated in tune with the impulses of the moment. They exist in the mind in that combination at the time. The cognitional existence is genuine existence, and where the person at the time is unable because of disturbed psychic conditions to compare and contrast it with real existence, it appears under the circumstances as existence *tout court*. The origin of each of the particular images used has to be probed, sometimes through difficult psychoanalysis, in the person's past experience. But no other natural origin than cognition through the external senses has been established. Phenomena classed under telepathy and extrasensory cognition merit careful study. Where they can be explained by natural causes they seem to remain within the ambit of cognition based upon what is attained through the external senses. Supernatural origin is of course not excluded, but appeal to it will raise the consideration out of the domain of philosophy into that of sacred theology.

The epistemological conclusion, then, must be that errors in one's percepts are possible in an astonishingly wide variety of ways. The traditional skeptical arguments, and the recorded psychic experiences and psychological experiments, have each to be taken seriously and explained in the light of established physical, chemical and psychological research. Every confidence seems guaranteed that they will be traced ultimately to no other natural origin than the objects of cognition by the external senses. Our interpreting procedure allows all sorts of errors to creep into our percept. Mistakes in arrangement and distance can be frequent. In practical life one readily adjusts oneself to ordinary situations, after a little experience. Other difficulties require the aid of experimental psychology or of related disciplines. But in either case a careful distinction between what is sensed and what is interpreted, and a close critique of the interpretation, will in principle furnish the means of understanding and controlling the errors. The details of the corrections can be left to the relevant sciences. For the present one need merely note that factual errors are a rather prominent phenomenon in human cognition when it is subjected to even a descriptive survey.

Sense Data. Attempts to account for cognitional errors through sense-datum philosophy were painstakingly made in the New Realism and the Critical Realism of the early twentieth century. In these philosophies what is immediately sensed was regarded as "given" to the senses, and in that perspective was called a "sense datum." The epistemological problem was then posed in terms of how and to what extent the sense datum was identical with or agreed with something in the real world. The prolonged controversies about the status of the sense data failed to achieve unanimity. The reason, as should be apparent from the preceding considerations, is that what the senses originally grasp is a material thing existent in itself. It has to be assessed basically in terms of its own substance and of its existence in its own self. To regard it as a sense datum is to conceive it basically in relation to cognition. So conceived it is understood as something *given in* sensation.[32] But in point of fact what is basically grasped in sensation presents, as has been seen above, its nature and its own existence in epistemological priority to the aspect of being sensed. It requires basic definition in terms of its own nature, and basic understanding in terms of its own existence. A "Wrong Road" sign should face any attempt to approach it as something originally existent through cognition, or as neutral to real and cognitional existence. From the start it is an existent in itself.

Physical Object. A similar difficulty arises from epistemological approach to the sense world in terms of "physical objects."[33] What sensation first attains is thereby defined in relation to cognition. Though introduced as physical in contrast to the abstract or universal, or to the logical or the mathematical or the metaphysical, it is conceived basically as the object of a cognitive act instead of as a real existent in itself. To avoid the difficulties that stem from this approach, the phrasing "a material thing" will help keep what is directly sensed from any objective admixture with the concomitant but reflexive awareness of the sensing. "Physical object" presents it as something "thrown before" one's cognition, rather than as existing in itself. Epistemologically, then, this expression is hardly satisfactory.

Résumé. You come to the study of epistemology with a mind already filled with memories and shaped by the training of experience that has gone on throughout a considerable number of years. Without for a moment ceasing to be keenly aware that everything you know is based upon things encountered in the real external world, you are able to reflect upon those things as they exist in your cognition. An examination of this content of your cognition reveals no other origin for it than the things you have come to grasp cognitionally through seeing, hearing, feeling and the other kinds of awareness they may be called external sensation.

Yet you find inevitably that your cognition becomes extended to objects beyond the entire sensible world. The sensible objects of which you are immediately aware present different facets. They manifest themselves basically as substances, but also as extended in space, as possessing qualities of many kinds, and as being related in various ways to numbers of other things. When one of these aspects, quantity, is considered apart from the sensible qualities with which it is penetrated in the real world, you have an object that gives rise to the world of mathematics. When substance and existence are taken in themselves apart from the way they are determined by particular natures, you have the object for metaphysical study that takes you into the realm of immaterial beings, beings that cannot be attained immediately by sensation. The distinction between these different facets of the sensible object provides the basis for reasoning to things beyond sensible experience, without requiring any other ultimate objective origin than sensation for the whole content of your cognition.

The same variegated composition in the immediately sensed object accounts for the multitudinous errors to which one's cognition is liable. The percept that we have habitually come to regard as the unit of our experience, such as an individual stone or tree or person, turns out to be built up from what is basically sensed as "something" into a definitely distanced three-dimensional agent or patient endowed with many qualities and relations, with a determined substantial nature, and with a history of its own. Confusions and errors easily creep into this combining of the various features. Colors can be different according to different conditions of perspective and of light, features taken from memory can be altered with the course of time, things remembered as really existent in the past can become mixed with imaginary events as fiction melds with fact in one's reminiscences. Motives of vanity, habits of exaggeration, prejudices against others, all combine to cloud our recollection of the data stored up in our memories. As a result our percepts often require careful scrutiny to distinguish the object of our enriched perception from the thing actually being sensed. All this suggests the need for a careful study of the genesis of the percept and the structure of the cognitive activity by which it is achieved.

Notes to Chapter 3

1. Cf.: "The first thing that appears when we begin to analyze our common knowledge is that some of it is derivative, while some is primitive; . . . the immediate facts perceived by sight or touch or hearing do not need to be proved by argument, but are completely self-evident." Bertrand Russell, *Our Knowledge of the External World* (Chicago, 1929), 72. See also Willard Van Ornam Quine, *Methods of Logic* (New York, 1950) xiii. On the other hand, for a case against any "foundations picture," see Bruce Aune, *Knowledge, Mind, and Nature* (New York, 1967), 263-367. Aune argues that any view of this kind will be "excessively restrictive" (265) in regard to knowledge and also will render the basic concepts immune to revisions. In reply, one may say that the possibility of deriving further knowledge from the foundations should be approached with an open mind and not ruled out *a priori*--rather, current notions in that respect should be left open to revision. Likewise the basic concepts can be revised continually, for there are different ways of conceiving what was originally perceived. Here again one's mind should remain open till the whole question has been thoroughly examined. On Aune's (266) contention that "all putative basic claims" have three background assumptions, see infra, c. 9, n. 13, where a corresponding Neoscholastic tenet is briefly discussed. A survey of differing views on the sources may be found in the chapter "The Sources and Construction of Knowledge," in Kelvin Van Nuys, *Is Reality Meaningful?* (New York, 1966), 77-106.

2. In this sense "phenomenology" does not mean the philosophical way of thinking that stems from Husserl. Rather, it is taken in the more general signification given in the College Edition of Webster's *New World Dictionary* (s.v.) as "the branch of a science that classifies and describes its phenomena without any attempt at explanation." In the present context "one is speaking phenomenologically, i.e. is describing how a thing looks without implying that it has or has not the quality in question"--Rodney Julian Hirst, *The Problems of Perception* (London, 1959), 33-34; cf. 36-37. In a phenomenology of this type, contrary to Husserl's procedure, there is no *a priori* reason for bracketing or excluding

existence. Rather, if *an object* appears existent should not the fact be noted along with all the rest? In the present chapter the phenomenology is restricted to the content of perception. In succeeding chapters the inventory will be gradually broadened to all that is found in experience, with "experience" understood as "the broadest term for whatever there is in mental life"--Arthur Campbell Garnett, *The Perceptual Process* (Madison, 1965), 27.

Even a more recent conception of phenomenology in its current philosophical sense should not be allowed to prejudice any issue here. This position claims that "phenomenology" is also a philosophy that put a essences back into existence, and does not expect to arrive at an understanding of man and the world from any starting point other than that of their 'facticity.'"--Maurice Merleau-Ponty, *Phenomenology of Perception*, trans. Colin Smith (London, 1962), vii. One should not *presume* that existence is ever separated in perception in a way that would allow it to be received back authentically into the essences. On the contrary, the way existence is involved in whatever appears should first be scrutinized in the initial phenomenological study. The exigencies of its relations to finite essence requires careful examination.

3. The term "percept" was introduced in the mid-nineteenth century by Sir William Hamilton. See *O.E.D.*, s.v. It was meant to signify as a whole the object attained in an act of sense cognition. In formation the word was intended to parallel the much older term "concept." It signified what was perceived, quite as "concept" referred to what is *conceived* in the mind. In general use, "perception" may mean any kind of mental apprehension. But, as Hirst notes in Paul Edwards' *Encyclopedia of Philosophy*, s.v., "in philosophy it is now normally restricted to sense perception." See also Hirst, *Problems*, 15. In this context, by way of generalization from inductive instances, one may accordingly find perception described loosely as "a certain generic mental activity or state of which, when we reflect, we think seeing, feeling or touching, hearing, tasting and smelling to be species"--Harold Arthur Prichard, *Knowledge and Perception* (Oxford, 1950), 200. So, "in the primary sense, 'perception' can signify any means whereby we come to recognize, identify, or characterize something by means of the senses"--David Walter Hamlyn,

Sensation and Perception (New York, 1961), 194. In this way the awareness of abstract objects, of *a priori* truths, of intellectual inference and of reasoning are excluded from the current philosophical use of "perception." Positively, however, the presumption that perception means "a single kind of experience" has, as Hamlyn (188) notes, "caused great difficulties." The possibility that it is constituted by different kinds of activity should be left open. The basic constituent, as is manifest in the above descriptions, is sensation. Without sensation there can be no perception. But if the objects of sensation are regarded as colors, heat, pain, sounds, odors, and so on, and the objects of perception as stones, trees, dogs, automobiles, and the like, sensation would be a necessary but not sufficient condition for perception. See Hamlyn, 196; Henry Habberly Price, *Perception* (London, 1932), 22-25; James Jerome Gibson, *The Perception of the Visual World* (Boston, 1950), 3; Erwin Straus, *The Primary World of Senses* (New York, 1963) 316-331. Yet universally recognized precision in the acceptation of the terms is not to be expected. On the one hand, Hirst (*Problems*, 120) can say "almost all philosophers have recognized that perceiving is more than just having purely sensory experiences and involves some non-sensory activity." On the other hand, Hamlyn (186) can conclude after a long and detailed historical study of the two notions: "an explicit distinction between sensation and perception has only rarely been made. It was made by Reid and Bergson, for example, but by few others." Even though in recent writing the distinction is present, the lack of clarity is notable: "In thousands of pages of writing there is barely an attempt made to define with precision what is meant by sensation, perception, or by the objectivity of either"--K. T. Gallagher, "Some Recent Anglo-American Views on Perception," *International Philosophical Quarterly*, 4 (1964), 138. For instance, "perceptual consciousness," introduced by Price (25) for the additional "non-sensuous mode of consciousness" and used by Hirst (*Problems*, 219) for "the mental activity or state in perceiving," does not seem to add initial clarity though it draws attention to the difference between perception and sensation. For a critique of the "traditional explanation" that sensations are "the raw material" and perceptions the "manufactured products" see Gibson, *The Perception of the Visual World*, 11-43.

4. E.g., Locke, *Essay Concerning Human Understanding*, Book I; Aristotle, *De anima*, 3.8.432a7-14; Aquinas, *Contra gentiles*, 1.3, Quod autem. So "all knowledge has an eventual empirical significance in that all which is knowable or even significantly thinkable must have reference to meanings which are sense-representable." C. I. Lewis, *An Analysis of Knowledge and Valuation* (La Salle, IL, 1962), 171.

5. For Plato (*Men.* 86A; *Phd.*, 75B-76E; *Phdr.*, 249B-250A), knowledge of the Ideas came through recollection (*anamnesis*) of what had been seen by the soul alone in a previous existence, and not through sensation (see *Phd.*, 65C-67A; 79CD). In the Augustinian tradition this source became the divine illumination, and in Descartes (*Notae in Programma Quoddam*, A-T, VIII^2, 357.26-358.11; cf. *Third Objections*, 10, in A-T, VII, 189.104, and IX, 147) knowledge of ideas and of eternal truths was "innate," while knowledge of God and of the soul could not come through the senses (*Discours*, 4; A-T, VI, 37.13-14). With Kant (*Critique of Pure Reason*, B 92-108), the primitive intelligible aspects were regarded as categories imposed *a priori* by the mind and on the sense manifold.

6. See Joseph Banks Rhine, *Extra-Sensory Perception* (Boston, 1935), and "Additional Reading" list in Rhine, *The Reach of the Mind* (New York, 1947), 225. Extrasensory perceptions, including clairvoyance and telepathy, are labeled ESP and classed under "Psi-phenomena." On the deficiencies in the results of this research, and its inability to establish any cognition that would come about independently of brain activity, see Hirst, *Problems*, 203-207. The propriety of using "perception" in its philosophical sense for these phenomena, including telepathy, is questioned in *Human Senses and Perception*, ed. G. M. Wyburn (Edinburgh, 1964), 213.

7. "The panorama is utterly and entirely a performance of the living organism." Gibson, 1. "The visual world is a response of the organism--amazingly complex but still a response." Ibid., 146. On the ambiguity of "stimulus" for the immediate cause (e.g., the pattern of light waves, and the like) or for an "inner aspect" instead of something physical, see Hirst, *Problems* , 246. On the absence of agreement in its use in the sciences, see Gibson, 63 and 215. The details of the sensory stimuli and receptors may be found in treatises

on experimental psychology, e.g., Frank A. Geldard, *The Human Senses* (New York, 1953).

8. See above, c. 1, nn. 12-14.

9. "Whatever may be an object of thought, or may occur in any true or false proposition, or can be counted as *one*, I call a *term*. . . . A term is, in fact, possessed of all the properties commonly assigned to substances or substantives." Bertrand Russell, *The Principles of Mathematics* (Cambridge, 1903), I, 43-44 (no. 47). For logical atomism, see Russell, "The Philosophy of Logical Atomism," *The Monist*, 28 (1918) 495-527; 29 (1919), 32-63, 190-222.

10. See above, c. 1, n. 7.

11. For discussion of the category of relation, see Leo Sweeney, *A Metaphysics of Authentic Existentialism*, (Englewood Cliffs, NJ, 1965. One may speak of "the perception of relations," e.g., Marjorie Grene, *The Knower and the Known* (London, 1966), 85. As Hamlyn (*Problems*, 188) notes, it is of great importance to realize that the objects of perception are not uniform in type.

12. On "where" and "when" as categories grounded on relations, see A. Krempel, *La doctrine de la relation chez saint Thomas* (Paris, 1952), 437-440.

13. See *O.E.D.*, svv. accident, II, 6-7; substance, 103. In spite of the disfavor into which "substance" has fallen--"the temporary eclipse of the category of substance," Wilfred Sellars, "Abstract Entities," *The Review of Metaphysics*, 16 (1963), 627, n. 2, and in spite of the misunderstanding to which it has been subject since the time of Locke, it still seems to be the established word for the notion at issue here. In consequence its use should be retained. Locke satirized substance as something "under" the accidents, like an elephant supporting the world and in turn resting on a tortoise, and the tortoise itself on "something, he knew not what" (Essay, 2.23.2; ed. Nidditch, 296.5-6). This caricature at least shows that substance cannot be explained through prior knowledge of the accidents, under pain of infinite regress. Rather, the substance is immediately

perceived along with the accidents.

As a technical term, "substance" came into the philosophical vocabulary to translate the Aristotelian *ousia*, a noun formed from the Greek word for "being." Morphologically its equivalent would be the obsolete English "beingness." So: "To my judgment there is a comparatively simple way into the categories according to which the word translated 'substance' means 'being' and the primary notion of being is existence." A. C. Lloyd, "Aristotle's Categories Today," *Philosophical Quarterly*, 16 (1966), 258. The type of distinction between being and substance, however, is a problem for metaphysics, and has been subject to centuries-long dispute. But wherever there is any object, there is being and there is substance. Even in the case of transubstantiation there is always substance present, though for the believer and the substance is not the body normally associated with the accidents here involved.

14. The notions of "thing" and "being" are not found in the same way in all their instances. In their full meaning they reside only in a primary instance. The other instances carry the meaning through various relations to the primary instance. Today this type of signification is usually referred to as "focal meaning," a phrase felicitously coined by G. E. L. Owen, "Logic and Metaphysics in Some Earlier Works of Aristotle," in *Aristotle and Plato in the Mid-Fourth Century*, ed. I. Düring and G. E. L. Owen (Göteborg, 1960), 169-189. Focal meaning is the warp and wool of characteristic Aristotelian philosophy.

15. E.G., being, goodness, friendship. In regard to being, the doctrine is explained concisely in Aristotle's *Metaphysics*, 4.2.1003a33-b17 and 7.1.1028a10-b7.

16. The use of the term "nature" in the sense of a *kind* of thing became established in the Latin philosophical tradition through Boethius (480?-524 A.D.), the early translator of Greek philosophical texts: "'Nature' pertains to things that, as existent, may be grasped in any way at all by a concept. Therefore in this definition both accidents and substance are defined; for all of them can be grasped by a concept" (Natura, est earum rerum quae, cum sint, quoquomodo

intellectu capi possent. In hac igitur definitione et accidentia et substantia definiuntur; haec enim omnia intellectu capi possunt). Boethius, *Liber de persona et duabus naturis*, 1; PL, LXIV, 1341B. Cf.: "Another term used for this is 'nature' . . . while 'essence' is used because through it, and in it, that which is has being." Aquinas, *On Being and Essence*, trans. Armand Maurer, 2nd ed. (Toronto, 1968), 1.4; 32.

17. "Even in the case of sensible beings we do not know their essential differences; we indicate them through the accidental differences that flow from the essential differences, as we refer to a cause through its effect." Aquinas, *On Being and Essence*, 5.6; trans. Maurer, 63. Cf. Aristotle, *De an.*, 1.1.402b16-403a2.

18. Locke, *Essay Concerning Human Understanding*, 4.12.8 and 9; Peter H. Nidditch (Oxford, 1975), 643-645.

19. The Latin version of Avicenna (980-1037 A.D.) noted that "being" (*ens*) and "thing" (*res*) and "necessary" (*necesse*) are at once stamped upon the soul in the initial impression of an object: "statim imprimuntur in anima prima impressione, quae non acquiritur ex aliis notioribus se." *Metaph.*, 1.6 (Venice, 1508), fol. 72r2 (A). The sensed object does not leave one free to regard it as nothing. Necessity is in this way seen in the object. It accordingly exercises its compelling force in sensation, even though there it is not given any separate status. But its basic role in every object of cognition is enough to prompt the remark: "The notions of existence and necessity have held the interest of philosophers longer than many other problems in the philosophy of logic." J. Hintikka, "Studies in the Logic of Existence and Necessity," *The Monist*, L (1966), 55. Similarly the need for every object to be "something" is spontaneously recognized, e.g.: "Whatever we are acquainted with must be something"--Russell, *The Problems of Philosophy* (New York, 1912), 186.

20. See Aquinas, *On Being and Essence*, 4.7; trans. Maurer, 56-67. So existence even in creatures may be called a thing, and has to be represented as a thing in order to be a subject of discussion. Hence Aquinas can refer to it as something: ". . . the act of existence of a

thing is, in a sense, something created"--*De ver.*, 1.4.ad 4m; Mulligan trans., *Truth*, I, 19. Here both "thing" and "something" translate the Latin *res*. Cf. infra, c. 6, n. 10.

21. On this topic see C. Fabro, "The Transcendentality of Ens-Esse and the Ground of Metaphysics," *International Philosophical Quarterly*, 6 (1966), 389-427. Fabro notes "the two-fold content of *ens*, essence and *actus essendi*. Therefore, the *notio entis* precedes them both"--426.

22. On some interesting evidence for the conclusion that "neither sight nor touch originally is capable of genuine spatial perception; that is, in each a learning process in indispensable," see W. S. Haymond, "Is Distance an Original Factor in Vision?" *The Modern Schoolman*, 39 (1961), 58. Nevertheless the beginnings in every instance can be found in the objects of sensation: "We do not have to learn that things are external, solid, stable, rigid, and spaced about the environment, for these qualities may be traced to retinal images or to the reciprocal visual-postural processes." Gibson, 186-187. The visual field in fact "is never flat, . . . never wholly depthless. . . . Nevertheless it has *less* of these qualities than the visual world." Ibid., 42. On the oversimplifications to be avoided, see ibid., 200. A short discussion of the evidence on what cataract patients blind from birth see on the removal of the cataracts, may be found in Gibson, 216-220. Indications are that what they see is "more nearly a visual world than a flat visual field, yet requiring a long process of learning to attain the "literal world which we see." Ibid., 218.

Cf.: "Paradoxical as it may seem, the perception of shape without depth is more difficult to understand than the perception of shape in depth." Gibson, 100. Gibson's (191) stand is that "the tendency to think of form as two-dimensional only" has been a stumbling block in psychology. Hirst's conclusion, after an extensive consideration of the evidence, is that "perceiving is a highly complex process far removed from simple awareness." *Problems*, 278. The difficulties here arise from the wish to conceive each sensible quality as a separate epistemological atom. These difficulties disappear through the realization that from the start the object of sensation is grasped as a substance and is accordingly able to be filled out in perception with other qualities and further accidents.

23. Together, sight and touch may be said to give the framework for the exact three-dimensional interpretations of the world: ". . . vision and touch formed a kind of framework for experiences of depth, a framework to which all spatial perceptions are constantly referred." Kai von Fiandt, *The World of Perception* (Homewood, IL, 1966), 227. Cf.: ". . . the immediate object of sight is a three-dimensional arrangement of visible surfaces." David Malet Armstrong, *Berkeley's Theory of Vision* (Melbourne, 1960), 102.

24. On this topic see J. Wisdom, J. L. Austin, A. J. Ayer, "Symposium: Other Minds," *Proceedings of the Aristotelian Society*, Suppl. 20 (1946), 122-197. Against the analogy argument, see Wisdom, ibid., 123-127. But the analogy does not at all mean that one "constructs" other people and the world in which one lives. Rather, one *interprets* in this way the immediate object of sensation. John Wisdom's discussion of the problem as a whole may be found in his book *Other Minds* (Oxford, 1965), especially 68-86; 111-115; 230-231.

On the general problem, see Charlie Dunbar Broad, *The Mind and its Place in Nature* (London, 1925), 317-349, and also the essayists in *Epistemology*, ed. Avrum Stroll (New York, 1967), 83-158. In the intersubjectivity approach, the perception of both one's own self and other selves depends with equal force upon the environmental condition: ". . . there is no means of isolating the concept of 'self' from the context of intersubjectivity apart from which it is a mere abstraction"--Margaret Chatterjee, *Our Knowledge of Other Selves* (Bombay, 1963), 217.

25. The case against "the traditional argument from analogy" may be found stated briefly in Don Locke, *Myself and Others* (Oxford, 1968), 49-50. For a defense of the argument, see N. Malcolm, "Knowledge of Other Minds," *The Journal of Philosophy*, 55 (1958), 969-978, and H. Feigl, ibid., 978-987. On the notion of "deductive analogy," see John Wisdom, *Other Minds* (Oxford, 1965), esp. 68-86; 111-115; 230-231. For "deductive analogy," see ibid., 211. One should keep in mind that analogy in this context need not mean a merely

probable argument. It can signify deductive reasoning, in cogent fashion, as in Aristotle's demonstration of the existence of primary matter in *Ph.*, 1.7.191a7-21.

26. Cf. supra, n. 5. Mathematicals were regarded as "intermediate" (*Republic*, 6.511D) between the objects of the highest type of intelligence and those of opinion. On their order in the "divided line," see 6.509D-511E.

27. See Aristotle, *Metaph.*, 7.16.1040b27-34; 13.9.1086b9-11. For Aristotle, on the contrary, the universal object was identical "severally" (4.26.1023b31; Ross trans., 2nd ed., 1928) with each of the instances, and in this way did not add another instance.

28. See supra, n. 25. On the lack of all formal determinations in the basic matter in the category of substance, see Aristotle, *Metaph.*, 7.1029all-26.

29. See the comparison of the two ways of receiving a form at *De an.*, 2.12.424a17-b12. The explanation if given through the examples of a ring receiving a device, of a lyre struck too violently, a thunderbolt splitting the timber, and so on. The immaterial character of the cognitional reception is established through contrast with the physical changes. In cognition the reception of the form does not change the object itself, but makes it identical with the percipient without producing any third thing.

30. On the problem in general, see George Boas, *The Inquiring Mind* (LaSalle, IL, 1959), 26-53. The examples of the oar appearing broken in water, and of the one color on the pigeon's neck appearing multiple, are mentioned as though standard by Cicero, *Academica*, 2.25.79-81. Cf. Sextus Empiricus, *Adversus mathematicos*, 7.159-165 and 402-414. Descartes in the *First Meditation* leans heavily on the argument from perceptual errors. Detailed discussions of the argument may be readily found, e.g., in Alfred Jules Ayer, *The Foundations of Empirical Knowledge* (London, 1958), 3-46; Hirst, *Problems*, 16-50; John Langshaw Austin, *Sense and Sensibilia* (Oxford, 1962), 20-54. Austin, 48 and 54, warns against an assumption that there is a basic dichotomy between "delusive" and

"viridical" perceptions. There is in fact no reason to presuppose that the two must have entirely different sources. The relativity of perception has to be taken into account in regard to both. Further, Gibson, 14, asks: "Why are the optical illusions of the textbooks actually the exception rather than the rule?" and K. T. Gallagher, art. cit., *International Philosophical Quarterly*, 4(1964), 137, notes among recent writers a repudiation of the argument from illusion in this epistemological problem. See also Hirst, *Problems*, 18.

31. So Aristotle, *De an.*, 3.3.427b1-2, observes that "error seems to be more natural to living creatures, and the soul spends more time in it" (Hett trans.).

32. Cf.: ". . . That ambiguous phrase 'the given.'" --Helen M. Smith, "Is There a Problem about Sense-Data?" *Proceedings of the Aristotelian Society*, Suppl. 15 (1936), 79. The feature stressed in the notion of being "given" is direct presence to consciousness: "This peculiar and ultimate manner of being present to consciousness is called *being given*, and that which is thus present is called a *datum*"-- Price, 3; cf. 5-6. Yet in the sense in which its proponents understand this "given," an opponent can argue that it just is not there: "So far then from its being, as Professor Price asserts, certain that there are sense-data, it is certain that there are not"--Harold Arthur Prichard, *Knowledge and Perception* (Oxford, 1950), 213.

33. On "physical objects," see Willard Van Orman Quine, *Word and Object* (Cambridge, Mass., 1960), 233-243.

CHAPTER 4

The Cognitive Agent

Integrated Object. The object upon which human cognition
bears immediately and directly is, as the preceding three
chapters have made clear, something that exists externally in
itself. It is not something that exists primarily inside the
cognition. Rather, it is contrasted with the cognition as
external. It is spontaneously interpreted as a world of
multitudinous individual existents. But whether or not the
interpretation of it as a vast plurality of separate things can
be sustained by close epistemological critique, the presence of
a graded yet integrated order in its being is at once manifest.
It has accidents that keep changing, while it itself continues
in existence. Always the object of our perception has that
twofold involvement. It is never a simple accident in itself, or
a substance that is just itself and nothing else. It is without
exception a substance that is characterized by accidents. It
may be a rock or a tree or a dog, but it is also colored, heavy,
and in place and time. The one basic thing, the substance, is
what all those different characteristics imply, but in different
ways. The object of our immediate and direct cognition is
thereby integrated into a single unit that is presented to our
perception as the one whole, in stone or plant or animal or
human person. In every case the object is one substance and
one existent, though made manifest in a wide variety of
accidents.

Unitary Percipient. In corresponding fashion, a single
percipient may be aware of the one external object through a

plurality of different faculties or powers. The many faculties are accidents, the one percipient is the substance in which they inhere and function. The gradated order of focal meaning corresponds on each side. The perceived accidents have their being in virtue of the substance in which they inhere. The faculties do the perceiving primarily because of the unitary percipient that is functioning through them. That is why Aristotle was so insistent on making clear that strictly speaking not the faculties nor even the soul did the thinking or feeling, but rather the *anthropos*, the man or woman who had the substantial form and the accidental faculties.[1] There is but the one cognitive agent throughout. To write that the eye sees or the ear hears or the nose smells is merely shorthand for the meaning that the human person is seeing or hearing or smelling by means of those organs. Accordingly there is no basic problem regarding how awareness through one sense can be shared by awareness through another sense. It is the same percipient in each case. In the act of awareness one and the same percipient becomes and is the one sensible thing in the different acts of cognition. There is no need to look for any deeper means of communication. What is seen may be felt and heard and smelled and tasted as the same thing by the same person. Mistakes may be made, as already noted (supra, c. 3, nn. 30-33). But the means for closer examination and correction are thereby guaranteed. Since in every case you yourself are the percipient, everything you come to perceive is brought into the unity of your own cognition. Correspondingly, the color, hardness, sound, odor and taste were shown to be accidents of one and the same thing. But since no finite substance is immediately active, the percipient will require faculties in order to perform the acts by which both the diversity and the unity in the things are sensed. From late antiquity these faculties have been called the external and the internal senses.

External Sensation. Sight, hearing, touch, taste and smell have been known traditionally as the five external senses. Their particular organs are investigated in detail in experimental psychology. The psychological study adds some other senses, by reason of experiments that isolate distinct organs for each. The distinct organs indicate particular senses for temperature, for pain, for kinesthetic feelings. They do not allow these sensations to be reduced to touch as the sense of resistance. Pain receptors, for instance, are found to be different from those of tactile sensations.[2]

What is meant in general by an external sense is a faculty whose exercise gives awareness of extended and qualified objects existent *outside* our cognition. With "external" taken in that meaning, the designation is sufficiently apt. The five traditional senses make us immediately aware of things that exist in themselves in the real world, things such as chairs and tables that we see and touch, food that we taste, perform that we smell, or the singing that we hear. Kinesthetic and pain sensations make us aware of what is going on inside our body. Yet the pain and the motion are occurring in reality and are not existent solely in our cognition. From that viewpoint the faculties that provide awareness of them may be classed with the external senses, because they bring us into immediate contact with what is external to our cognition. The fact that all the external senses are faculties internal to the percipient and his or her perception need not cause any distraction.

In every case, then, external sensation makes us aware of something that has existence in reality, in contradistinction to something that exists merely in our cognition. As has been already noted, the type of existence that is encountered in sight, hearing, touch, taste and the other external senses can be sharply distinguished from an existence solely in our cognitive activity. A well-done juicy steak that is actually being seen and tasted manifests a different kind of existence from that of a steak that is just being dreamt of. It is sensed as existent in itself, in the real world. The difference between the two ways of existing is crystal clear when they are confronted with each other under undisturbed conditions. In saying that the real existence is perceived by the external senses there is no question whatever of representing the existence as itself a substance or even a thing, quite as there is no question of representing the external sense as a cognitive agent just in

itself. As already stressed, there is but the one existent thing
that is perceived together with its accidents, and the one
existent agent that perceives through the senses. On each side
there is but one existent whole, with the existence functioning
not as an added *what* but as bringing about the fact *that* the
thing really exists. The existence of the sensible thing could
never be made to appear as a separate object for perception. It
remains integrated in the existent whole, quite as the activity
of perception is integrated into the one existent percipient.
Existence goes with everything on each side. In ordinary
conversation there is no need to say that an existent cat is
observing an existent mouse. The existence on both sides is
implicit in the overall conception of the things concerned.
Only later in the course of intellectual scrutiny do existence
and thing become represented as separate objects of
consideration.

This rather boring insistence has been necessary on
account of a tendency to claim that the senses never perceive
existence, and that only the intellect does. This claim is
occasioned by the fact that the senses never bear on existence
as upon a separate object, in the way intellection does. Yet the
senses undoubtedly grasp the whole existent thing, with the
existence strongly included. The cat not only perceives the
substance on its dish as food, but also *that* the food exists here
and now before its sight and smell. The reaction shows that
the cat is distinguishing definitely between the existence and
the non-existence of the food. If the food were not there, the
cat would let you know at once. In either case it has the same
awareness of *what* the substance in question is, but a
drastically different perception in regard to its existence on
the platter.

The importance of this consideration should be apparent
from the conclusions in the preceding chapters about the
origin of human cognition. For the Aristotelian empiricist
traditions there can be nothing in the intellect that was not
previously attained by the senses. Real existence can be no
exception. If it were not grasped by the senses it could never,
with us, become an object of intellectual scrutiny. The
cognitive agent could not know even itself as a real existent. It

would be aware only of an unsubstantial flux without any self, as in Hume's phenomenal flux, even in the supposition that such a situation could be rendered intelligible. But also where the percipient's self is represented in terms of something sensible, as shown in the two preceding chapters, its real existence has to be grasped as the existence of a sensible thing, no matter what conclusions may be later drawn about that existence as primarily the existence of a spiritual substance. As first known in reflexion, it is the existence of a sensible composite.

In full solidarity, then, with the axiom that nothing comes under the intellect's scrutiny unless it was first attained by the senses, the grasp of real existence in the external sensible thing takes place first on the level of sensation. In external sensation, as in any other cognition, the percipient becomes and is the thing perceived. What is sensed is a real existent. What the percipient becomes *cognitionally* is in consequence a really existent thing. In fact, it might not be going at all too far if one applies to the object of sensation what Aquinas remarked about the object of intellection.[3] What is attained primarily and by way of actuality in absolute fashion is the thing's existence. What strikes the sense primarily in the thing and as most actual is the existence. Without the existence, there would be nothing to be sensed. Though other than the existence, the thing itself is not attained by the external sense except as really existent, and in fact primarily as really existent. In this fashion all human cognition originates in really existent sensible things.

Common Sensation. The various kinds of external sensation are distinguished from one another by reason of the special sensible quality under which each attains its object. Sight is specified by color, touch by hardness, hearing by sound. But common to all these particular objects is extension in space and time. Color and hardness are spread out over a surface, sound is measurable in terms of pitch and duration. As examples of objects of common sensation (*koine aisthesis*) Aristotle listed movement, rest, figure, size, number and unity, mentioning that these could not specify a further particular sense without thereby ceasing to be common.[4] These are contained within the objects of the other senses. They are accordingly sensed in the proper meaning of the word. You literally see the size and shape of a building. You are not adding size and shape from the recollection of former associations, as when you say you are seeing the birthplace of a great-grandparent. That type of "enriched" perception was called by Aristotle "incidental" sensing. His example was the assertion that you are seeing Cleon's son. You do not literally see the filial relationship, but merely add it from past knowledge. But the size and figure are actually being seen at the moment. They are being sensed in the proper meaning of the word.

By the very fact that these sensible objects are common to different senses, they become adaptable to the varying conditions under which the particular senses operate. What appears as a tiny luminous speck to a terrestrial observer may be a galaxy billions of miles in extent. The common sensibles have to be checked by the data obtained through other particular sensations and often by scientific reasoning based on the information given by those further sources. But when left uncontrolled, they can easily be the occasion of errors.

We are also aware of a very different type of common sensation. We recognize our own seeing, hearing, touching and so on, in common as sensations. We distinguish them from one another, and compare them them with one another. We thereby distinguish their objects as things seen, touched, tasted, heard, and the like, and as able to be compared with each other under those respective characterizations. This means, as Aristotle (*On Sleep and Waking*, 2.455a15-25) pointed out, that we have a "common faculty" (a15-16) for looking upon those objects together under the one common aspect of sensations and things sensed. The situation is therefore very different from that in which each particular external sense observed characteristics that are common to all their own objects. For that, no new particular sense was necessary or even possible. Each of those common sensibles was necessarily attained already in the act of the particular sense. But here a further and distinct sense is required. None of the external senses attains its object as something already sensed and already congitionally existent in the percipient for distinction from and comparison with other sensations. Although when you see or hear or touch you are concomitantly aware of your activity, you are not holding up the sensation or its object before your gaze to distinguish it and compare it. For this a new and distinct sense is required, a sense that bears fully upon the external sensations and their objects as upon a common object in which they can be assessed and related. If you wish to use the term "reflexion" to designate this further cognition, insofar as in it your cognition is "bending back" upon something already sensed, the notion implied is brought out with sufficient force. But it is reflexion only in the meaning that through a new and distinct faculty your cognition is bending back upon what it has attained through other faculties, here the external senses. It is not the case of a faculty bending back completely upon its own activity, as occurs in intellection. Yet it enables even irrational animals to be aware of themselves and their own activities as distinct objects of their cognition.

This consideration reinforces the tenet that the external sensations and the things so sensed constitute in common the specifying object of a distinct and very important sense. There is no common sensation of that object by the particular external senses as each attains its own object. Rather, as in the passage of Aristotle to which reference has just been made, it requires for its activity "a common faculty that follows upon" all the particular senses. Elsewhere Aristotle (*On Youth and Old Age*, 3.469a12) looks on it as having for its activity a sensorium that is "common", in contrast to particular sense organs. In any case, we are aware of our capacity to observe and coordinate the date of the separate senses. To determine the parts of the nervous system or brain in which this activity takes place is a task for psychological experiments. The concern of epistemology is to show that the observing and coordinating require a specifically distinct faculty, and to investigate the function it exercises in building up the totality of our cognition.

In each particular sensation a substance and several of its

accidents are grasped together in the one whole thing. You see a small piece of wood, with its color, length, width, shape, position and so on. In cognitional being you become and are the wood under those aspects. Through touch with your fingers you simultaneously become and are cognitionally a solid substance with a definite weight and resistance. Is it the same substance that you are attaining in both cases, in the first under the aspects that correspond to your faculty of sight, in the second under those that correspond to your sense of touch? When you strike a match you have from long habituation become accustomed to regard as one and the same thing what you see as colored and small and flaming, and that you feel as solid and light, hear through the crackling noise, and smell through the pungent odor. Under all those varied aspects you look upon yourself as sensing one and the same substance, namely the small piece of wood, the match. In every particular sensation you are sensing a substance. But that particular sensation in itself gives no information that the same substance is being sensed by another faculty.

When watching the massed choirs on the opening day of a gala sporting event, you easily take for granted that you are hearing them singing here and now. Only later you learn that the singing was recorded under ideal conditions, and that what immediately produced the sound to which you were listening was a tape and not the choirs you were looking at. As with the common objects attained by the particular senses, the conditions under which each particular sense operates have to be taken into consideration. In identifying the substance attained by each particular sensation, the sense that overviews them all does not itself go beyond what the media for the particular senses allow. These allow the substance attained in different sensations to be regarded as identical by the overviewing sense. But also they can occasion errors, though providing means for correction. In this way the common aspect functions quite similarly to the way size and distance are erroneously gauged in particular sensations. Always some size is seen in the particular sensation of sight, but not always the right size is identified. Correspondingly a substance is grasped in each object in front of the overviewing sense. Yet it is immediately sensed only as a substance, and not as the same substance attained under other sensations. However, it provides the cognitional framework in which the identity or non-identity can be worked out. No sense attains a thing's specific substantial nature.

In Aristotelian tradition this overviewing faculty has been known as "the common sense" (*sensus communis*). From the time of Avicenna it has been classed with the "internal senses," in contradistinction to the external senses just considered.[5] The designation and classification seem apt enough. The act of sensing in the overviewing sense is that of a single faculty, and not something belonging in common to the particular sense faculties. Its object bridges the external and the internal, the sensations and the things sensed. In consequence the faculty itself is rightly called "common." The label "internal" may cause a bit of difficulty. In the context it should imply that its objects are internal to one's cognition, just as the things perceived by the external senses are outside it. But this is only partly true. The common sense is directly viewing the things perceived by the external senses. It is distinguishing their color in reality from their hardness or taste in reality. It is looking upon its objects in their real existence, and not as represented in a cognitional image. It does not express any image at all. It thereby differs from the other internal senses, for these bear upon their object as it is represented in our cognition. The common sense in contrast bears upon its objects in their real existence, but now as visible, tangible, and so on, namely the objects as they are attained by the external senses. In this manner it itself is attaining both the various sensations and the things that are their objects. Its overall sweep gives awareness of a one externally existent thing as seen, touched, felt, tasted, smelled in the actuality of external sensation.

Through the common sense the sensations are in this way attained as distinct from one another, and able to be compared and contrasted as different types. In those sensations the respective objects are grasped in corresponding fashion, for the objects are their whole content and provide the specifying factors by which the types of external sensation are distinguished. In this combined way the "sensations and the things sensed" present together a common aspect that specifies the common sense.

The object of the common sense, then, remains always in the real external world confronting the percipient here and now. But it is filtering through the cognition of that world that has been given by external sensation. From this angle the common sense may be classed with the internal senses. It does in fact always bear upon the external thing in that thing's real existence, but under aspects recognized in the thing through external sensations.

This is an important consideration when one is facing the question whether colors, sounds, hardness, odors and so on really exist in the external thing or just come into being in our sensing of them. Locke had maintained that the primary qualities were existent in the external thing, but that the secondary qualities existed only in our cognition. Berkeley showed that since the primary qualities cannot be known except as extended under some secondary quality, the same arguments that do away with the external reality of the secondary qualities likewise show that the primary qualities exist only in the mind.[6] The end result is that the whole material world disappears. Through the proper sensibles, then, the common sensibles and the substances are attained. To regard the proper sensibles as not real will cut off our access to any reality in the material universe. Painters and other artists whose work depends on intense awareness of colors, sounds and other sensible qualities are very cognizant of their reality. To everyone, in fact, the secondary qualities appear fully as real, if not more real, than anything else in the external thing. Only through later arguments is a case brought against their reality, and it turns out to be a case that would destroy the reality of all else in our cognition of the material world. Yet as we come to know the sensible qualities, and distinguish, compare and discuss them, it is as they have already been presented and rendered distinct through the activity of the external senses. Aristotle, accordingly, could speak of the sensible qualities as existing in the percipient, while at the same time refuting the "earlier philosophers" who thought that "white and black have no existence without vision, nor flavour without taste."[7]

Also important is the way the common sense, in its type of reflexion upon the cognitive activities of one's own external senses, gives the awareness that all these activities are proceeding from one and the same agent, namely oneself. It thereby furnishes the model for regarding every thing as an agent endowed with accidents. It does not penetrate into the specific natures of the substances, nor does it immediately see the identity of the seen substance with the felt or sounding substance. In consequence it does not show immediately a substantial identity of the seen and the felt thing. It does not show that the piano you are seeing before you is the piano you are touching and hearing. But it does provide an instance of different sensible activities functioning together as accidents of the same substance, namely oneself. It thereby provides a model for regarding other objects as substances endowed with different accidents, with the one substantial existence synthesizing them into a single thing and agent. It can give occasion for error, but it provides the means for correction. By giving awareness of the unity of the percipient, the common sense provides the framework for inferring the integrated unity of substance and accidents in other groups of phenomena.

Two very different types of common sensation, then, appear clearly articulated in the phenomenology of the agent's perception. First, the common sensibles, or primary qualities, are attained directly by each of the external senses. The direct perception of them does not require, nor allow place for, any new and distinct faculty. Secondly, the sensations themselves and the external things as sensed separately by them, present together a common object that *does* require a new faculty in the percipient. It is a common object that on the sense level spans real and cognitional being. It allows the same content to be sensed at once in real existence in the external world and in cognitional existence in each of the sensations by which it is grasped through the external senses. It thereby makes possible, on the sense level, both comparison and contrast of the sensations with each other and with the things sensed. This common object specifies the distinct faculty that has traditionally been known as the common sense and been classed with the internal senses.[8]

Imagination. Cognition by means of the external senses and the common sense is set afoot by the activity of external things upon the sense organs. The distant star or the nearby advertisement board acts upon the percipient through the medium of light waves. The cannon welcoming the official visitor, and the person talking alongside you, act upon you through the medium of sound waves. In these respective ways they bring you into their own forms in immaterial fashion, that is, they make you aware of them. They do not make you be themselves physically or materially. But they do bring about identity in a new way of being, since form is the cause of being. In this immaterial manner they make you be themselves cognitionally. Cognitionally you become the things exactly as they are there in their real existence. That is the way you are aware of them, and from the fact of that awareness you infer the causality they are exercising upon you.

But you are also aware of cognition within yourself that is not being brought about by the activity of external things upon you here and now. You can conjure up at will the representations of persons long dead or houses years since demolished. You can indulge in daydreams of things that never happen, or tell tall tales or compose short stories or novels about events that have not taken place in reality. In every case, however, you will find that the components of these representations or phantasies have come to you originally through the cognition of the external senses. You are merely reviving within yourself the cognition of these components, or are arranging them in new order and new combinations under the inspiration of your own genius. In a word, the forms originally obtained through external sensation are being revived and made active in new life.

This means that the forms into which you as sentient subject were originally brought through external sensation have remained present all along within you in habitual fashion. You remain *informed* by them. At will, you bring them into activity when you cast back your internal glance at events of the past. Very frequently physical or psychic happenings trigger the revival. But now it is not the original external things that are acting upon you by themselves through external media. It is rather your own will or the physical or psychic causes acting within yourself that now set afoot this new cognition. The faculty that enables you to retain these forms and to reactivate and combine them anew is called the imagination. This faculty is internal in the full meaning of the term. It is not grasping things as they are in their real external existence, but only as they exist cognitionally within your own awareness.[9] Just in itself it presents them only in cognitional existence.

Instinct. A third internal sense is known as instinct. It gives awareness of what is beneficial or harmful to the percipient. The infant is instinctively impelled towards its nourishment, the lamb is filled with dread at its very first sight of the wolf. The object of this faculty has tended accordingly to be looked upon as something not already attained by the external senses. It antecedes the experience of nourishment or of the wolf's voraciousness. Nevertheless it is in fact based upon a type of sensation already shown to come under the range of what is external to cognition even though the object is internal to the percipient's body. Quite as sensations of attraction or revulsion are brought about by the way one's constitution reacts to favorable or unfavorable situations, or the kinesthetic sensations to muscular exertions, so a percipient's nature is constituted to react sensitively to the sight of nipple or predator. The instinct gives awareness of this natural reaction. From the epistemological viewpoint, therefore, nothing is found in this instinctive awareness that does not originate in external sensation, combined with the reflexion of the *sensus communis.*

In human beings, the instinctive sense works in conjunction with intellectual reaction, and has been traditionally called the estimative or cogitative faculty. With

Islamic philosophers especially it played an important role in doctrines of cognition, and was given the Arabic designation *wahm*.[10]

Memory. In revivifying past events cognitionlly you are also aware of the ability to date them in relation to other events, and to recall, sometimes with great effort, the circumstances and surroundings that accompanied them. This requires another faculty on the internal sense level. The traditional name for that faculty is memory. It bears immediately on the time element.[11]

Beliefs. Besides the things you perceive through your own external senses, or invent through your imagination, you find your memory replete with things and events that you have learned from others. You recognize other people as independent sources of experience and observation. You profit by what they communicate to you. Travelers who have seen places and witnessed happenings on other continents tell you about them. Newspapers, radio and television are constantly operative in extending your cognition to myriad details that you do not encounter at first hand. Modern means of communication have intensified to an astonishing degree this way of learning about things. With regard to the past, people tell you about their own life history. Written records communicate the story of bygone ages. Since all this consists in accepting data on the word of another, in contrast to what you yourself attain immediately with your own external senses, it is a type of cognition tradionally called "belief." In a case like Aristotle's example about incidentally seeing the son of Cleon, your acquaintance with the filial relationship comes from what others have told you or what you have read in the records. In recent use, however, "belief" means any judgment to which one gives assent. It is added to enrich the percept.

Interpretation. From these various sources what is originally sensed as merely something in human shape and dimly colored, for example, may be greatly enriched with numerous other characteristics. In the evening dusk you may be seeing only the vague outline of a human figure in the garden next door. Confronting your vision is something that is indistinguishable from what you would see in the figures of hundreds of other men. Yet spontaneously you associate that figure with much of what you know from years of acquaintance with your neighbor. You project the observed figure as a man of sixty years with glasses and greying hair, a chartered accountant of high reputation, an amateur gardener of only moderate skill, and you clothe him with many other details from long memory. The comparatively meager object of sensation is at once constructed into a thing or a person enriched with a wealth of qualities and accomplishments.

In a corresponding way the visible world in front of us is interpreted mainly as made up of three-dimensional objects, each with its own real existence and accidents, and with its real activity. What is present on the retina as a flat image is projected in depth, and through spontaneous interpretation the perceived world is peopled and furnished in rich detail. Extension in two dimensions is immediately seen. The third dimension is added through contours attained by touch.[12] Accidents grasped through the other senses are associated with the same substance, usually on account of identity in place. The notion of two really different things simultaneously occupying the same space, with the one having the color and the other having the hardness, proves unacceptable. The spontaneous interpretation, when the colored thing and the solid thing are compared and contrasted through the common sense, is that one and the same thing is being seen and felt simultaneously.

In that way what is grasped through a single external sense is enriched into your completed percept of the object. Some of the added characteristics may be grasped simultaneously through other external senses. Further additions are drawn from memory and imagination. Unified action is generally taken as indicating a unitary thing as the agent. But that is not enough, just in itself, to show that all the observable accidents belong to the one substance. All movements observed in the typewriter converge on printing a unified message. Yet on the basis of perceptible configurations and properties a further division can be made into the pieces of metal out of which the machine is composed. In consequence the basic metals are habitually interpreted as substances, the typewriter in turn as an artifact. A tree, on the other hand, exhibits a combination of movements and changes that center upon its growth and conservation as a definitely maintained configuration. It is accordingly interpreted as a substance in itself. Mosquitoes, cats, elephants are marked off by the same type of interpretation. Other sensible configurations, exhibiting in themselves the indefinitely richer manifestations of speech and social life, are grouped together by you as human beings like yourself. In these ways the everyday world in which you live is represented in your cognition. Activity, immediately expressed in your own perceiving and reflecting, is automatically transferred to other substances. They are interpreted as the agents producing the observed movements and changes.

All this is interpretation that has become habitual. The external changes are immediately observable, the activity is not. Yet the interpretation is practically instantaneous, and can be surprisingly penetrating and far-reaching in certain types of people, such as the born gambler or detective. From a philosophical viewpoint, at least after Hume's time, it is not too hard to see why different types of Skeptics have thrown doubt upon the presence of efficient causality in the observable world, or how Malebranche came to restrict it to God. Yet one has immediate experience of causal activity in one's own planning and striving. On this there follows a natural tendency to attribute proportionate causality to other substances. This tendency may well be grounded in an instinct or *wahm* required for meeting the needs of practical living.

Through spontaneous interpretation, then, one rounds out into full-blown percept one's particular sensations of something colored, or felt, or heard, or sounding, or tasted or odoriferous. Likewise the self of which one is concomitantly aware in every act of cognition is filled out in terms of a body seen and felt, and experienced in kinesthetic and pain sensations. The existent percipient, and the other things existent in themselves, are in a corresponding way represented in distinct percepts and as spatially separate from each other in the real external world.

This separation immediately gives rise to the problem how the external thing, if spatially separated from the percipient, can impress its own form upon the cognitive agent in the way required for sensation. The causality exercised by the sensed thing is what makes the percipient take on the form of that thing and thereby become cognitionally the thing itself. The problem can be intensified where the thing is no longer really existent when the sensation is taking place. In Longfellow's poem,

> Were a star quenched on high,
> For ages would its light,
> Still traveling downward from the sky,
> Shine on our mortal sight.[13]

But can a long extinct heavenly body still be seen? Further, how can the causality transmitted to the retina by the light waves be continued into the nerve and brain centers as required by the neurophysiological data concerning the act of sight?

Cognitional Media. Psychological experiments and detailed studies show cogently enough that what immediately excites and brings about sensation is the end product of two factors. One of the factors is a stimulus from outside. The other is a reaction of the organic sensory apparatus. Time-lag and artificial stimulation of sensory centers in the brain indicate that the determining product, a complex of highly encoded signals, is located in the interacting of the cerebral cortex and the nerve systems from the sense organs to the brain.[14] The conclusion, then, is that the immediately operative instrument enabling the external thing to bring the sentient agent into that thing's own form is the product of the stimulus and the reaction. Accordingly the thing immediately sensed as really existent outside the cognition is so attained just to the extent its form is purveyed through the interior neural activity. Only subsequently is the thing interpreted in terms of distance and multiplicity and other features added in the percept.

What ultimately determines you to perceive the hard, brown, varnish-smelling desk one foot in front of you is therefore a product of the action and reaction that take place within your neural activity. In that product you are the recipient of the form that makes you cognitionally identical with the thing you are sensing. You see something really existent, something that you interpret as the desk with real hardness and color. It is perceived as a unit and as present there in itself, in marked contrast to a desk read about in a novel and existent only in human cognition.

The details of these psychological and neurophysiological conclusions pertain to their respective sciences. But they highlight facts that need consideration in an epistemological study. They require that perception be explained in function of an encoded complex brought about in one's own neural activity. As in television, there is color in the distant object. There is color in the retinal image. But there is no color in the neural activity through which the external thing's form is immediately received by the percipient. This lack of immediate physical contact with the retinal image need not be any more disconcerting than was the distance through which the causality of thing had to travel to reach the sense organ. Air and water were the external media through which the signals travel from the distant object to the eye or ear. Through those media the distant thing exercises its efficient causality upon the percipient, impressing its own form in immaterial fashion upon the cognitive agent. The same type of reasoning holds in regard to the use of the interior media. Through them the efficient causality of the external object brings the percipient immaterially into the form of the thing perceived, just as the wood is brought materially into the table's form.

There is in consequence no requirement for a replica, with one-to-one correspondence to the thing in observable features, that would travel from the thing through the external media and then through the interior neural media, in order to account for perception. There is no interior television screen on which the object is reproduced in its own colors and shape for the percipient to gaze upon. Rather, through the activity of the percipient, who has already been determined and specified by the form of the thing perceived, the object comes into new existence in cognition.

The problem is therefore in principle no different from that of the transmission of efficient causality through media in which there is no observable point-to-point correspondence in detail with the efficient cause itself. The conception in the mind of the sculptor passes through hands and chisel into the marble without requiring any exact replica to go through those media. What passes through them is the efficient causality that works the form of Churchill into the marble or bronze. What counts is that the percipient is brought into the form of the thing perceived, in the immaterial fashion that enables him to perform the act of perceiving the distant thing.

In this same regard, moreover, the genesis of one's acquaintance with the ultimate cerebral product is not to be forgotten. That product is not something observed through immediate reflexion. Its presence, rather, is deduced as a conclusion from the observable effects produced by colored, hard, sounding, ill-smelling or bitter things, in the course of experiments. The pointer readings in the experiments are themselves external, extended, and really colored in at least black and white. These external things are the foundations called upon to support a hypothesis of internal location for the object immediately sensed. The descriptive details about the internal object have to be deduced from them. So any interpretation of the conclusions in a meaning that would do away with the already known real existence of the sensible things would be self-destructive. It would be sawing off the bough on which it itself is sitting. Eddington's two tables are really one and the same thing, known in two different ways, with the scientific way dependent on the ordinary way for its data.[15]

By the same token, these observations set aside any

simplistic interpretation of sensible awareness on the model of photography or tape-recording. The percipient is not making a film of the end product located in the cerebral cortex. The end product does not present even a replica for the filming. Rather, by means of that product the percipient is brought into cognitional identity with the really existent objects through the immaterial reception of their forms. His awareness is indeed his own activity. But it is formed and fashioned instrumentally by the cerebral product in a way that makes the percipient be cognitionally identical with other really existent substances. The epistemological problem is not what the cerebral product looks like, but how it is able to make one aware of things to which it does not have exact correspondence in terms of either secondary or primary qualities, and only the vaguest correspondence in terms of substance. In fact, one might ask, if what is thereby sensed is immediately the cerebral product itself, how could it ever come to be interpreted genuinely as something not produced by the cerebral activity but as really existent in independence of that activity? How could it ever be metamorphized into our world of stones and trees and animals?

Finally, how is the perception of self as cognitive agent to be explained in terms of the cerebral data? Much less than in the case of external objects can there be question of envisaging its activity after a photographic model. Its activity is not something that is sensed as a direct object. It is grasped only in a concomitant awareness that is not at all articulated in any terms of its own. It could exhibit nothing that would *confront* the alleged internal camera in the attempt to focus on the aspect of the active self as looked for within the cerebral product. Immediate presentation of itself as a definite figure can hardly be expected.

Psychological findings, rather, seem to show that what is first sensed is something indefinite, grasped neither as external nor as internal. Then one's own self is gradually distinguished from the surrounding mass.[16] At first a confused but unitary object is basic in one's awareness. Only later is oneself as cognitive agent distinguished from the opposed ambient. Through kinesthetic sensations and feelings of pain and hunger and thirst the cognitive agent is located in a particular body. The body is readily definable in terms of sight and touch and other external senses, for instance in the obvious difference in sensations when an ice cube is touched to one's own skin and when it is slipped down somebody's else's neck. In this way the self is separated from the ambient not only as the concomitantly grasped percipient but also as an object with definite three-dimensional extension and secondary qualities and as existent in the panorama that confronts one's sight and is likewise perceived through the other external senses.

From the psychological viewpoint, then, internal status was not at all manifest in the vague unarticulated object first grasped by an infant's cognition. Rather, an ensuing process was required to extract the self from the ambient. There is no evidence of starting from awareness of self and then projecting the rest as external. The effort was to get from something indefinite to a definite self. It was not a process of going from the inside to the outside. Psychologically the indefinite appears to have had at the beginning a certain priority in human cognition. Epistemologically, however, the problem still is whether the primitive indefinite object and the concomitant awareness have real rather than merely cognitional existence. Here as elsewhere percipient and thing perceived have to be one in the actuality of cognition. Both are perceived as existing. But whether the existence is real or cognitional remains undistinguished in the general vagueness of what is grasped. A closer look, followed on more experience, will show that the existence of both was grasped as real from the start, even though it had been recognized only indefinitely as existence. The relevant distinction is not that of one's own body from the ambient that is external to it. It is rather the distinction of what exists outside cognition from what exists only internally in the cognition. Each of the two types of existence has to be perceived immediately. No amount of reasoning from your imagining of the Loch Ness monster can be the basis for concluding to its real existence. Likewise it could have been in real existence for centuries without implying its existence in any human mind. Neither the external nor the internal can be originally inferred from the other.

In using the psychological findings, therefore, one needs to keep carefully in mind the two types of external status that are at issue. One type concerns what is external to the human body. That is the type seen in the ambient when one's own human body has been distinguished from it. The other type is that of existence that is external to cognition in contrast to existence within cognition. Attempts to reach an outside from this latter type of the internal have from Descartes' time on invariably ended in failure.

Vocabulary. In the foregoing discussion on the human cognitive agent, clarity and precision have at times required a use of words that is somewhat different from ordinary speech. Distinction of "sensing" from "perceiving" has been necessary to account for the enriched percept. Yet we do not usually say that sight senses colors, or that hearing senses sounds. Further, imagination and memory and instinct are not ordinarily referred to as senses. Nor do we assert that imagination or memory senses something, though we may say at times that instinct does. "The common sense" is no longer used in ordinary English for the faculty known in Scholastic Latin as the *sensus communis.* To make oneself understood in regard to that faculty, one has to use the Latin phrase.[17] So in regard to focusing on the important difference between what is immediately attained by the human cognitive agent and what is then presented in the enriched percept, "sensing" has to be used for what is actually and immediately being grasped in external sensation and in common sensation, while "perceiving" covers also what is added from other sensations or from imagination and instinct and memory. Likewise we do not ordinarily say that past percepts are stored in the imagination. Rather, we speak of them as being kept in our memory. Finally, "cogitative" and "estimative" have gone out of use as English designations for instinct in humans.

In Scholastic terminology the form that the sensed thing impresses upon the percipient is called the *species impressa,* the impressed species.[18] *Species* is taken here in the philosophical meaning of "form." These impressed forms determine the imagination to produce an image or representation of the thing, an image in which the thing itself is held before the percipient's internal gaze. The Scholastic designation for this image is the *species expressa*, the expressed form. In that image the thing can be examined and remembered, and be recognized as an object of dread or of utility.[19] Hence instinct and memory as well as imagination require an expressed species. The external senses and the common sense do not express any image, since they bear directly on their object in its real existence. These forms or species are conserved in an habitual state in the imagination, and can bring the percipient again and again into the actual cognition of their object as often as they are "expressed" anew by the percipient's own effort or by events that occasion recollection of them. In Scholastic terminology the impressed species belongs to the order of first actuality, insofar as it functions in habitual fashion as a form in the percipient. The expressed species, in contrast, pertains to the operation in which the thing was actually being perceived, and accordingly belongs to the order of second actuality.[20]

Further, is it correct to say that you "see" or "hear" a distant object? Are you really seeing here and now a star that has been extinct for millions of years? What you are seeing in the pinpoint of light is something shining. But what is that "something"? It is certainly not the relatively inverted image in the visual field on the retina.[21] That image is something you come to know only through scientific investigation. It is not the light wave itself, for that is something you do not see but only learn about through study. It is hard to locate what you see as anywhere else than in the galaxy itself. The galaxy is the "something" you are seeing. It may no longer be there, but it was there when it emitted the light waves that are now reaching your eye. Through their instrumentality it is still working here and now on your sense organ, and is transmitting to nerves and cortex the signals that impress the form of the galaxy upon your cognitional potentiality. It thereby makes you identical with the galaxy itself in cognitional existence, that is, it makes you aware of the really existent galaxy itself. The cognitional identity is with the really existent galaxy, as attained through an extremely enriched percept.

The galaxy, then, is what you are literally seeing. You are seeing it as it really existed millions of years ago. If you disregard media and time lag, and make the judgment that it is still really existent, you can be in error through neglecting to consider the conditions of transmission. But to say that what you are seeing is the galaxy is an indubitably correct statement. Similarly you are hearing the distant thunder in the clouds, even though the crash was finished several seconds earlier. Likewise you are hearing the birds singing and the band playing, and seeing the mountains and the moon and the planets. The same considerations hold correspondingly in the case of other external senses.

Finally, you have no real trouble in distinguishing externally existing things from what has existed only in your cognition. You recall the Challenger (1986) disaster as a tragic event that really took place in the outside world. You do not confuse that real existence and the mourning it caused with the existence you are now giving it as you think about it. But if you imagine yourself to be a member of the first crew to land on Mars and to be exulting in the triumphal reception on the return from the Martian voyage, you know that you are dealing with a different type of existence. Where one sees definitely, one need not restrict oneself to the term "appear" when speaking about perception. The thing not merely appears to exist when it is perceived. It is definitely perceived to exist, either really or cognitionally. Most of the time your perception clearly distinguishes the one type of existence from the other. Only when you are not sure do you need to settle for the term "appear." When you are not sure whether a distant object is moving or stationary, you may use the language of appearance. But once you are certain, you definitely say that it *is* moving or that it *is* staying still. This remark has its relevance in an epistemological study of perception. One approach has been that the start should be made from the way things appear, withholding judgment about whether or not they exist. A thing is thereby basically understood in relation to our cognition, namely as an object that appears to us. So understood, it would be doomed to stay that way. But we first grasp things definitely as existing in themselves, and then we reflect upon them as existing in our awareness. On this account "existing" rather than "appearing" is the epistemologically correct term in their regard.

Résumé. The epistemological study of your perception shows that you are the one percipient throughout all your various acts of sensing and imagining. The unity of your perception through its whole course is thereby assured. Your lifelong perceptive activity has not been just a succession of self-sustaining acts in Humean fashion. Rather, close reflexion shows that those acts were performed by one and the same individual cognitive agent, yourself, the individual now reflecting upon them. The images produced by the acts, images in which things other than the acts themselves are perceived, remain habitually in your *one* memory. They are recalled into actuality by you as the percipient. In this way your reflexive consciousness manifests yourself as the one percipient who unites all your perceptive activities into one global whole, quite as the one substance unites all the generic and specific and accidental characteristics of the percept into the one perceived thing.[22]

In the same vein, you find your perception is structured in substantial and accidental grades through your different abilities or faculties and their corresponding acts. Just as the one percept is structured through generic and specific and accidental differentiae, so your unitary act of perception is structured through its external and internal sensation on the sense level, and on the intellectual level through its understanding of the percept in terms of universality, and of the percipient in terms of will. These intellectual aspects have yet to be considered. But on the sense level the external senses correspond in structural terms to the proper and common sensibles in the object, as sight, touch, hearing and the other external senses grasp the object in their respective ways. The common sense distinguishes these sensations from one another, but by the same token can point to their bearing on one and the same object. The imagination expresses internal images or representations of the things attained in sensation, conserves in habitual status their forms or species, and unites them in new combinations. In those images the things sensed are gauged by instinct as to utility of harmfulness, recalled by memory, and brought to the fullness of "enriched" or "transformed" percepts by the cognitive agent. In this way the distant object that has impressed its form on the percipient merely under one sensible aspect is rounded out into the thing or person that confronts our everyday perception.

Notes to Chapter 4

1. "It is doubtless better to avoid saying that the soul pities or learns or thinks, and rather to say that it is the man who does this with his soul." Aristotle, *De an.*, 1.4.408b13-15; Oxford trans. Cf. ibid., b25-27. Similarly Aquinas, *De veritate*, 2.6.ad 3m. Likewise today: "People, not their eyes, see." Norwood Russell Hanson, *Patterns of Discovery* (Cambridge, 1958), 6. Similarly Rodney J. Hirst, *The Problems of Perception* (London, 1959) 280. E. L. Mascall, "Perception and Sensation," *Proceedings of the Aristotelian Society*, 64 (1963-1964), 272, aptly notes the virtual impossibility of avoiding in ordinary language the phrasing that the senses perceive and the intellect apprehends; cf. 264 and 267. A discussion from a psychological viewpoint that the man, not the brain, does the thinking may be found in Erwin Straus, *The Primary World of Senses* (London, 1963), 184-186.

2. On the modern classification of the senses, see Frank Arthur Geldard, *The Human Senses* (New York, 1953). The traditional classification of five senses, accepted by Aristotle, continues in popular speech. Muscular or kinesthetic sense was added in nineteenth century psychology. On the weight of evidence in favor of two thermal senses, see Geldard, 211-232. Separate stimulation for pain (ibid., 198-199) marks off another distinct sense. For further discussion of the whole topic, see G. M. Wyburn, R. W. Pickford and R. J. Hirst, in *Human Senses and Perception*, ed. G. M. Wyburn (Edinburgh, 1964), 15-133; and James Jerome Gibson, *The Senses Considered as Perceptual Systems* (New York, 1966), with bibliography 322-329. On the "five senses" in Greek times, see John Isaac Beare, *Greek Theories of Elementary Cognition* (Oxford, 1906), 9-201. Current psychological discussions on topics relevant to sensation may be found in periodicals such as *Cognitive Psychology* (1970--), *Cognition* (1972--), Perception (1972--) and *Cognitive Science* (1977--).

On the extent of the notion "kinesthetic sensations," see Geldard, 234-235, and on the kinesthetic receptor organs, 235-239. On the pain receptors, see ibid., 191-208. The topic, however, remains highly complex. Smell and taste, called "the chemical senses"

(Geldard, 233), quite apparently include in their object much of the percipient's bodily reaction, since they can differ so widely with the body's disposition. On these two senses, see Geldard, 270-323; Wyburn (editor), *Human Senses and Perception,* 114-133 (with short bibliography); Gibson, *The Senses Considered as Perceptual Systems,* 136-153 (with designation "chemical *sense*" rejected, 139).

3. "It primarily signifies that which is perceived in the mode of actuality absolutely; for 'is,' said simply, signifies *to be in act . . .*" Aquinas, *In Peri hermeneias,* 1.5.22; trans. Jean T. Oesterle, *Aristotle: On Interpretation. Commentary by St. Thomas and Cajetan* (Milwaukee, 1962), 53. In the sense judgment, the perceived existence is not distinguished from its subject, as is done by verb and noun in intellection. Yet the existence is what is primarily attained. Otherwise there be nothing there to grasp.

4. Aristotle, *De an.,* 3.1.425a27-30. On the topic of common sensation, see D. W. Hamlyn, "Koine Aisthesis," *The Monist,* 52 (1968), 195-209; J. Owens, "Aristotle on Common Sensibles and Incidental Perception," *Phoenix,* 36 (1982), 215-236. The Aristotelian common sensibles correspond to Locke's "primary qualities," and the proper sensibles to his "secondary qualities." In opposite perspective, Scholastic terminology regarded the proper sensibles as sensible *per se primo* and the common sensibles as sensible *per se secundo.* See Joseph Gredt, *Elementa philosophiae aristotelico-tomisticae,* ed. 7a (Freiburg, 1937), I, 379 (no. 487). Cf. John Locke, *An Essay Concerning Human Understanding,* 2.8.23; ed. Peter H. Nidditch (Oxford, 1975), 140. For Locke, the primary qualities were in the things, with the power to "*produce in us*" (ibid.) ideas of secondary qualities.

5. On the origin and history of the "internal senses," see Harry A. Wolfson, "The Internal Senses in Latin, Arabic, and Hebrew Philosophic Texts," *Harvard Theological Review,* 28 (1935), 69-133. The phrase "internal sense" is of Latin origin, with the meaning that the location of an internal sense is inside the brain. See Wolfson, 70; 96. On Avicenna, see ibid., 95-100. Aristotle himself designates as "senses" only the five traditional ones and the primary or fundamental sense later known as the *sensus communis.* He has no

classification that would group the latter with imagination, memory and instinct. Later classifications went as high as seven. Locke, *Essay*, 2.1.4, ed. Nidditch, 105, noted the expression "internal Sense," but preferred "*Reflection*" as contradistinguished from "*Sensation.*"

6. See Berkeley, *A Treatise Concerning the Principles of Human Knowledge*, 1.15; in Works, ed. A. A. Luce and T. E. Jessop (London, 1948-1957), II, 47.11-14. *Three Dialogues Between Hylas and Philonous*, 1; II, 194.20-26.

7. Aristotle, *De an.*, 3.2.426a20-22; Hett trans. Cf. *Metaph.*, 9.3.1047a4-6.

8. See Bernard J. Muller-Thym, "The Common Sense, Perfection of the Order of Pure Sensibility," *The Thomist*, 2 (1940), 315-343. "The object of the common sense is not the common sensibles, *communia sensibilia*"--321. For other treatises, articles and references concerning the *sensus communis*, see George P. Klubertanz, *The Discursive Power* (St. Louis, 1952), 19-22, nn. 7-16. While it attains its object under the unitary aspect of "sensation and thing sensed," it is not at all the faculty that unifies all the data into one's experience-- see Robert W. Schmidt, "The Unifying Sense: Which?" *The New Scholasticism*, 57 (1983), 1-21. That unifying sense, Schmidt shows is rather the discursive or cogitative power. On the early Greek background of the *sensus communis* and the other faculties later classified as "internal senses," see Beare, *Greek Theories of Elementary Cognition from Alcmaeon to Aristotle*, 250-336. For the topic in Aquinas and preceding medieval philosophy, see Edmund Joseph Ryan, *The Role of the "Sensus Communis" in the Psychology of St. Thomas Aquinas* (Carthagena, OH, 1951).

The problem of organ for the type of sensation ascribed to the *sensus communis* is not a concern of epistemology, but rather of natural philosophy and psychology. The epistemological consideration bears on object, activity, and percipient. In this perspective the location of different qualities in the one subject has interested modern writers without being attributed to the traditional *sensus communis*. E.G., "We have argued, on the contrary, that the qualities perceived by touch qualify the very same space as that immediately perceived by sight." David M. Armstrong, *Berkeley's Theory of Vision* (Parkville, Australia, 1960), 102. See also Maurice Merleau-Ponty, *Phenomenology of Perception*, trans. Colin Smith (London, 1962), 235. On "common sense" in this meaning in English, see *O.E.D.*, s.v. 1. However, it is not a topic in Paul Edwards' *Encyclopedia of Philosophy* II, 155-160, though it is recognized by Baldwin, *Dictionary of Philosophy and Psychology*, s.v. (3), and in French (*sens commun*) by Lalande, *Vocabulaire technique et critique de la philosophie*, s.v. A, and in the *Enciclopedia filosofica* is listed first among the meanings of *senso comune*. Yet its role in connecting the cognitional with the external has exercised a certain fascination in accord with the prevalent trends of various backgrounds. John of St. Thomas, *Naturalis philosophia*, 4.8.1, in *Cursus philosophicus thomisticus*, ed. Reiser (Turin, 1930-1937), III, 242a, attempted an association of the *sensus communis* with the "animal spirits," and Mercier, *Psychologie*, 6th ed. (Louvain, 1903), I, 240-248 (nos. 100-102) with the *sens intime* and muscular sensation. In any case, the common object here is not something that is acting upon any of the external senses. It specifies a distinct faculty.

9. On imagination, see Aristotle, *De an.*, 3.3.427a17-429a9. For a discussion on the topic, see Michael V. Wedin, *Mind and Imagination in Aristotle* (New Haven, 1988), 23-159. On the stand that "imagination is not a full faculty," see Wedin, 48. In the Aristotelian context, however, a faculty (*dynamis*) is an ability to do something, and was listed as the second species of quality in the *Categories*, 8,9a16. The Scholastic term in Latin was *potentia*. It may be rendered in English as potentiality, capacity, capability, power or faculty. "Potency" in English does not seem to carry this precise meaning. The question whether a faculty is really distinct from the substance in which it inheres is an entirely different problem. But the fact that one actually imagines is sufficient to show that one has the faculty of doing so, in the Aristotelian meaning of "faculty."

The images are stored in the imagination, and can be dissociated and associated anew by it. But the externally sensed things remain always the cause of the images. On this, see Aristotle, *On Dreams*, 2.459a23-b1.

10. For a coverage of this faculty, see Klubertanz, *The Discursive Power* (St. Louis, 1952). An early name for it classed it as *dianoetic* (see Wolfson, 71) and in that way "discursive." On the Arabic *wahm*, see Wolfson, 89-95.

11. Memory in this Aristotelian sense does not store the images. It shows the location in time for the things remembered. Since intellectual objects are always presented to our cognition in sensible images, they are *incidentally* subject to memory--Aristotle, *On Memory and Recollection*, 2,451a25-29. "Recollection" in this context refers to the rational effort made towards recalling events, with the time element the distinguishing character of memory.

12. See Gibson, *The Perception of the Visual World* (Boston, 1950), 15-24.

13. Longfellow, *Charles Sumner*.

14. The "stimulus," in the strict sense, should mean the cause that immediately acts upon the sensory organ, for instance the pattern of the light waves that strike the eye. The immediate reaction of the organ with it produces the inverted colored image on the retina, and then the impulses traveling along the optic nerve, and finally the product in the cortex. The cortical activity and its result are a necessary condition for sensation, and quite possibly, in the opinion of neurologists, may if adequately stimulated be sufficient to account for it. However, "present ignorance of the details of cerebral activity" (Hirst, *Problems*, 252) does not allow a satisfactory neurophysiological explanation of the exact happenings in the context in which they are approached by the epistemologist. For a philosophical discussion of the data, see John Raymond Smythies, *Analysis of Perception* (London, 1956), pp. 3-74.

15. A fragment of Democritus (5th century B.C.) expresses this truth vividly: "Miserable Mind, you get your evidence from us, and do you try to overthrow us? The overthrow will be your downfall." *Fr.* 125 (DK; trans. Kathleen Freeman, *Ancilla*, 104.) So: "Empirical Science can never be more trustworthy than perception, upon which it is based." Henry Habberley Price, *Perception* (London, 1932), 1; cf. 36-

37. On the two tables, see Arthur Stanley Eddington, *The Nature of the Physical World* (Cambridge, 1928), ix-xi; Stephen Toulmin, *The Philosophy of Science* (New York, 1953), 12. Cf.supra, c. 1, n. 23.

16. Cf.: "The child is a realist, since he supposes thought to be inseparable from its object, names from the things named, and dreams to be external. His realism consists in a spontaneous and immediate tendency to confuse the sign and the thing signified, internal and external, and the psychical and the physical." Jean Piaget, *The Child's Conception of the World* (London, 1929), 124. So "what we speak of as internal and what we speak of as external are for a long time equally regarded as common to all." Ibid., 129. Cf. Piaget, *The Construction of Reality in the Child*, trans. Margaret Cook (New York, 1954), 350-357; Josef Ernest Garai, in *Perceptual Development in Children*, ed. Aline H. Kidd and Jeanne L. Rivoire (New York, 1966), 344-352.

17. The difficulties in calling this faculty the "common sense" in English have been discussed above, n. 8.

18. The term *species* in this context covers both sensible and intelligible forms. In English the word "image" can be used regularly for the Latin *species expressa*, provided that "image" is extended to include the notion of an intelligible representation. "Representation" can always be used for both the sensible and intelligible *species*. Where no representation is expressed, the thing is being perceived or known in itself. But where the thing is not being immediately attained through external sensation, and also where it is attained in its intelligible aspects, an expressed *species* is required. It is perceived or known in that representation. ". . . The life of a perfect animal requires it to apprehend a thing not only in its sensible presence but also in its absence. . . . It is therefore necessary that through the sentient soul the animal not only receive the forms (*species*) of sensible things, when it is altered by them, but also that it retain and conserve them." Aquinas, *ST*, 1.78.4c. An expressed species is required for all human intellectual cognition, since the intelligible object does not exist in universal fashion in the sensible thing. This expressed *species* in the intellectual order is called in Latin the *verbum* or the *verbum mentis*.

19. Dread and utility are not aspects attained by the external senses, but rather through one's natural reaction to the things so perceived. Only from this angle may they be regarded as aspects that are not sensed--"intentiones, quas non percipit sensus exterior," Aquinas, *ST*, 1.78.4c. Here John of St. Thomas *Naturalis philosophia*, 4.8.1, ed. Reiser, III, 251a24 (cf. 249a38,b25, b29,b46; 250a15,a46; 251a1; 252a24, a31, a34) attributes to Aquinas the notion of *species insensatae* and (a28) that of *ratio insensata*. Busa's *Index thomisticus*, svv. insensatus, etc., does not list any instances in the works of Aquinas. J. Gredt, *Elementa philosophiae aristotelico-thomisticae*, I, 394 (no. 503.3) nevertheless reads "intentiones insensatas" into the Thomistic text. The expression seems very inept, since the aspects are perceived through internal sensation, which is regarded as genuine sensation in this context.

20. "First actuality" is used by Aristotle (*De an.*, 2.1.412a27) to denote mere possession in contrast to exercise, as in sleep one still possesses knowledge that one is not exercising at the moment. Against this background "second actuality" became the standard Scholastic phrase for the exercise of a faculty, as contradistinguished from possession of it. First actuality was existence, second actuality was operation.

21. The notion that "a retinal *picture* is transmitted to the brain by the optic nerve" is characterized as "naive" by Gibson, *The Perception of the Visual World*, 9a. Cf.: "It is an event composed not of light, but of nerve-cell discharges, and if a surgeon exposed the brain to view, there would be nothing to see"--ibid., p. 50b. Regarding the general agreement today on the causal chain from object to cortical activity, see Hirst, *Problems*, 279. On the inverted ocular image, see Irvin Rock, *The Nature of Perceptual Adaptation* (New York & London, 1966), 15-33.

22. On the correspondence of structure in percipient and thing perceived, see Aristotle, *De sensu*, 7.449a14-20; *De an.*, 3.7.431a22-b2.

PART TWO . . . . INTELECTUAL COGNITION

CHAPTER 5

Abstraction

Intellection. External sensation, as noted in the preceding chapter, is limited in scope when compared with the totality of one's cognition. True, it is the origin of all subsequent awareness in the natural order of things. Yet a moment's consideration is enough to show that in everyday life one's cognition is not restricted to its bounds. Countless images keep arising in one's cognition, images of houses and stores and schools long since demolished, of streetcars superseded years ago by buses, of baseball and football and hockey teams of former days. Through them cognition is focused upon the external things themselves, not as having real existence here and now, but rather as enjoying cognitional existence in the images. As they exist in the images they can be combined in new ways, for instance in unicorns and gremlins, in daydreams, in cars and yachts planned for the future, or, through your reading, in the characters and events of a novel like *The Brothers Karamazov*. Imagination, as in novels and plays, can travel far beyond the real existents grasped in immediate external perception. But in imagination the objects are still limited to definite time and place, for example to nineteenth century Russia or to King Arthur's Camelot. The spacious and luxurious home of one's daydreams takes on a definite size and location that set it off against other houses. Likewise it is envisaged as being built within one's own lifetime. But one has also the notion "a house" that can be applied to any house whatsoever, to a house in ancient Babylon as well as to the houses along one's street, in fact to every house that was ever built or will be built or could be built. In a word, you are facing an object that oversteps the conditions of space and time. Individual differences are effaced as it is predicated of your own bungalow or the White House or the Kennedy residence at Hyannisport. Each individual building is one by one, that is, severally, "a house."

The disregarding of temporal and spatial conditions and of the individuating features has from medieval times on been given the technical name "abstraction."[1] Today it is common enough to speak of discussing themes in abstraction from time and place and individual circumstances. The term accordingly seems acceptable enough. It implies that something has been "drawn away from" time and space and individuation. What, then, is the object that has been drawn away or abstracted in this fashion? It seems to be the *kind* of thing that each of the individual objects is. In the examples just used, each is a house. Correspondingly, Moses, Plato, Caesar, Genghis Khan, Mozart, Tennyson, Churchill, or Bertrand Russell is each a man. That is the kind of being each is. If the term "nature" may be used to designate the kind of thing an individual is, it will allow one to say that the object abstracted is the nature that the individuals are seen to share in common.

The process by which the nature is abstracted from the individuals is not a concern of epistemology. It gives rise to difficult questions treated in metaphysics and in the philosophy of nature.[2] What does matter for epistemology is that one in fact possesses these abstracted notions and is continually using them in predication. Their importance is obvious on account of the way in which they allow human cognition to extend itself beyond the limiting temporal and local framework of the things perceived. They have made possible all the sciences studied so far in human history, by permitting classification and prediction. They have enabled us to pursue the epistemological investigation up to the present, by providing the common tools such as the conceptions of object, thing, sensation, perception, imagination and other relevant notions. For epistemological purposes, then, it is the abstracted natures themselves that will call for detailed scrutiny, along with the cognitive activities they immediately specify.

The broad difference between awareness on the level of abstract nature and awareness on the level of perceived individuals ushers in a new type of cognition. This new type may be conveniently called intellection or understanding. Etymologically the term "intellection" denotes insight into something, as though one were penetrating into the deeper recesses of the individual things.[3] "Understanding" may be used as a synonym for it, as though one were placing oneself underneath the surface characteristics in order to attain a more profound cognition of the thing.

In any case, this new type of cognition can readily be assessed as an advance over mere sense perception. The vast panorama of the sciences that it has made possible, and the benefits accruing to the civilization built upon its accomplishments, are sufficient testimony here. Prima facie, at least, this advance spells out the difference between people and lower animals. However, although one is introduced to it through the fact of abstraction from individuals, solid grasp of the individual is by no means excluded from its capacity. Rather, a sharp cognition of the individual is implied in its seeing the abstract nature as identified with the individuals one by one, and its consequent ability to predicate the common nature of each of them severally. Its advance over sense perception consists in its capacity to attain the abstract nature as well as the concrete individual, and to work in function of the relations of the one to the other. The full scope of intellection will remain open to immediate judgments or intuitions, as well as to mediate judgments or reasoning, with gradual development into the sciences. But the introduction to it is through abstraction, and the basic kind of abstraction is the type just mentioned. In this type the abstracted object maintains identity with the whole individual, allowing you to say that Socrates *is* a man, an animal, a living thing, and so on.

What calls for emphasis in this expanding of knowledge through intellective activity is the real identity of the one individual with everything predicated of it in the same category. Aristotle's approach in the *Metaphysics* and the *Posterior Analytics* was from the obvious plurality of individuals.[4] The scattered individuals were the starting point. They were regarded as seen primitively in disorder. Then the presence in them of a common intelligible object, namely the specific nature of human beings, was discerned. After that a still wider object, the animal nature that they shared with other sentient beings, was seen in them, and so on till the highest genera were reached. That is how the procedure from individual to highest genus was described by Aristotle, though without attempt to show how the human mind could be capable of accomplishing it. In accord with his method of defining faculties through their activities and the activities through their objects, Aristotle needed only to delineate the distinct objects.[5] "The soul is of such a nature as to be capable of being affected in this way"[6] was the sole explanation here required. Traditionally the metaphor of illumination, which goes back to Aristotle himself (*De an.*, 3.5.430a15-17), has been used to bring out the activity involved. The content in the one real individual is illumined in the intellect in order to make manifest what the individual has in common with others. But however one cares to explain the fact, the important point epistemologically is that in all these instances of abstraction the one human knower becomes cognitionally identical in differing ways with the one real thing. The single individual is a man, an animal, a living thing, a body, a substance, an existent. One real thing is being known throughout by one real knower. It is not the eye that sees, nor the intellect that understands, but rather the one cognitive agent, the man or woman, through eye and intellect. Likewise, in man, animal, living thing, body and substance the same real thing is being known. The one real individual *is* each of these abstract objects.

From that angle, then, there is no problem of the content of sensation traveling from the sense into the imagination, and from the imagination into the intellect. There is but the one real cognitive agent throughout. Correspondingly there is but the one real thing, which is being attained under all the various facets. From the start the same cognitive agent is identical in the actuality of the cognition with the same real thing. There is no question of traveling from one faculty to another. The one real thing is identical throughout with the one real agent.

Just as little is there any procedure from what in logic has been called a "bare particular" to a raiment that could be really different from the individual itself. The extremes, namely the fullfleged individual and the most abstract predicate, are never prescinded from one another in this basic type of abstraction. In point of fact, the most primitive notions we have of anything are thing and existent, and anything in the real world is individual.[7] That is the way the thing is first attained in perception. There is in consequence no difficulty in seeing how the start may be made from the way things are presented in the percepts, when one is aiming at this progress to deeper knowledge about them. Nothing is found to interfere with the observation that when the same things are considered as objects of intellection they are immediately regarded under the widest aspect of all. The result is that either their sensible appearance as individuals, or their intelligible status as things and beings in the widest possible signification, can be taken as a starting point for drawing conclusions. In starting with the bare particular, you are not cutting off anything that the particular does not contain within itself. The abstraction is not exclusive. It does not prescind anything. It retains the whole content of the thing, though indistinctly and implicitly. In this way the one knower is cognitionally identical with the whole thing from the start.

In the texts just cited, Aristotle commences with the individuals and goes on to the highest genera. Nevertheless, the process of acquiring exact knowledge may be from the most general to the particular in the case concerned. Each individual percept presents itself as "something," and may prompt further inquiry into just what it is. On a hunting trip, for instance, you are very careful not to fire your gun until you have convinced yourself of the real identity of your target. A vague object scarcely discernible in the distant rushes appears at first as a body of some kind, motionless and without clear distinction from the environment. It begins to move about, and is recognized as something living, either animal or man. You still do not fire. It stands erect, raises a gun, and is identified as a human being and a hunter. A still closer look enables you to recognize him as your next-door neighbor who had come along with the hunting party. Each of these notions--something, body, living thing, animal, human being, hunter, neighbor, your good friend Jones--signifies just by itself the one and the same substance that confronts your cognition.

However, there is a gradation. "Something" is extremely vague and gives no inkling about the kind of substance present. "Body" is somewhat more definite. It indicates a kind of substance, namely corporeal substance, the kind that is extended in length, breadth, and thickness. It is accordingly understood as a nature, a corporeal nature. It gives the substance upon which you are concentrating your attention a nature held in common with all the other things in the panorama. "Living thing" means a further nature, a vital nature common at least to all vegetative life, for instance, the surrounding rushes. "Animal" expresses a common nature restricted to sentient life, and "human" a nature still more limited in extent as common only to people. Further distinction has to be made on the basis of accidental characteristics, such as "hunter" and neighbor."[8]

How the accidental features are brought into the unity of the known things is a topic that belongs to the metaphysical study of the existential synthesis of accidents with substance. For the moment, what is under consideration is unity in one and the same category. In the category of substance, whether you start from the bottom or the top of the familiar Porphyrian tree, all the predicates are ways in which the one real thing is represented. The only way the objects predicated are found in the real world is in the individual. Socrates *is* a man, an animal, a living thing. Each predicate is a different expression of what Socrates is. Each is a whole that is identified in reality with Socrates and with each of the other predicates. What this basic abstraction takes from the individual is therefore not a part of the individual. It is the whole individual, represented in a distinctive way.

There is accordingly a twofold problem of identity in the expansion of human knowledge through abstraction. From one angle there is the requirement of strict cognitional identity of knower and thing known. In the actuality of the cognition the two are one. The difficulties, arising from the complex natures of both knower and thing known, find solution in the unity of substance and accidents in the thing on the one hand, and on the other hand in the unity of knower and faculties. It is the one knower that becomes and is cognitionally the one thing. Intellection is the further penetration into what the cognitive agent had already become through sensation. But from the angle of the real unity of abstract object with individual thing, the problem of unity is notably different. It is the question how one object signifying the whole thing can be abstracted from the individual in such a manner that it contains the whole individual and can be predicated of the individual without reservation, in the meaning that the one is the other. It is the abstraction of a whole from a whole, whether you go from Socrates to "something," or start from "something" and add predicates till you get to "your neighbor Jones." Yet the identity has to be on a one by one basis, without identity of individual with individual or of species with species. Socrates and Plato are severally "a man." But that does not make Socrates be Plato.

Non-Precisive Abstraction. The basic abstraction, in consequence, is the abstraction of an intelligible whole that is identical with each individual in turn. One sees that Socrates is a man, Napoleon is a man, Wyeth is a man. The one object "a man" is seen successively identified with each individual. The identity of the abstracted nature severally with each individual existent means that nothing in the individuals is being positively excluded from the nature. True, the individual differences, among them place and time, are not made explicit in the abstracted nature considered just in itself. They are taken on by it inevitably when it is applied to an individual, one set of differences for instance in the case of Socrates, another set in the case of Napoleon, another set in the case of Wyeth. The abstracted nature remains open to all individual differences. It excludes none of them. If it may be said to include them in some way, it certainly does not express them or contain them explicitly. If the object "a man" explicitly contained the individual differences of Socrates, it could never be applied to Napoleon, for it would make Napoleon identical as an individual with Socrates. At most, consequently, it may be said to contain the individual differences implicitly, allowing them to be clearly different in each instance when they are made explicit.[9]

What technical name may be used to denote this abstraction of a nature that does not exclude any individual differences and does not explicitly include any of them, yet in a way includes them all implicitly? Objects of this type are continually present before one's reflexive gaze. Their role in human thinking is of prime importance. For epistemological study, then, they require apt designation. A technical term that has been used for the exclusion of the traits from which the nature abstracts is the very "prescind," with "precision" and "precisive" as the corresponding noun and adjective. "Prescind," it is true, has been used in a dominant Scholastic tradition as a synonym for "abstract."[10] With its etymology of "cutting off," however, it serves much better for designating a positive exclusion of the differentiating traits from the abstracted nature, as it does in the technical vocabulary of Aquinas. Rather than weakly substituting on occasion for the main term "abstraction," it can function in its own right in the further and epistemolgically important role of a technical term reserved for the positive exclusion of the differentiating features. The cognitive activity that takes the nature in itself as an object, but without excluding the differences, can then be called, technically, non-precisive abstraction.

What is immediately abstracted from the individuals, in the sense of what is most proximate to individuation, is called the specific nature. Man, iron, water, are instances. But further abstraction may take place. In men, horses, elephants one may see a common object that is named animal, or in iron, silver, and gold the one notion of metal. Common to more than one species as well as to the individuals in the species, these are known as generic natures. Abstracting from all sentient traits in men and other animals, one goes on further to the wider generic nature of a living thing, a nature common to plants as well as to animals. Still wider is the notion of body, which is seen in inorganic as well as in organic things.

Can one abstract still further? One can indeed compare a body with its accidents, such as its size and its color, and in this perspective regard it as a substance. But is this the same process of abstraction? Is it possible to suppress the characteristic of body in one's notion of substance, just as one can leave the notion of man out of one's notion of animal? Or is a different process required? This question will require careful consideration later on.[11] For the present, however, one can merely note that one is aware of a notion of substance that can be identical in turn with bodies and with the basic natures in any non-corporeal things. In the Aristotelian tradition substance so conceived has been regarded as the supreme generic nature in the category. Its two-pronged reach takes in spirit as well as body.[12]

Correspondingly in an artifact such as the desk at which one types, there is first the individual desk, then the specific nature of a desk, then the notion of artifact, then that of shape or figure, and finally that of quality. In this case there seems to be no special difficulty in regarding the supreme generic nature of quality as abstracted from the generic nature of shape or figure, as long as it is not applied to incorporeal qualities. As an object, quality can be found in colors or tastes without at all involving in its content any definite shape, and spiritual qualities are incorporeal. The other categories likewise have appropriate generic gradations.

Finally, all the natures, both substantial and accidental, seem to come under notions like those of a thing, of a being, of a unit, of a good. These notions are predicated of individuals and natures as identical with them, at first sight in much the same manner as the abstracted natures. But can they actually be regarded as natures? If "nature" involves the notion of a *kind* of thing, how can it be applied to thing or being in general, where no *kind* of thing is meant? Here one must look for a distinguishing characteristic that is not present in the merely conceptual notion of a thing or a being. Yet these most universal notions are observable in one's reflexive cognition, and are regularly used of anything that can be an object of one's awareness. They have the widest range of all. They call for investigation therefore from the viewpoints of the way they are obtained, as well as of the reason why they can function in the manner of notions apprehended through non-precisive abstraction, in spite of the fact that they themselves are not isolated by merely abstractive activity. But first, a different type of abstraction requires attention.

Precisive Abstraction. Besides notions taken non-precisively, one is also reflexively aware of others that are abstracted in a definitely precisive way. Humanity, animality, corporeality, circularity, are examples of natures that positively exclude some factor or factors of the percept from which they are abstracted. The humanity of a person, for instance, represents the totality of the aspects, including materiality, by which he or she is human. It is contrasted with the subject into which it is received, the individual. In that manner it is set apart in cognition from the subject as though it were a closed unit in itself. Accordingly it prescinds from its subject, and allows the way in which it is abstracted to be termed precisive abstraction.

Abstracted precisively, human nature has in this way the role of one part, a part that combines with a subject to constitute a third thing, namely the thing perceived. As a part, it is not identical with the whole. It cannot be predicated of its subject, in the way a nature abstracted non-precisively can. You cannot say "Socrates is his humanity," in the way you can assert "Socrates is a man." The non-precisive abstraction was the abstraction of a whole from a whole, merely by allowing the differences to remain implicit in the abstracted nature. "Socrates" represented the whole percept, "a man" represented the whole percept. "A man" merely left out of express consideration the individual differences, without positively excluding them. But precisive abstraction sets up the nature as the formal part of the whole percept. It may in consequence be regarded as the "abstraction of a form," in contrast to the "abstraction of a whole." Further, the different aspects are represented precisively as forms constituting the nature, when human nature is regarded as composed of animality and rationality, or of body and mind. In that setting, ascetic literature can speak of the struggles between body and soul, or flesh and spirit, even though physically body and soul are one real being. Each form is represented as something just in itself.

Yet the activity remains solely cognitional abstraction. It is not at all the discovery of any physical distinction between a nature and the subject that possesses the nature. It does not show that a man or other material thing is composed of two physical principles, form and matter. That is knowledge reached only in natural philosophy, and is acquired solely by those who have studied the discipline. Notions like humanity or circularity, on the contrary, are available to all. Humanity means the whole nature of man, as immediately recognizable. It does not mean one of the physical parts of his nature. In this perspective the physical form, as reached in natural philosophy, informs the other physical part, the primary matter. From that standpoint the physical form has been termed "the form of a part." In contrast, humanity informs the whole man. It does not inform just a physical part. The whole man is the subject in which it is present, and from which it is cognitionally abstracted. It is "taken away" from the whole percept, while physical form is taken away, in substantial change, from the primary matter. For this reason the whole nature, when abstracted precisively, has been called "the form of the whole."[13]

Humanity, then, or human nature as ordinarily understood in expressions like "the dignity of human nature," is a man's nature abstracted as though it were a form that is present in the whole individual composite of physical matter and form. It abstracts from the individuality found respectively in Socrates, Plato and Plotinus, and in every other individual human being. It retains in formal fashion the whole of human nature that is common to all and made up of physical form and matter. As the *whole* nature, taken formally, it includes the matter. The terminology is complicated, but is required for the understanding of the topic. Precisive abstraction has to be understood as the abstraction of form from subject, not of a whole from a whole. Nevertheless the form here is the form of the whole percept, and not just the form of one of its parts.

The manner in which this prescinding takes place can be readily observed through reflexion on our way of thinking. The prescinding obviously follows the scale of generic grades that is apparent in the non-precisive type of abstraction. Precisive abstraction is seen to be based upon them. The process can be observed in detail. Things are grasped first in global fashion as existents, insofar as in sensation one is immediately aware that they exist. On the intellectual level this means, when analyzed, that their existence is represented through precisive abstraction as the first actuality to which they are related and through which they are known. The ever-present relation to existence will hold beyond the corporeal order, and will apply to purely spiritual beings such as angels. Hence it leaves open a place in the categories for incorporeal substance. Substance is thereby seen as a wider notion than body. It extends to anything whatsoever that exists in itself instead of existing in another in the way accidents exist. So Porphyry was able to distinguish substance as a higher grade than body, even though Aristotle in the *Categories* (5.2a11-4.b19) had shown no interest in a substantial grade higher than the corporeal. All objects of human intellection are known in sensible images, with the result that the sensible feature cannot be left out merely by abstraction. It has to be separated through the judgment that some things exist in non-sensible fashion. Hence substance at once appears as superior to body and spirit.

On the other hand, things perceived through the senses are lined up in specific and continually widening generic groupings, as illustrated in Aristotle's (*Posterior Analytics*, 2.19.100a15-b3) rout simile. You see that the people around you are humans, sentients, living things, as well as bodies. But you can look at the notion of something bodily and go on to consider the generic characteristic just in itself. You thereby positively exclude from the notion the further characteristics of living or non-living. In this way of taking it, you cannot predicate it of a concrete subject by way of identity. You cannot say "Socrates is corporeity" in the way you could say "Socrates is corporeal." Socrates is indeed the whole of himself, but he is definitely not a physical part of himself. This holds for all the genera.

Further, each of the accidents can, quite as in the case of existence, be represented as something in itself. A strawberry is red, and redness is a color. In this way the notion of the accident is prescinded from that of the substance in which it inheres. The accidental characteristic is represented then as a substance standing in itself and is expressed grammatically as a noun. This process is necessary if the accident is to be the subject of study and discussion, as Aristotle pointed out.[14] But that does not mean that one can regard the accident as ever subsisting in itself in the real world. No matter how it is abstracted, it always has to be defined and understood as a modification of something else. The point for the moment is that the two types of abstraction are applied in all the categories of being.

But what happens when one goes above the categories and tries to abstract precisively a notion that would be common to them all? In non-precisive fashion one can predicate "a thing" and "a being" of anything whatever. But, as already noted, there is difficulty in directly seeing any content in that notion.[15] For some keen thinkers all content has become dissipated in it, leaving it the equivalent of "nothing." With them it does not present any distinguishing feature that would make it recognizable as a nature. It leaves no content that could be prescinded from the subject. Moreover, any alleged prescinding of it would involve an internal contradiction. Being and thing are predicated of everything. If prescinded, each in its own content would embrace all things, including the subject from which they were supposed to be prescinded. The notion, accordingly, would be self-contradictory. It is difficult, moreover, to express the notion in English. "Beingness" is long obsolete, "thingness" would sound rather odd. It has traditionally been recognized, from Aristotle on,

that being, if represented as something in itself, would in
Parmenidean fashion have to contain all its differentiae.
Hence arose the difficulties in predicating being even in non-
precisive fashion. Being could not be predicated univocally,
as the genera in the categories are. For Aristotle it had to be
predicated through focal meaning, and for the Scholastics
analogously. The Eleatic monotone would blend all notes
into the single sound of being. All these considerations point
to the conclusion that being and thing and the other notions
that transcend the categories arise from a cognitive activity
different from mere abstraction. To demonstrate that
conclusion, the way being is grasped in judgment has to be
carefully considered. But first, the study of abstraction needs
to be rounded out through inquiry into the conceptualization
it necessarily involves.

Conceptualization. As should be obvious from the facts
already noted, abstraction consists in presenting to your
cognition, under one aspect only, something that was grasped
globally in perception or imagination. It makes the thing
knowable just from the viewpoint of one substantial or
accidental characteristic, without the rest that accompanies
that feature in the percept or in the image. But as projected
just under this one feature, apart from all else that
accompanies it in reality, the thing cannot be sensible
perceived and it cannot be imagined. It cannot be presented in
this non-individualized isolation in either the percept or the
image. In consequence it has to be *re*presented in its new
status, just as a thing that is not being sensed externally at the
moment has to be *re*presented in an image when one is aware
of it through imagination. In the imagination the
representation of the object is individual and concrete, and is
called an image. In abstraction, however, the corresponding
representation is no longer individual and mixed with the
other features, but expresses the one aspect only. It is called
the concept, in the sense of an expressed species. But the thing
itself, as presented in the concept, is what one knows through
abstraction. "Concept," as something *conceived* in the mind,
is a traditional designation. "Percept," coined in

correspondence to it, was meant to denote something *perceived*. Through the percept, thing and existence are grasped globally. The concept, on the other hand, attains the thing in abstraction from its exercised existence.

In late Scholasticism the intellectual representation tended to be called the formal concept, to mark it off as the concept produced by the mind. Contrasted with it was the conceived object, under the designation "objective concept."[16] This notion paved the way for the Cartesian doctrine of ideas as the proper object of the mind's consideration. The notion of an "objective concept" does not fit very well into an epistemology in which real sensible things are the direct object of our intellection. Rather, the object of the concept is the thing itself as known in abstraction. In this way the human nature, the animal nature, and the vegetative nature of a perceived object are represented in separate concepts. They are represented apart from each other, even though in reality they are never found in separation from the really existent individual. The existence these objects have in separation from one another is accordingly cognitional existence. As abstracted they cannot be sensibly perceived or imagined, though they are always known in a sensible image. The notion of "objective existence," as contrasted with real existence, would seem wrongly to endow the abstracted nature with a kind of being in between cognitional and real existence.[17]

Universals. In abstraction, one and the same nature bears an identical relation to all the individuals from which it may be abstracted. Human nature is the same nature and is represented in the same concept whether it is abstracted from Alexander the Great, Calpurnia, Julius Caesar or Ronald Reagan. The concept, taken just in itself, represents in equal fashion all the individuals from which it is abstracted or can be abstracted. In itself it is something one, yet it represents any and all of the instances that come under it. This relation to the many instances is expressed by calling it a universal. The etymology of the Latin term "*universale*" is "turned towards something one," implying that the nature found separately in each of the individuals or instances is a single whole in the concept. The notion of a single whole bearing upon all the individuals was uppermost in the original Greek designation *katholou.*[18]

In being known in a concept a nature is automatically universalized; insofar as it is abstracted from all individuating traits. So abstracted, it can come to exist, in the concept, only as a universal. But by the same token, it is not found as a universal anywhere outside the concept. Wherever human nature is encountered in the sensibly perceived world or in an imagined world, it is always individualized. This means that the universal has only cognitional existence. It cannot be a predicate of any real existent. The universal "man" is a unit in itself, related equally to all men, and precisely as universal cannot be identified in predication with any one of its instances. The universal, then, is not what is predicated of the individual. Socrates is not the universal "man," any more than he is "humanity." He is not the whole of human nature as a unit.[19]

The Common Nature. But what is predicated when you say that Socrates is a man? The same nature is found both in the real world as individualized in the concept as universalized. The identical nature, say of iron, is found really existent in magnetite and is known in human cognition. It is an object that is common to both ways of existing. Whether existing in reality or in cognition, it remains the same nature. In this perspective it is designated as the common nature.[20]

The common nature differs in crucial respects from the universal. It is not a unit itself, as is the universal. It is spread out in all its different instances in reality, and is identical with each in turn, as well as with the nature that is universalized in cognition. It is the same nature throughout. It is multiple in real existence, but a unit in the universal. So of itself it is neither one nor many, and adapts itself to either condition. This allows it to be represented in the universal and really exist in the singulars. It is therefore able to be predicated in real identity. When one says that Chomski is a human being, and Lévy-Strauss is too, it is not the universal that is being predicated. It is the common nature that is found really identified with each individual severally, or one by one. But no real individual can be something universal.

Further, the universal is an object of immediate awareness in reflexion. It can be held before one's reflexive gaze and patiently studied in logic and epistemology. It is there in its own kind of existence, cognitional existence. But the common nature, on the contrary, can never have the role of an immediate object of cognition. It cannot be placed as such before the mind's immediate gaze. What is neither one nor many can be found nowhere among the *objects* of either perception or intuition. As common, then, the nature is nowhere found to exist. Wherever a nature comes before one's cognitive gaze, it is either individualized in reality or universalized in a concept. As an object common to both ways of existing it never comes before one's immediate gaze. Like the square root of two, it is something that can be reasoned to but not visualized. That the nature is common both to different individuals and to the universal is a conclusion that is drawn. One can reason to the conclusion, but one cannot represent the result as an object of cognition just in itself.

This means that a nature, just as a nature, is not an existent, either really or cognitionally. Where the nature exists, it is either individualized in a thing or an image, or universalized in a concept. As common to all, it does not exist. Yet of itself it is not a non-existent. Of itself it does not call for non-existence, since it is able to exist both in reality and in cognition. In the language of Aquinas (*De ente*, 3.68-70; XLIII, 374), it abstracts from every way of existing, yet prescinds from none. Of itself, then, the nature is neither existent nor non-existent, just as it is neither one nor many. In this "absolute" consideration only, that is, as "freed from" the modes of individuality and universality and from real and cognition existence, is the nature understood to be common, even though it is always grasped in either the one or the other of those two ways of existing. But it remains an inference from the viewpoint of its status as common.

The common nature, in its abstraction from both existence and non-existence and from unity and plurality, is as important for epistemology as the zero figure has been for mathematics. It makes possible the type of human cognition that extends beyond the limits of the individual and beyond what is immediately attained in perception and imagination, even though all our cognition originates in sensible things. Yet despite its penetrating significance in the expansion of human knowledge from everyday sensible experience into the vast domains of the sciences, the common nature does not seem to have achieved epistemological justification outside the doctrine of Aquinas. Where it has been given attention by others, as in Avicenna, Henry of Ghent and Duns Scotus, it has been assigned a being of its own that keeps it from functioning convincingly as the solvent for the problem how universal knowledge can be of singular things. That problem has been alive since the time of Plato's Ideas. In the logical order the problem is now met with a theory of quantification. Nevertheless it still calls for epistemological explanation.

Mathematical Abstraction. Finally, there is another type of abstraction, the abstraction in which the objects of mathematics are known. This type is not of immediate concern for the present stage of our epistemological investigation, except as a reminder that it was what originally gave rise to the term "abstraction" in Aristotle. It may be left for detailed consideration to the treatment of the mathematical sciences.[21] In it, things are represented in abstraction from all the special sensible qualities, such as color, sound, odor and so on. The thing is represented as something quantitative only. As quantitative it has to include substance, which is contained in the notion of every accident. But in this abstraction, substance is regarded as only the subject of quantity. Thereby one has mathematical extension and mathematical units and numbers. This abstraction can be either non-precisive or precisive, for instance in the notions of two and duality, circle and circularity, sphere and sphericity.

****

When asked how the cognitive agent is able to undertake these various abstractions, one has only the answer given by Aristotle in regard to the non-precisive type: ". . . the soul is of such a nature as to be capable of being affected in this way."[22] Acts are specified by their objects, and powers as faculties by their acts. As potentialities the faculties of the human agent make their nature manifest solely through their activities. The study of the activities is the one means we have for knowing what the faculties are. They respond to the nature of the things themselves, from the viewpoint of intelligibility.

Résumé. Through intellection the things that the human cognitive agent has become through perception are penetrated in greater depth and known in far wider extent. In this further cognition the natures of the sensible things are abstracted, both non-precisively and precisively, from spatial and temporal limitations. This makes possible the consideration given them in the sciences and in philosophy. As abstracted objects, the natures are *re*presented to the mind in concepts for study and investigation. Just as absent things are made present to the imagination and memory in sensible images, so the natures of concrete individual existents are held abstractly before the mind in intelligible representations. The intelligible representation itself is the concept. In it the abstracted nature has cognitional existence, and is universal in its bearing on all its instances, while in its real existence it is individual. This means that in itself the nature is neither universal nor singular, neither existent nor non-existent, but open to all these possibilities. Those conditions allow it to be predicated of its instances one by one, or severally, without thereby bringing the instances into the strict unity possessed by the universal in cognitional existence. As a result the common nature, and not the universal, is what is predicated of the individual thing. In this way the same nature that has universality in cognitional existence is the nature that is predicated of the individual thing in real identity. But the nature as common is not immediately present to the mind's gaze. The nature itself is grasped either as singular in the individual or as universal in the intelligible representation, and is then inferred to be something common to both. In a third way of abstraction, namely that of mathematics, the special sensible qualities can be left out of consideration, in either non-precisive or precisive fashion.

Notes to Chapter 5

1. As a technical philosophic term, "abstraction" has its origin in Aristotle's use of the Greek word *aphairesis* for the way in which the objects of mathematics are represented to the mind. They are "drawn away from" the special sensible qualities in which they are found in really existing things. In Scholastic tradition the simile of stripping the individual successively of its various predicates was used: ". . . naturam generis vel speciei denudatam a principiis individuantibus"--Aquinas, *Summa contra gentiles*, 2.75.Nec tamen; ". . . naturam universalem denudatam ab omnibus conditionibus individuantibus"--ibid., 2.77.Si quis. This simile should help emphasize the consideration that abstraction bears principally upon the positive content remaining, rather than upon the traits that are "taken away." So in modern times Alfred North Whitehead could insist that it is completely wrong "to ask how concrete particular fact can be built up out of universals." On the contrary, "The true philosophic question is, How can concrete fact exhibit entities abstract from itself yet participated in by its own nature?" Whitehead, *Process and Reality* (New York, 1929), 30.

2. See Aristotle, *De anima*, 3.5.430a10-25; Aquinas, *SCG*, 2.76-78. The status of the abstracting intellect as a "part of the soul" (Aristotle, *De an.*, 3.4.429a10) remained highly controversial. On the problem from the standpoint of the singular and the universal, see G. P. Klubertanz, "St. Thomas and the Knowledge of the Singular," *The New Scholasticism*, 26 (1952), 135-166. On medieval viewpoints, see my brief survey in *The Cambridge History of Later Medieval Philosophy*, eds. Norman Kretzmann, Anthony Kenny, Jan Pinborg (London, 1982) 442-455.

3. On the etymology, see A. Walde and J. B. Hoffmann, *Lateinisches etymologisches Wörterbuch* (Heidelberg, 1938), I, 352, s.v. *diligo*.

4. See Aristotle, *Metaphysics*, 1.1.980a27-982a3; *Posterior Analytics*, 2.19.100a14-b5.

5. Aristotle, *De an.*, 2.4.415a14-22.

6. Aristotle, *Post. An.*, 2.19.100a13-14; Apostle trans.

7. See Aquinas, *De ente et essentia*, Prooemium; trans. Maurer, *On Being and Essence*, 2nd ed. (Toronto, 1968), 28 Cf. " . . . it is of the nature of stone that it should exist in this or that particular stone, or of the nature of horse that it should exist in this or that particular horse, etc. Thus the nature of stone or any other material reality cannot be known truly and completely except in so far as it exists in a particular thing." Aquinas, *Summa theologiae*, 1.84.7c; Blackfriars trans. (New York, 1963), XII, 41-43.

8. "Because everything is individuated by matter and located in a genus or species through its form, accidents that derive from matter are accidents of the individual and they differentiate individuals within the same species. On the contrary, accidents that result from the form are properties belonging to the genus or species, and consequently they are found in everything sharing the nature of the genus or species." Aquinas, *De ente*, 6.6; trans. Maurer, 69.

9. See Aquinas, *De ente*, 2.5-13; trans. Maurer, 37-44.

10. As in Suarez, *Disputationes Metaphysicae*, 2.2.16; ed. Vivès (Paris, 1856-1877), XXV, 75b.

11. See below, n. 15. A discussion of the problem may be found in my article "Metaphysical Separation in Aquinas," *Mediaeval Studies*, 34 (1972), 287-306.

12. See the Porphyrian tree, as illustrated in Boethius, *Commentaria in Porphyrium*, 3; *PL*, XLIV, 103B.

13. See Aquinas, *De ente*, 2.285, Leonine ed. (Rome, 1976), XLIII, 373; trans. Maurer, 44. On the contrasted *forma partis*, cf. Aquinas, *In Boethii De trinitate*, 5.3c; ed. Bruno Decker (Leiden, 1955), 185.21. On the background in Albertus Magnus, see M.-D. Roland Gosselin, *Le "De ente et essentia" de S. Thomas d'Aquin* (Paris, 1948), 172-173, n. 4. On "total abstraction" and "formal abstraction" in Cajetan, with change of meaning, see Cajetan, *In De ente et essentia*, ed. M.-H. Laurent (Turin, 1934), 6 (no. 5). For a discussion of this latter topic,

with stands opposed to each other, see Edward D. Simmons, "In Defense of Total and Formal Abstraction," *The New Scholasticism*, 29 (1955), 427-440, and L. Ferrari, "'Abstractio Totius' and 'Abstractio Totalis,'" *The Thomist*, 24 (1961), 72-89.

14. See Aristotle, *Metaph.*, 4.2.1003a33-b17; 7.1.1028a10-b2. Cf. ". . . accidents as well as substances have their *intima*, their intelligibility." R. B. Gehring, "The Knowledge of Material Essences according to St. Thomas Aquinas," *The Modern Schoolman*, 33 (1956), 181.

15. See Hegel, *Logik*, 86-87, trans. William Wallace, *The Logic of Hegel*, 2nd ed., reprint (Oxford, 1959), 158-163; Robin George Collingwood, *An Essay on Metaphysics* (Oxford, 1940), 12-15. Hence the wish to "banish the term being from the vocabulary of philosophy"--Sydney Hook, *The Quest for Being* (New York, 1961), 147. Thus the comment: "Those who, in spite of all, have tried to look upon being naked and unadorned have been struck with intellectual blindness. And those who have attempted to express it in clear and distinct ideas have sinned against intelligence . . ."--Gerard B. Phelan, *Saint Thomas and Analogy* (Milwaukee, 1941), 8. The basic philosophic reason is that the human mind can know *that* subsistent being does exist, but not *what* being in the category of substance is.

16. See Suarez, *Disp. metaph.*, 2.1.1; ed. Vivès, XXV, 64-65. John of St. Thomas, *Ars Logica*, 2.2.2; ed. Reiser (Turin, 1930), I, 290b30-291a25. On the notion of "object," see Louis-Marie Régis, *Epistemology* (New York, 1959), 176-221. As objective concepts, the ascending natures in the Porphyrian tree came to be regarded as "metaphysical grades" (*gradus metaphysici*)--see John of St. Thomas, *Ars logica*, 2.3.6; I, 337a40-b2. But it is hard to see how the differences between these conceptual grades merit the designation "metaphysical." Moreover, their continuity is not entirely regular. "Living" is a higher grade than "corporeal" in the tree, yet it applies immediately to spiritual substances without the mediation of corporeity. Intellectual cognition is likewise in them without the requirement of sentience. Further, substance is not divided into corporeal and incorporeal on the ground of any new abstraction, but

rather through separation by the propositional denial of corporeity in one type. On the "continuation" of human intellection with sense cognition in this regard, see André Hayen, *L'Intentionnel dans la philosophie de Saint Thomas* (Brussels, 1942), 249-250.

17. Aquinas speaks of the concept as intermediate between the intellect and the thing understood, but in the sense that the concept is a means by which the intellect attains the thing: "The intellectual conception is a medium between the intellect and the thing known, because through its mediation the intellectual operation attains the thing." Aquinas, *De veritate*, 4.2.ad 3m; trans. Robert W. Mulligan, *Truth* (Chicago, 1952), I, 179. In this regard the terminology "cisobjective subject" and "*transobjective* subject" was used by Jacques Maritain, *The Degrees of Knowledge*, trans. Gerald B. Phelan (New York, 1959), 93-94. That terminology does not at all mean that the concept is known as a separate object in itself in epistemological priority, with knower and thing known located respectively on either side of it. Rather, "Philosophical reflection has to affirm that the *thing* is given with and by the object, and that it is even absurd to wish to separate them" (93). It refers to "a transobjective subject, which is one with that object" (94).

18. The Greek expression is adverbial, referring to *things* taken in a certain way, namely as whole. It does not imply any new existent over and above the things themselves, as Platonic Idea would. It means knowledge on the basis of formal cause, holding severally for each individual. In this way Aristotle can speak of the common definition as being "of the universal and of the form" (*Metaph.*, 7.11.1036a28-29; Oxford trans.), and say that the formal aspect is related to the thing "in the same way as a bent line to itself when pulled out straight" (*De an.*, 3.4.429b16-17; Hett trans.). It is in fact identical with the thing. But when it is "pulled out" straight in formal fashion by the intellect's consideration it allows the items in the thing's nature to be read in detail, quite as the line when straightened can be measured against a ruler. What is opaque and illegible in the concretion is drawn out in an even line for reading, and can be applied to all the instances. So in chemistry, for instance, the formula H_2O expresses the nature of water and applies to every drop. In that way universal knowledge in terms of form differentiates our intellectual cognition from sensation, even though both are of the

same individual things. Aristotle can accordingly use the notion of "form" with explicative force in saying that the definition is of the universal. Whatever belongs to a thing in virtue of this formal aspect may be predicated truly of each instance. As *able* to be so applied, the universal is *potential* knowledge of them all, as Aristotle asserts at *Metaph.*, 12.10.1087a15-17. In this respect he equated knowledge through the universal with knowledge through cause (*Metaph.*, 1.2.981a28-30). Knowledge through the universal makes possible the sciences, with their ability to infer and predict: "For if there is no universal, there will be no middle term, and so no demonstration" (*Post. An.*, 1.11.77a7-8; cf. *Topics*, 8.14.164a8-11).

19. The reason is that as a universal the concept is a single whole, an *unum quid*: ". . . non inuenitur in indiuiduis natura humana secundum unitatem ut sit unum quid omnibus conueniens, quod ratio universalis exigit"--Aquinas, *De ente et essentia*, 3.85-87; Leonine ed. (Rome, 1976), XLIII, 374.

20. On the introduction of the notion "common nature" into Scholastic philosophy, and the role played by it, see my papers "Common Nature: A Point of Comparison between Thomistic and Scotistic Metaphysics," *Mediaeval Studies*, XIX (1957), 1-14, and "An Appreciation of Professor Turnbull's Views on Aristotle," *Philosophical Inquiry*, 7 (1985), 158-176. The common nature has been mistakenly called the "direct universal," or "universal *in re*" in contrast to the "universal *ante rem* (Platonic Idea, or idea in the divine creative mind) and the "universal *post rem* (logical universal). For Suarez (*Disp. metaph.*, 6.8.3-4; XXV, 232-233) it was the "physical universal," with the universal *ante rem* regarded as the metaphysical universal. For John of St. Thomas (*Log.*, 2.3.5.; I, 333a42 ff.) the nature itself (334b41) was the metaphysical universal, or fundamental universal, while the logical universal was a second intention. In Duns Scotus, the common nature was what the intellect first grasps in sensible things, and therefore was metaphysically basic in its own being and unity. In the present century, Joseph de Tonquédec, *La critique de la connaisance* (Paris, 1929), 156, phrased the situation as "*l'universel direct, nature absolue, est dans les choses, quant à ce qu'on en conçoit,*" even though acknowledging that these designations are applied "moins proprement' (154), and

that the absolute nature "n'est pas l'universel, mais elle en est la matière" (160). Nevertheless he writes: "Elle est l'objet d'un acte direct, d'une simple intuition abstractive: *prima intentio*" (155).

The designation "intention," as used in these writers, stems from the medieval Latin translation of an Arabic term for "notion" or "idea." On this point, see Amélie-Marie Goichon, *Lexique de la langue philosophique d'Ibn Sina* (Paris, 1938), 172-173 (no. 353) and 253-255 (no. 469). That is all it means. In subsequent Scholastic tradition, "first intentions" became a technical phrase for direct look at whatever could be seen in things in their real existence. "Second intentions," as though by way of a second look at the same things now in cognitional existence in the mind, bore upon the logical relations between the various ways in which the things are conceived, such as "an individual," "a species," a "genus," a "predicate." In late Scholasticism, however, the etymological nuance of "tending towards" the object was read into the term: "tendit in illud, scilicet in obiectum"--John of St. Thomas, *Log.*, 2.2.2; I, 291a3-4. Aquinas, *De ver.*, 21.3.ad 5m, carefully distinguished the technical sense of the term *intentio* in the present context from what its etymology seemed to imply. On the topic, see H. D. Simonin, "La notion d'"intentio' dans l'oeuvre de S. Thomas d'Aquin," *Revue des sciences philosophiques et théologiques*, 19 (1930), 446-448.

21. See below, c. 11, n. 11. Mathematics abstracts from sensible matter, but not from intelligible matter or the corresponding substance. "Materia vero intelligibilis dicitur substantia secundum quod subiacet quantitati. . . . non tamen possunt considerari sine intellectu substantiae quantitati subiectae . . ." Aquinas, *ST*, 1.85.1. ad 2m. See also Hippocrates George Apostle, *Aristotle's Philosophy of Mathematics* (Chicago, 1952), 51-52.

22. See above, n. 6. For Aristotle's doctrine of specification of faculties by acts and objects, see *De an.*, 2.4.415a14-22. On the traditional Scholastic way of distinguishing the science on the basis of three ascending "degrees of abstraction," and the current objections against it, see Robert J. McLaughlin, "Abstraction as Constitutive of Science according to Aristotle and Saint Thomas" (diss., Toronto, 1965), 1-57. On the medieval background of that

doctrine in Giles of Rome and Robert Kilwardby, see McLaughlin, 33-39. In Kilwardby the term "degree" and the ascending scale with its threefold numbering are explicit.   See Kilwardby, *De ortu scientiarum*, 25.195-206; ed. Albert G. Judy (Oxford, 1976), 76-79. The internal difficulties with the doctrine do not lie in the use of the term "abstraction" for all three types.   Aquinas can use the word for metaphysical separation: "Quaedam vero sunt quae possunt abstrahi etiam a materia intelligibili communi, sicut ens, unum, potentia et actus, et alia huiusmodi. . ." *ST*, 1.85.1.ad 2m. Cf. *Super Boethii De trinitate*, 5.3; trans. Maurer, 32-46. But the danger is that the notion of abstraction may be taken to be univocal in all three cases.   See the comments by Maurer (xxiv) in introducing his translation. To look upon the "degrees" as progressive applications of the same notion is misleading.   The fact is that in the philosophic tradition the term "abstraction" bristles with ambiguities.   Just as the word itself can mean "leave out of consideration" or "retain for consideration," so the ways in which the intellectual separation of notions takes place can be radically different, giving rise to difficulties that in each instance "un peu de réflexion suffit à expliquer, à faire comprendre par sa raison d'être"--Nicholas Balthasar, *L'abstraction et l'analogie de l'être* (Barcelona, 1924), 5. See also Jacques Maritain, *Existence and the Existent*, trans. Lewis Galantiere and Gerald B. Phelan (Garden City, NY, 1958), 37-40 (no. 14). "What is common to the three degrees of abstraction is only analogically common to them." Ibid., p. 40. The terminology may remain flexible, but the thinking has to be firm.

CHAPTER 6

Judgment and Reasoning

Knowledge of Existence. Besides knowing *what* a thing is, as the abstract concepts represent it, you can also know whether or not it exists. Through external sensation you perceive that the desk in front of you and the chair on which you are sitting exist in the real world. You are aware that the castles you build in your daydreams exist in your own cognition though not as yet in reality. Even a cat perceives the difference between the existence and the non-existence of his food on the platter, and is instinctively aware of danger in the presence of an angry dog. But you have also an intellectual awareness of the existence of things. You can form a concept of their existence. You can reason about it and talk about it. Existence is an object of knowledge as well as of perception.

But how do you know that something exists? You cannot get that knowledge just from the nature of the thing as you know it in abstraction. You know well enough what an intramercurial planet is, but that knowledge just alone does not tell you at all whether such a planet exists. You have to examine the evidence gathered by the astronomers and then draw your conclusion. You know what a tunnel under the English channel is, but you had to wait till the work on it was finished before you knew that it exists. The standard medieval example in this regard was the notion of a phoenix. It was a bird that rose rejuvenated from its own ashes. But no amount of knowledge about what a phoenix is will tell you whether one ever existed. Even the knowledge that it exists in your own cognition while you are thinking about it does not follow from the abstract nature of the phoenix. Nothing in its nature requires that you or anybody else should be imagining it here and now. Only the immediate awareness of your own cognitive activity lets you know that it is actually existing in your imagination.[1]

These considerations show clearly enough that existence is not originally known through abstraction. It calls for a different type of intellection. In sense perception you have to look out and see, if you wish to know whether the day is fine or whether the trees are in blossom, or else actually touch or feel or taste or smell the things. So on the intellectual level you may direct your gaze definitely to the existence of the things you already know in abstraction. In this way, whether a thing exists or not is an object of knowledge. You know that the Eiffel Tower exists, and that the Colossus of Rhodes no longer exists. But this definite knowledge is not abstraction. In ordinary language it may be designated as knowledge that a thing exists, in contradistinction to knowledge of what a thing is. The difference between the two types of knowing is sharp and clear.

However, it is not too easy to get an acceptable word for this further kind of knowledge. In medieval Scholasticism it received the designation of "second operation of the intellect," along with other suggested names.[2] These did not prove satisfactory. The "second operation" was suitable enough in logic, where the subject and predicate terms were regarded as basic. Those two terms were treated as known first, through simple apprehension, and then as joined together in a proposition by way of a second act of intellection. But epistemologically the nature cannot be regarded as having a priority over the existence. If the things did not exist in some way they would be nothing at all. They could not be known. Here existence has to be regarded as primary and most basic. In the terminology of Aquinas the verb "is," even as a copula, signifies the actuality of every form both substantial and accidental. It is what strikes the intellect by way of actuality in absolute fashion.[3] In a word, even though what the intellect knows is always globally an existent thing, what it attains first and foremost in the thing is the existence.

Consequently the designation "second operation of the intellect" does not prove satisfactory.   Of the other designations, the one that finally came to predominate was "judgment." A "judgment" was an alternative expression for a "proposition," and in logic the knowledge of existence was expressed in propositional form. "Judgment" was not entirely congenial.   On account of its courtroom connotations it tended to imply careful consideration of all the facts before it could be given.[4] Here it may mean immediate cognition of its object, without having to presuppose any antecedent knowledge. It expresses what strikes the mind immediately. It turns out to be the most convenient word for conveying what is meant in the intellect's grasp of existence. But one has to keep carefully in mind what it stands for here. It signifies the awareness that something exists.

In English, however, this notion is expressed by two different verbs, "is" and "exists." With a predicate term following, the idiom requires "is." We say that the water is warm and the air is cool. Where no predicate term follows, the verb "exists" is used. We say that dinosaurs no longer exist, that ospreys still exist, that we hope universal peace will eventually come to exist. English idiom does not countenance "dodoes no longer are," or "whooping cranes still are," or "peace is," although by placing a "there" before the verb one can also use "is," as in "there is peace" or "there are blue whales." In Latin (*esse*) and Greek (*einai*) the one verb suffices, making it easier for us to understand that the same actuality is meant regardless of the verb used. Further distinctions are made in logic, such as existential "is," the predicative "is," the "is" of identity, and the veridical "is." But in every case it can be shown that what is meant is an actuality over and above the nature that is isolated and grasped through abstraction.[5] Epistemologically "being" and "existing" are the same.

Synthesis. The function exercised by existence can perhaps be best understood when it is approached through accidental existence. The fact that your friend Jones is a neighbor and a gardener and a hunter does not follow from his essential nature.   He could be a man without having any of those accidental characteristics. Yet you say he *is* all three. The "is" expresses their synthesis in the one real existent. The synthesis is something over and above the abstract natures involved, and is not required by them. So the actuality that brings them together and synthesizes them into the one real existent is at stake here. In the case of accidents like these it is comparatively easy to see that the synthesizing factor has to lie outside the abstract natures. But likewise in the category of substance the abstract natures are not sufficient to account for their union in the one individual. Jones is a man, an animal, something living, and so on. He is each of them, in the strongest of unions, namely identity. Yet the identity is not accounted for by any of the abstract natures. The abstract natures are all much wider than Jones. None of them just in itself requires identity with Jones. But here and now they exist together as synthesized in the one individual. The various components exist combined, and in real identity, even though as abstract natures they differ from each other. Existence turns out to be the synthesizing factor quite as in the case of the existential identity with accidents.

Yet the synthesis in these cases does not presuppose that the components are already there. Individual, man, animal, and the rest, are not first there as constituted elements waiting to be joined together like the separate automobile parts on the assembly line. Rather, a Jones not already synthesized with man and animal and living thing and body could not be what he is. The existential synthesis is presupposed by the components. The synthesis is here the basic actuality. It is the actuality that, as seen above, at once strikes the intelligence in absolute fashion. It is the actuality that is grasped by the intelligence in knowing that Jones exists, and it individualizes all the characteristics into the one real thing.

Existence, then, is known first and foremost as the thing's basic actuality. On close investigation it is found to be a synthesizing of the specific and generic natures into the individual in the category of substance, and of the accidental features into the one existent thing. It is not at all an added nature, and accordingly cannot be grasped through the

intellect's abstracting activity.   It escapes that type of
knowledge. It requires a synthesizing rather than abstracting
kind of cognition.   It is in consequence proportioned to
knowledge through judgment, which, as its propositional
structure shows, is a synthesizing of its two terms in a unity
expressed by the copula "is" in judgments like "Socrates is a
man" or 'The tree is green." Where "exists" is used in English
without a further predicate notion, the composition of the
thing with its existence is expressed.   But while logic is
interested only in the relation between subject and predicate
that is expressed by the copula, epistemology is concerned
with the type of knowledge given by the synthesizing. From
the epistemological viewpoint, judgment is primary an act of
knowing. It is the knowledge that the thing is or exists. It is
an intellectual look at a thing's basic actuality.

From these considerations one may also see that real
existence is what individuates all the natures. Of themselves
the natures are open to a multiplicity of instances.   Real
existence individuates them into a singular thing. In the real
world the existence that is imparted to new beings by their
causes is always individual. What is produced or engendered
is an individual house or machine or plant or person. You
cannot give a universal, or a nature as common, any real
existence.[6]

Ways of Existing. But real existence is not the only way in
which a thing can have existential actuality. Universals exist
in our cognition, and individuals can have cognitional
existence in our minds over and above the real existence they
enjoy in the external world.   Two very different ways of
existing are therefore readily discernible.   The friends with
whom you associate, the houses in which they live, the streets
on which they walk, and your own self as well, all have the
type of existence that is called real. It is existence in things
themselves. On the contrary, Hythloday and the other people
you remember from More's *Utopia*, and the persons and
events in Dickens' *Oliver Twist*, have existed only in human
minds. The existence they possess was never real. It was just
cognitional. But that does not mean that it was not genuinely

and authentically existence. To say a thing exists only in the mind is not a roundabout way of saying that it does not exist at all. The great characters of fiction endure from generation to generation down the centuries. Surely that merits the designation of existence. Likewise when the thing is in the mind it is more than nothing, and in consequence has some kind of existence. But though both ways of being are genuine and authentic, epistemologically the things in their real existence come first. They are what is first known, and the imagined things are modeled on them. Cognitional existence ranks accordingly as a secondary type, a type that is truly existence but focally dependent upon a prior type.

The same thing, of course, can have both kinds of existence simultaneously. The desk on which you are writing has real existence in front of you, and has also cognitional existence in your mind as you think about it. When you deliberately confront the one way of existing with the other, you cannot help but be aware of the difference between them and of the fact that the one need not exclude the other. But anything immediately perceived or known has to have at least one of the two kinds of existence. The immediate object of any human cognition is composed of a nature and its real or cogitional existence.[7] The existential actuality just by itself, or the nature just by itself, can never be immediately attained. As separate objects the two are inferred from a metaphysical study of the existent thing, and each of them has to be represented as an existent something. Only in this way can each be held before the mind's gaze and be investigated philosophically.

The things themselves, however, are remembered as having the kind of existence in which they were first attained. The companions and events of your early school days are conserved and remembered as objects that were actuated by real existence. The characters and happenings in fiction are retained and remembered as having had only cognitional existence. In consequence when you recall the one or other type of existent you represent it as having its original kind of existential actuality. To both types of existent you are giving new cognitional being as you think about them here and now.

But that does not interfere with the kind of existence you remember them to have had at your first acquaintance with them.

There might seem to be something of a paradox in saying that you are giving cognitional existence to a real existent as you perceive or remember it. But what was originally perceived or known was definitely an existent, and not a nature apart from existence. A nature common to real and cognitional being is, as has been seen above, only an abstraction open to both ways of existing. In that status it is just the conclusion of a reasoning process. It is not an object immediately attained. The nature as immediately known was already actuated by one or the other type of existence. When recalled in memory, the nature is represented with the type of existence it had when it was previously known. That original composite of nature and existence is what now receives new cognitional existence when you think about it. Hence a real existent can be given cognitional existence when it is recalled in memory. The remembered object does not have to be first stripped of its real existence and then given cognitional existence as though in its stead. No, what is remembered is something that was synthesized by real existence and is now being represented as it once was in that real being. You are not giving existence to a nature previously known as common. You do not know that the nature in itself is common until you have studied philosophy. You know it only as something existent either really or cognitionally. What you are now recalling is not something first known as existentially neutral. It is something that was actuated by the one or the other type of existence. The nature as common was a conclusion that existed in your reasoning, and there its existence was that of a universal. You recall it as existing in that way in your mind. So in every case what is immediately known and remembered is an existent.

Further, substantial existence and accidental existence may be regarded in their own ways as different types of being. But here the difference is rooted not in a diversity that springs from existence *qua* existence, but rather from the specification given by the categories of substance and accidents. These specify their respective existential actualities in formal though potential fashion. This is very different from the way the form specifies its matter. The form specifies its matter by functioning as an actuality in regard to a potentiality. The form makes the building materials a house, or the appropriate matter a metal or a plant or an animal. It is the actuality, and the matter is the potentiality. But in regard to existence the nature is the potentiality, and as a potentiality it specifies its existence as material, vital, animal or human.[8] These considerations involve intricate metaphysical problems. But a quick glance at them is in order for rounding out the present topic. Existence can be a nature in one primary instance only. There it subsists. Elsewhere it is participated as real and as cognitional in accord with the causality at work. This distinction pertains to existence itself as participated. But its further distinction into substantial and accidental existence comes from the specification by the nature it is actuating, a nature that may be either substantial or accidental.

Concept of Existence. If existence is to be considered and discussed as a distinct topic, it has to be held before the mind's gaze in a concept or expressed species. It is not something that lies before human intellection in separate status, like a stone or a tree. According to what has been previously seen about the requirement of *representing* in an image or concept anything that is not really existent in itself and attained that way by the senses, existence as a distinct object of consideration will have to be presented in a concept expressed by the intellect. Here the content, then, will be that of a judgment. Your awareness that winter is cold remains impressed on your mind and can be expressed at will or on occasion as you recall the fact. In that representation the existential actuality is known and considered. In English this composite representation is not usually named a concept. In Scholastic Latin, however, the technical term *conceptus* may be found used for the representation of the judgment as well as of the abstract nature.[9]

But besides this propositional representation of existence

as functioning in a judgment, a representation of it in static form as though it were a nature is also in use by the mind.[10] This is what actually occasions the trouble about the concept of existence. As seen earlier, this concept has been regarded as totally void of content. The conclusion drawn has been that the term "being" should be banished from philosophy.[11] If an attempt is made to attain this concept by continuing the process of abstracting grade after grade in the natures of sensible things, the result will inevitably be an empty concept. But if attention is given to the actuality attained in judgment, over and above what is attained through abstraction, the result is very different. The abstract natures of things can be graded in terms of actuality or perfection. Life is more perfect and more actual than mere corporeality, sentience than vegetation, rationality than sentience. But all these formal characteristics require actuation by existence. Existence can accordingly be defined as the actuality of all actualities and the perfection of all perfections.[12] It is thereby defined by use of concepts drawn from sensible things through abstraction, but combined in a way that focuses the mind's attention on what has been attained through a different intellectual act, namely judgment.

As might be expected, this concept of existence is not without anomalies. Of itself it does not inform you whether the thing to which it is applied exists or not. You can think of a really existent dodo or crane, without being given to know whether the one or the other really exists. In knowing that both are birds, you know that both share that type of animal nature. But as regards existence, you still have to look and see. You cannot represent dodoes or phoenixes without implying ornithic, vital and corporeal natures. But you can represent them as really existent without thereby implying that they do exist or ever did or will exist. The most notorious instance is the case of the ontological argument for the existence of God. The argument is based on what has been called the logic of perfection. God is by his nature the most perfect being. But the most perfect being must have real existence, or else be lacking existential perfection and no longer be most perfect.[13] The fallacy there is that the two types of perfection are known by two different types of intellection. As far as human cognition is concerned, perfection in the order of nature is known through abstraction, while existential perfection is known through judgment. Perfection based on a nature, even if expanded to the infinite, will never include the least existential actuality.

Formed in this way, the concept of existence can function in the manner of an ordinary abstract concept. In non-precisive fashion it can be applied in predication in the case of each of its instances. It allows each to be called a being or an existent. You say that a stone is a being, a house is a being, a tractor is a being, a tree or a cat is a being. The term "existent" could be used as a substitute in any of these instances. As already noted, existential actuality is expressed in English by either "to be" or "to exist," as the idiom requires. So in the concrete what is actualized by it is a being or an existent. The Latin *ens*, just as the Greek *to on*, will usually suffice for either of the English words. But whatever the term used, the predicate so expressed has the widest possible range. It can be predicated of anything that exists.

But the concept of being or existence can also be taken in precisive fashion. It then denotes the existential actuality as set off against the potency that corresponds to it. The potentiality is the nature it makes exist. Regarded in this relation to existence the nature is called an essence.[14] As the potentiality that accompanies existence, essence has accordingly the same universal range in applying to all things when it is taken in non-precisive abstraction. Everything that exists is an essence when essence is taken in this non-precisive way. From this viewpoint essence so taken is synonymous with "thing," even though it gives expression to the thing's relation to existence. But essence can also be taken precisively. In this case it is not predicated of the individual but functions as any precisively abstracted nature. As a result Aquinas could conclude that in one sense (non-precisive) Socrates is his essence and in another sense (precisive) he is not his essence.

Another consequence for the Porphyrian tree is involved in the way the concept of being has been formed. It explains how substance can be immediately divided into the corporeal and the incorporeal. That division was familiar to the Greeks in the wake of Platonic and Aristotelian philosophy. But the division is not attained through abstraction. Human cognition originates in sensible things, and on account of that origin cannot abstract from corporeal nature. Through judgment, however, it can separate the notion of substance as a potentiality for existence from the notion of it as a body. By this process of separation it reaches the concept of a substance that is not a body, and therefore the concept of incorporeal substance. Insofar as substance is a notion that extends to both the corporeal and incorporeal, then, it is not a concept reached just by abstraction. Rather, it requires the separation that takes place in a judgment denying that substance is limited to corporeal being.[15]

From these considerations one can readily see how the structure of human intellection accords with the constitution of the sensible thing. That object is composed of its nature and its existence. Without the existence it would be nothing. Correspondingly, the existential actuality cannot occur without a limiting subject, for existence can subsist in one instance only. Wherever it is imparted, it is making something else exist. The result is that in sensible reality existence is never found without a limiting nature, and a nature is never found apart from its existence. On the one side of the couplet lies the thing's essence--namely what the thing is. On the other side of the couplet is the thing's being or existence--namely that the thing is or exists. When you are in doubt about the kind of existence the thing has you can take a closer look, but it will be at the existence already grasped in the original act of cognition. So what you become cognitionally in any intellection is an existent thing. Abstraction and judgment can no more be separated in intellection than can existence and essence in the thing.

Immediate Judgments. When you see that traffic light ahead of you has turned green or that the road in front of you is curving, your judgment about those facts is immediate. It requires nothing else to serve as proof. You see at once that those situations exist. This holds for whatever else is being directly perceived by the external senses. The judgment is grasping its object without intermediary. The same will hold for things existing at the moment in your imagination or in your mind. You are immediately aware of their cognitional existence. Without any other aid you grasp the fact that they are there in your awareness.

Likewise in the order of essence you are immediately aware that some notions are necessarily implied in others. Socrates could not be a man without being a sentient and living corporeal substance. What you mean by man is just that. Your judgment that Socrates is each of these does not require help from anything outside these notions. Similarly in mathematics your knowledge that one and one are two is immediate, because what you understand by two is exactly one unit with another. The predicate is immediately seen to be in content what the subject is, either reciprocally or by way of non precisive abstraction.

Immediately judgments, then, can be of two orders. When things are actually being perceived, their real existence is grasped directly in the concrete as being exercised here and now. In reflexive cognition their existence in the percipient or knower is concomitantly attained. But in abstractions a necessary connection of predicate with subject is required for an immediate judgment. The existence of an abstraction apart from its concrete instantiation is existence in the mind and is universal in character. Whatever it is has to hold for all its instances. All animals are living things. That immediate predication can be made, for it holds universally. But not all living things are animals. The mediation of the notion "sentient" is required in order that a living thing be an animal. A maple tree is a living thing, but it is not an animal. A particular living thing may well be an animal, as is the squirrel in the tree, but the further notion of sentience has here to be added to the subject as a mediating factor to ground a particular judgment. The premises thereby allow only a particular conclusion, for the subject notion in one of the premises is not taken universally.

From these considerations one can understand how all our

immediate judgments have their origin in one way or another in sensible things. No other source is needed. Descartes, in setting aside sensible experience as the starting point for philosophy, sought in the mind itself the source of all axioms as well as of all ideas. The axioms for him were established by God and implanted by nature in our minds.[16] The first principles of knowledge were understood as given to us in that way, the rest of the structure was built upon them.[17] Procedure on this basis was widespread in the wake of Descartes, and might be regarded now as "foundationalism."[18] But in the Aristotelian tradition the principles as well as the concepts originate in sensible things, with the immediate judgments regarded as evident in themselves (*per se nota*), that is, as known just through themselves without any mediation. The things are immediately seen to be in the way expressed by the judgments.

Mediate Judgments. Human intellection, however, does not stay content with just immediate judgments. It seeks continued expansion of its knowledge through mediated conclusions. In every immediate judgment a predicate is synthesized in existential union with a subject. The one is the other. For instance, this jacket is white. That is known immediately in what is seen. But the predicate also has its own characteristics. The color white, from independent knowledge, is understood to turn back the sun's full ray and the accompanying heat. So when the second premise is subsumed under the first, one knows that the jacket is appropriate summer wear. That conclusion was contained in neither premise taken separately. It is further knowledge. The jacket's existence, which before had synthesized the accidental characteristic "white" with the subject in question, now is seen to synthesize also with the subject the characteristic "cool." The same jacket that *is* white is now known also to be cool, according to what is otherwise known about the characteristic "white." Through the union of the two independently known premises one's knowledge has been increased.

This situation may stand out even clearer in our knowledge

that the outer galaxies are receding from us at a tremendous speed. We know from the physics of the Doppler effect that a shift to the red in a spectrum means recession at great speed. From study in astronomy we know of the shift to the red in the spectra of the outer galaxies. Neither of these premises taken alone contains the knowledge that the outer galaxies are receding from us. But with the one subsumed under the other we do have that knowledge. We can predicate in existential synthesis that the galaxies *are* receding. That further predicate is joined in the existential synthesis to what we already know of the subject.

Often conclusions so drawn can be verified by direct observation. The planet Neptune was seen in the location previously indicated by Leverrier's conclusion that another planet was causing the perturbations in the orbit or Uranus. The bending of the sun's rays according to Einstein's reasoning was verified when they were observed during the 1919 eclipse. Cures for various maladies are reasoned to and then verified by experiment, as in the boiling of water to prevent dysentery, or vaccination for immunity from smallpox. Knowledge that the diseases are caused by bacteria and that bacteria are killed at a certain degree of temperature or by antibodies comes from two different sources. With one premise subsumed under the other, the synthesis expressed in the concluding judgment becomes evident. The process of drawing the conclusion from the premises is called reasoning, and the rules for correct procedure in it are studied in logic. In logic the notion that is common to both premises is called the middle term. Through its mediation the conclusion is known, and on that account is named a mediate judgment. In contrast to the *per se nota* aspect of an immediate judgment, mediate judgments were regarded as *per aliud nota*, the *aliud* being the other premise.

Résumé. Through intellection the human cognitive agent knows not only *what* sensible things are but also that they *exist* in their substantial natures and accidental features and activities. The natures themselves are grasped through abstractive cognition. In contrast, their existence is known through a synthesizing type of awareness that cannot be expressed assertively in English by just a single word. It is represented in a complex intellectual structure that is conveyed verbally in a proposition. You know "that the thing exists," or "that it is of such and such a nature" substantial or accidental. In that composite type of representation, the existence is known as surely as the nature is known in a quidditative concept. The complex representation may be technically called a judgment.[19] The representation is required for intellection, since neither the nature nor the existence confront the mind as objects present immediately in themselves. As known on the intellectual level they are understood in their appropriate representations or expressed species. What is grasped first and foremost through the judgment is the thing from the standpoint of its existential actuality, the actuality that strikes the intellect most prominently in the thing, namely the fact that the thing exists or is something. Cognitional activity and expressed species function only in instrumental fashion in enabling the cognitive agent to know that the thing itself exists or is what the predicate signifies.

Even the present way of talking indicates that existence can be conceived under the general notion of actuality and thereby be expressed in a quidditative concept pinpointed to the primary actuality grasped in judgment. Existence is accordingly defined as the actuality of all actualities and the perfection of all perfections. But unless the genesis of the concept is carefully kept in mind anomalies will arise, and the concept of existence may end by appearing totally devoid of content. Existence is not immediately known in the abstract, but is attained originally in the complex representation of a judgment. It itself is a synthesizing actuality.

The substantial existence of a thing, then, synthesizes all the essential traits into the individual. Socrates *is* human, sentient, living and corporeal. The same substantial existence synthesizes the accidental characteristics and their accompanying existential actualities into the one real thing-- Socrates is pale, snubnosed, walking and talking. All are

Notes to Chapter 6

1. The problem of the grades in existence and their relations to each other is profoundly metaphysical, and the various views on the topic differ radically. From the standpoint of quantification in modern logic, "grades of existence are uncongenial"--Quine, "Thoughts on Reading Father Owens," *Proceedings of the Seventh Inter-American Congress of Philosophy* (1967), I, 62. Traditionally, however, existence in cognition has been referred to as existence in the mind or in the soul (Latin, *in anima*). Existence in the outside world has in contrast been regarded as the existence of the thing in itself (*in se*) or in reality (*in re, in rerum natura*). This explicit philosophical contrast goes back as far as Plato (*Parmenides*, 132BD) on the question whether the Ideas exist in nature or only in souls. Aquinas (*Quaestiones quodlibetales*, 8.1.1) recognizes three ways in which a thing may exist. The primary way is in the divine creative essence. The second way, dependent upon that primary instance, is in the thing itself. The third way, dependent in the case of human cognition upon those two preceding grades, is in the finite cognitive agent. The relevant point in the present question is that cognitional existence depends upon a really existent cognitive agent. But no matter how existence is gauged metaphysically, the epistemological concern is to show that it cannot be originally known through quidditative abstraction. On the phoenix example in Aquinas, see *De ente et essentia*, 4.100-101; trans. Maurer, *On Being and Essence*, 2nd ed. (Toronto, 1968), 55.

2. See Aquinas, *Scriptum super libros Sententiarum*, 1.19.5.1ad 7m; ed P. Mandonnet (Paris, 1929), I, 489. There, *fides* is an alternate term. At *Sent.*, 1.8.1.3 Solut. (I, 200), *credulitas* was used.

3. ". . . that which is perceived in the mode of actuality absolutely." Aquinas, *In Peri hermeneias*, 1.5.22; trans. Jean T. Oesterle, *Aristotle: On Interpretation* (Milwaukee, 1962), 53.

4. See F. A. Cunningham, "Judgment in St. Thomas," *The Modern Schoolman*, 31 (1954), 207. On his objection to taking "judge" here in

the sense of "to apprehend mentally" (*O.E.D.*, s.v., 16), cf. "The Second Operation and the Assent vs. Judgment in St. Thomas, *The New Scholasticism*, 31 (1957), 23.

5. "Almost all twentieth-century philosophers in English-speaking countries have followed Frege and Russell and claimed that the words for being in natural languages . . . are ambiguous between the *is* of predication, the *is* of existence, the *is* of identity, and the generic *is*." Jaakko Hintikka, "The Varieties of Being in Aristotle," in *The Logic of Being*, ed. S. Knuuttila and J. Hintikka (Dordrecht, 1986), 81. Hintikka finds this claim "completely anachronistic" (ibid.) in the Aristotelian context.

6. Cf. supra, c. 5, nn. 7 and 19.

7. See above, c. 3, n. 21. But what is attained only as a concretion in sense awareness, is grasped intellectually in the twofold way proportionate to the existential composition in the thing. Cf. "But our intellect, whose cognition takes its origin from things that have composite being, does not apprehend that being except by synthesizing and dividing." Aquinas, *Sent.*, 1.38.1.3ad 2m; I, 904. See also ibid., 1.19.5.1.ad l7; I, 490.

8. See Aquinas, *Contra gentiles*, 2.52.Si enim; *De potentia*, 7.2.ad 9m. ed. P. M Pession, in *Quaestiones disputatae* (Turin: Marietti, 1949), II, 192.

9. See the observations of L.-M. Régis and Gilson's reply to them in the "Appendix" to the second edition of Etienne Gilson, *Being and Some Philosophers* (Toronto, 1952), 217-218 and 221-223.

10. ". . . esse rei quaedam res creata est." Aquinas, *De ver.*, 1.4.ad 4m; XXII, 14 (1. 237). To speak about existence, or even to think about it as a subject for discussion, one has to represent it as "something," for instance as the perfection of all perfections, or the actuality of all actualities, with the notions of actuality and perfection taken from the natures of things and pinpointed to the highest perfection, a perfection found as a nature only in the primary efficient cause of all beings.

11. See supra, c. 5, n. 15.

12. "Unde patet quod hoc quod dico *esse* est actualitas omnium actuum, et propter hoc est perfectio omnium perfectionum." Aquinas, *De potentia*, 7.2.ad 9m; ed. Pession (Marietti), II, 193.

13. On the formulations of this argument from perfection, see Charles Hartshorne, *The Logic of Perfection* (Lasalle, IL, 1962), 3-132.

14. "Sed essentia dicitur secundum quod per eam et in ea ens habet esse." Aquinas, *De ente*, 1.50-52; XLIII, 370. See trans. Maurer, 32.

15. See above, c. 5, n. 13. Cf. ". . . secundum operationem, qua componit et dividit, distinguit unum ab alio per hoc quod intelligit unum alii non inesse. In operatione vero qua intelligit, quid unumquodue, distinguit unum ab alio, dum intelligit, quid est hoc, nihil intelligendo de alio, neque quod sit cum eo, neque quod sit ab eo separatum.   Unde ista distinctio non proprie habet nomen separationis, sed prima tantum." Aquinas, *In Boeth. de trin.*, 5.3. Resp.; ed. Bruno Decker (Leiden, 1955), 183.24-29. See trans. Maurer, *Thomas Aquinas: The Division and Methods of the Sciences*, 4th ed. (Toronto, 1986), 37.

16. See Descartes, *Principia philosophiae*, 1.49; ed. Adam and Tannery (Paris, 1897-1910), VIII, 23.25-24.6, and IX, 46. Cf. letter *à Mersenne*, April 15, 1630; *A-T*, I, 145.7-22.

17. See Etienne Gilson, "Les causes et les principes," *Revue thomiste*, 52 (1952), 39-63. In particular, on the principle of sufficient reason see John Edwin Gurr, *The Principle of Sufficient Reason in Some Scholastic Systems, 1750-1900* (Milwaukee, 1900), and on the principle of causality, my article "The Causal Proposition--Principle or Conclusion?" *The Modern Schoolman*, 32 (1954-1955), 159-171, 257-270, 323-339.

18. Cf.: "The classical foundationalist divides our beliefs into two groups: those which need support from others and those which can

support others and need no support themselves. The latter constitute our epistemological foundations, the former the superstructure built upon those foundations." Jonathan Dancy, *An Introduction to Contemporary Epistemology* (Oxford, 1985), 53.

19. Viewed in this way, a judgment is an expressed species, a concept in the sense referred to above, n. 9. "Judgment" in this meaning of a formal proposition is of course not to be found in judgment by the external senses, for the sense for sense attains the object immediately in itself. No re*p*resentation is needed. When a judgment is taken in this formal and static signification, the traditional Aristotelian "sense judgment" becomes assessed as not properly a "judgment": "'Judgment' (improperly so-called) of the external senses and the aestimative, such as it is found in animals, and bearing upon a sensible existent given to perception. This is . . . the 'blind' equivalent of what we express in saying, 'this exists.'" Jacques Maritain, *Existence and the Existent,* trans. Lewis Galantiere and Gerald B. Phelan (New York, 1948), 27, n. 13.

CHAPTER 7

Truth

Standard for Judgment. In everyday life, long before one's approach to epistemology, has not cognition kept seeking a standard of its own? Has it ever been content with accumulating or tabulating unassessed items? In point of fact, it not only organizes the individual items in manageable fashion, but also in every judgment regarding them it spontaneously strives to have them attain a distinct and generally recognizable qualification. The qualification is commonly called truth. People naturally want to get to the truth about things. Just as the only currency sought is the genuine and not the counterfeit, so the judgments desired are the true ones, not the faulty or false. There is quite apparently a definite standard to which they are required to conform. To investigate that standard is the task of the present chapter.

But how do the notions of "standard" and "genuine" enter the epistemological scene? In the wake of the "philosophy of values" that became formulated with the turn of the present century, they may be called evaluative in contrast to the merely existential. But they intrude themselves ubiquitously. Experience of the sudden salty taste in what you thought to be sugar, of the cracking ice that you took to be solid, of the red pencil marks through answers you believed to be correct, of betrayal by a trusted friend, keep showing how your insufficiently examined tenets may be defective. The previously accepted judgments turn out, precisely as cognition, to be bogus, counterfeit. There is apparently a standard by which they are gauged. If they do not meet that standard, they are not what they offer themselves to be. They are not genuine cognition, insofar as they are faulty or deficient in filling the demands spontaneously made of them. When on the other hand cognition satisfactorily meets the standard, it is called knowledge in contradistinction to belief or opinion or conjecture of guesswork.

Knowledge, then, is understood in this context to mean "true cognition."[1] Examples can easily be multiplied. In the course of one's lifetime one deliberately discards dozens, hundreds, perhaps thousands of tenets that one had accepted without thorough examination--beliefs in Santa Claus, in the omniscience of one's teachers, in the reliability of one's companions, in the natural superiority of one's race, and perhaps even the temporal chauvinism of belief in the all-round superiority of one's age. One has made countless mistakes in the process of learning the various disciplines. One continues to make them in taking one person for another, in attributing colors, sounds, tastes, odors, pains to objects or areas that do not have them, and in misjudging distances and shapes. The whole study of epistemology has been motivated, as already seen,[2] by this so prevalent encounter with error. A standard is spontaneously set for one's cognition, and this standard is commonly called truth. To the extent that the cognition does not attain the standard, the cognition is recognized as bogus, or not genuine, or as less worthy or less desirable even from the viewpoint merely of cognition.

The term "knowledge" has of course many meanings, like most epistemic terms in ordinary use. It is often used loosely in a range as wide as that of cognition or awareness in general. But in its strong sense it carries in everyday use the very special meaning that is associated with truth. For instance, having reached the gates just in time to find them closed and see the train pulling out, and being asked as you dejectedly leave the station: "Do you think the train has left yet?" you reply "I don't just think so, I know it." similarly, you testify in court to what you know, not to what you guess or surmise or are doubtful about. What you know you swear to as the truth. Truth seems somehow to characterize knowledge as distinct from other types of cognition.[3]

The problem of knowledge, in this strong sense of the term, is accordingly to be approached in terms of truth. What truth is, becomes the preliminary query. Pilate's question has given it its best-known formulation. But the problem itself had long been facing the attention of Greek philosophers. It has continued to evoke different answers. In the present century the notion of "theories of truth," paralleling the use of "theories of knowledge" for epistemologies in general, has come into vogue. These "theories of truth" are intended to include Greek and medieval doctrines as well as the modern ones. The Greeks, clearly enough, systematized their various views against the background of Skepticism. The medieval conceptions, especially those based upon the notion of divine illumination, have not been sufficiently studied to allow any satisfactory survey of their contents.[4] The current classification of theories of truth is, however, clearly articulated. It provides a comprehensive background against which one can examine the meaning of truth and the nature and location of the standard that truth sets for knowledge.

Theories of Truth. What has been called the "Existence Theory"[5] of truth has its roots in the poem of Parmenides. There (*Fr.* 1.29-30, DK) the unshakable heart of truth is contrasted with the unstable opinions of mortals, insofar as it declares what exists while they express merely what appears. The ensuing Greek tradition distinguished in that way the true from the doxastic, with the *doxa* meaning the world set up by appearance. As an account of knowing, this meaning of truth was attacked by Plato[6] on the ground that to assert what is not is not to assert anything. It would accordingly leave no room for any distinction between the two kinds of cognition, the true and the false. However, the label "existence theory" may still be found used for any explanation of truth in terms of seeing what exists.[7]

The "correspondence theory" of truth is the name now given to a conception that also is traced back to Greek origins. It is described by Russell as meaning that "truth consists in some form of correspondence between belief and fact."[8] But just what is the kind of correspondence? In Aristotle it was correspondence from the viewpoint of being: "By the fact of the thing's being or not being, the proposition is called true or false."[9] The correspondence between the subject and predicate notions and the reality may be very analogous, as in the case of propositions made about the underlying matter in substances. But if there is correspondence in the being that is asserted by the verb, there is said to be truth. Aquinas speaks in terms of "commensuration" or "adequation" of judgment with thing, using a definition attributed to the early tenth century Isaac Israeli: "Truth is the adequation of thing and notion."[10] The terms "commensuration" and "adequation" are awkward in English. They carry the notion of measuring truth against some standard, and of requiring that it exactly fit the measure. As with Aristotle, the conformity has to be from the standpoint of being. Accidents may be represented as substances, and existence represented as something, and true propositions formed about them even though the correspondence in predicate and subject notions may be very remote. Taken in its widest meaning, though, the "correspondence theory" seems to be the most persistent and most generally accepted view. The basic objection against it is, in Russell's words, "the feeling that, if truth consists in a correspondence of thought with something outside thought, thought can never know when truth has been attained."[11] Where "beliefs" are the absolute starting point of one's epistemology, this objection can be serious. Yet where existents are the basic objects of cognition, and beliefs are set up as separate objects only through subsequent reflexion, the comparison between the two can be accounted as a normal course in the scrutinizing of relations between objects.

Another well-known view is called the "coherence theory" of truth. It regards tenets as true to the extent they fit into a system. It has as its background the comparatively modern (from the seventeenth century on) notion of a "system" of philosophy. It allows degrees of truth, insofar as the coherence is greater or less. It encounters serious objections because of its assumption without proof that there is an overall coherent system, and that truths of fact can cohere with reality in some other sense than that of the correspondence theory.[12]

The "pragmatic theory" regards truth as that which works in practice. The common characteristic of true notions is that they pay. The existence of God, for instance, is true for the believers whom it helps.[13] The objections to this theory are the relative nature it gives to truth, and its understanding of the term in a way different from the regular use. When one claims it is true that an external world exist, for instance, one is not claiming that an external world works in one's own case, or pays, or is useful.

The "semantic theory" places truth not in any particular language but in a metalanguage that discusses the sentences of the language.[14] Against it the "performative theory" maintains that truth is not descriptive at all, but performs an act in the sense of endorsing or underlining a statement.[15]

Judgment and Existence. What notion of truth, though, emerges from the analysis of cognition undertaken in the preceding chapters? Quite obviously, truth will apply in the cognition introduced by judgment and expressed verbally in sentences. You do not speak of the cat as true, or the mat as true, or even of "the cat on the mat" as true. Nor do you speak of "is" or "is not" as true. Only when copula or verb is added to subject to form a sentence does the question of truth arise. You can ask if it is true that the cat is on the mat. Mere conceptualization or simple apprehension does not suffice to bring in the notion of truth. The activity of judgment has first to enter.

But what exactly do you mean when you say that it is true the cat is on the mat? In perceiving the cat on the mat here and now, your intellectual penetration of that percept is rounded off in the synthetic understanding that the cat exists there. The synthetic apprehension is expressed in the sentence "The cat is on the mat." In that synthesizing cognition you are immediately aware of the fact. But someone in the adjoining room might question your assertion, on the ground that the cat could not have walked past him into the room without his noticing it. You look again at the cat on mat, and reply to the effect that the assertion is true. "It is true that the cat is on the mat."

What has been taking place? Your judgment is an act of intellection that has to be made in a representation.[16] It is an immediate and direct apprehension of existence, yet on a level that allows the object grasped to appear divided into subject, copula, and predicate. The object does not exist that way in reality, as perceived, but only in the intellectual representation, as it is attained in judgment. You express it in a sentence that displays the representation through the three different parts of speech used. In that way you have communicated it to the friend in the next room. He questions it in that form. To answer, you hold your judgment before your reflective gaze in the way you have communicated it, take another look at the reality before your eyes, and on the comparison of the two you see what you call the truth of your assertion.

What is it that you see? Through your direct judgment you are immediately aware of the existence synthesizing both the substantial components and the accidental location of the cat. The existence you cognize there is not originally grasped through any conceptualization. It is conditioned through and through by time, and is taking place in the present. But in the representation upon which you reflect, it is not synthesizing anything. It is grasped in a concept, the concept expressed verbally by the copula. It is static. You can represent it at any time in your mind in the same fashion. "The cat is on the mat" is a notion released from temporal conditions. It is used over and over again as an illustration for logical and epistemological tenets. As a representation in which the judgment takes place, it itself is not the object of judgment but of reflexive simple apprehension.

The dynamic existential actuality of the cat being on the mat is accordingly represented in static fashion in the judgment upon which you reflect. The two senses of "judgment" now begin to stand out in sharp contrast to each other. The apprehending of the real existence is the synthesizing act of judgment. The representation in which it takes place, and which expresses it, is also called the "judgment." The judgment in this second sense may in a logical context also be called a proposition. Judgment in the first sense is not a proposition but an activity. Because you can see the external existence in its concrete synthesizing of subject with predicate, and at the same time see it represented statically and distinct from subject and predicate in the representation, you can compare the two. If from the one viewpoint of existence there is a strict equation between the concrete reality and the representation as spread out in subject, copula, and predicate, you say that your judgment is true. But if in the meantime the cat has jumped up on the sofa, the judgment "The cat is on the mat" no longer can be equated in that fashion with the existence on the sofa that you are apprehending through your activity of judgment, and you see that this judgment or proposition is no longer true.

The static timelessness of judgments in the sense of propositions or representations can readily be seen in judgments made in the past. When Pershing uttered the words "Lafayette, we are here," he was immediately aware through judgment in the sense of cognitional activity that he and his soldiers were there on French soil. The judgment was true, for there was strict equation from the viewpoint of the existential factor. Today, the real being of Pershing and of his army on French territory has long since disappeared. But the representation is revived in exactly the same form every time we think about it. But "we are here" is no longer true in the sense that those who utter it in America are standing on French soil.

What do these instances show truth to be? From one angle, they are far-fetched. They are not the type of thing about which one ordinarily asks "Is it true?" Ordinarily one asks the question about reports where one cannot immediately or readily obtain cognition of the situation itself. On reading a report that the Soviet *Glasnost* has become fully as open as American free access to information, one may well ask if it is true. The situation in its real existence is not open to one's immediate inspection. A long study of the facts is necessary. But if that study could be satisfactorily completed, it would set before the mind's gaze the situation as it really exists. The procedure would then be the same as with the cat on the mat.

A comparison of one's own representation of the reported judgment with the facts reached through one's investigation and thereby apprehended immediately or mediately through acts of judgment, would show whether the representation accords with the reality from the viewpoint of existence. The verification of judgments about which the question of truth or falsity is usually asked is accordingly quite complicated, and adds very many factors to the basic considerations in the present problem. An instance familiar to all students of epistemology, such as the cat being on the mat, has to be used if tangents and distracting complications are to be avoided. All that needs first to be shown is that in pertinent characteristics the stylized example parallels the situation in which one ordinarily asks if something is true. It may then be conveniently used to illustrate the epistemological considerations involved.

The parallelism makes clear that in every case the question of truth is being asked about a static mental synthesis. The existential synthesis grasped through the act of judgment is not spread out in subject, copula and predicate. Only in the mental representation are these found distinguished. One asks directly "Is the cat on the mat?" The answer is what one directly grasps through the act of judgment: "The cat is on the mat." That is a judgment merely of existence or of fact. The further question "Is it true that the cat is on the mat" bears not directly upon the real existential situation of the cat, but upon the mental representation that is expressed verbally in the sentence. It is the judgment, in the sense of the representation, that is true or false. Truth and falsehood, consequently, are properties or characteristics of judgments in this sense of representations. The judgment is called true if it accords with the existence attained in the cognitional activity by which the object is originally grasped, the activity that is also named judgment in the epistemologically first and basic sense of the term. Since the synthesis of property with representation is seen through another judgment, just as any synthesis of property and subject is grasped through a judgment, the cognition of truth consists in a judgment (in the sense of an activity) about a judgment (in the sense of a representation).

Truth, then, presupposes an apprehension of existence that is actually synthesizing, through a judgment, and a reflexive cognition of that same existence as represented in the mind where it is not synthesizing anything but is the static concept expressed by the copula or verb. These two are objects of two different mental acts, of judgment and simple apprehension respectively.   If the two objects are in accord, the representation is judged to be true.

Need there be fear of an infinite regress if the cognition of truth consists in a judgment about a judgment? The further judgment of truth is made when some reason occurs for questioning the mental representation.   The reason your friend in the next room asks if it is true that the cat is on the mat, is that he did not notice the cat pass through. He has in his mind the representation that you have communicated to him in your assertion.   He wants to be informed if that judgment (the representation) is in accord with the situation in real existence.   Directly apprehending the real existence, and (reflexively) also the representation as it is in your own mind, you see that the judgment is true and communicate your new judgment to your friend. While you are directly seeing that the cat is on the mat, you experience no inclination to ask if it is true. Only when the judgment (as representation) is present apart from the synthesizing apprehension of the existence that is being represented, does the question of truth arise. In regard to the truth judgment itself, no reason for questioning occurs in ordinary mental discourse. Both the object of the truth judgment and the representation in which it is made, are sufficiently present before the mind's reflexive gaze.   No further pertinent evidence can enter the consideration. So, while for sheer delight of following an infinite regress one could keep asking "Is it true that it is true that it is true, etc.," the need for the query does not extend beyond the occasion of the first truth judgment.

Once truth has been seen as a property of a judgment (as mental representation), the standard by which it is measured becomes apparent. The standard is existence. If the judgment (the representation) is in strict equation with the existence apprehended as it actually synthesizes, the standard is met. The measure of truth, accordingly, is existence.17 It is the existence that was originally grasped in the synthesizing cognition of judgment.18 Each instance of existence stands on its own feet. As with a mirror in front and at back, each of the indefinitely receding representations is sufficient in itself, and does require new support from the others.

This standard of truth can be any kind of existence that synthesizes an object. In things perceived, such as the cat on the mat, it is real existence. It is the substantial existence when a cat is said to exist, accidental existence when the cat is said to be in a certain place. In the activity of cognition, and in any images and concepts and propositions in which it takes place, the thing represented has cognitional and not real existence. The cognitional existence is here the standard of truth, for instance with the assertion that Auschwitz still exists in many memories. As real accidents of a real cognitive agent, on the other hand, the activities and images and concepts and judgments have the real existence of accidents. This real existence is then the standard of truth about them, as in the assertion that I am now thinking of Auschwitz and that a concept of Auschwitz is at present in my mind.

The standard by which the truth judgment is measured is accordingly the cognitional existence by which an intellectual representation is seen synthesized with a relation that likewise exists only in the mind. Reflexion on the truth judgment itself (as distinct from the original existence judgment that it states to be true), is a new act of simple apprehension. It exhibits strict agreement with the cognitional existence grasped when the truth judgment was actually made. In this way, because the existence by which the truth is measured here is cognitional, an infinite regress could be projected even though no practical occasion for any attempt to follow it out will ever arise. The different mental acts, of course, are not to be imagined as existing in staccato fashion as though each meant a separate photographic plate. What is going on is the one continuous cognitive activity. It focuses attention now on one feature, now on another. The cognition itself is from this angle like the vital reality in

Bergson, while the cinematographic procedure occurs only in our philosophical analysis. In practice, one universal reflexive glance suffices, without need to parade the instances.

That consideration has its importance for the notorious paradox of the Liar, from the viewpoint of logical analysis, the assertion "What I am now saying is false" is self-refuting. It is alleged to be true if it is false, and false if it is true.[19] The shift to a different existence, as the standard by which the truth or falsity is here being measured, seems to escape the attention of the logician whose interest is centered only on content. From an epistemological viewpoint, however, the reason for the incipient regress is apparent. What I am now saying can mean, for instance, "Touching toads causes warts." That judgment is declared to be false, because it does not equate with the facts in really handling toads. But in a further act of reflexion, what I am now saying can mean "My assertion 'Touching toads causes warts' is false." This new representation is compared with the cognitional existence grasped in the previous falsity judgment, and is seen to be in accord. The *truth* of the new representation is what is being asserted. Further truth judgments could then go on reflexively *ad infinitum*. But no occasion to make them arises. Ordinarily not even the occasion to make the second judgment occurs. "What I am now saying is false" is judged by the standard of the original existence that is involved, and is let go at that. Only the logical analysis, which does not advert to the new existential standard that is introduced in the further reflexion, gives occasion for the incipient regress. The assertion about *causing* warts is false, but the assertion that this statement *is* false is true.

The External. How does this notion of truth apply in questions actually asked in epistemology? Before the study is approached, the sensible world is spontaneously judged to exist outside one's cognition. But that judgment may be questioned after the reading of Berkeley and the Idealists. The external status may be regarded as literally false, or as metaphorical.[20] Accordingly one may ask: "Is it true that the sensible world is external to human cognition?"

The question bears on the judgment (as representation) that is expressed in the sentence "The world is external." To answer, one compares this judgment with what is apprehended through the judgment by which the existence of sensible things is grasped. Upon close scrutiny that existence is seen to be the existence of sensible things in themselves. The other alternative, that it may be existence in cognition, is brought in. But existence in cognition is clearly seen to be existence in a human activity, and not existence in the sensible thing itself. It is not the type of existence that one is intellectually apprehended as one is gazing on sensible things. It is not the kind of existence originally grasped in perception. Existence in the sensible thing itself, however, is the basic existence that confronts human cognition. No more basic kind through which it might be cognized is ever experienced.[21] Through subsequent reflexion one confronts it with existence in cognition, and from that viewpoint calls it external. Epistemologically, however, it is the prior type of existence.[22]

External existence, then, means existence in the thing itself in contrast to existence in a human activity. The existential synthesizing takes place in the thing perceived, instead of a cognitive act. Since this is the type of existence apprehended in percepts, it becomes the standard or measure by which the judgment "The world is external" is assessed. The judgment is seen to be true. It includes the real existence of self as concomitantly attained, for in this context one's own real existence is external to cognition.[23] What is sedulously to be avoided is the placing of oneself first within one's own cognition and then asking how a world outside it may be projected, and how that world can be reached when the start has been made from the content of the cognition. That is the way the problematic has been framed in the wake of Descartes. Great difficulty is still experienced in trying to cut oneself loose from it. A deliberate effort has to be made to keep aware that the real sensible world is epistemologically prior. Though both the externally existent object and one's own cognition of it are known simultaneously, the cognition of the external thing is direct and the cognition of oneself is only concomitant. In consequence the starting point of the discussion should be located in what is directly known, namely the external things. The concomitantly known self can then be probed in reflexive cognition.

Distant Things. Sensible things, including one's own body with its innermost organs and activities, are seen in this way to be truly external to cognition. It is *true* that things perceived exist in an external world. But what is immediately sensed does not appear immediately as distant.[24] Is it true, then, that distant objects are perceived?

The answer may at first seem to be even more difficult to focus upon than in the reply to the preceding query. When from a mile or so away you are watching a military salute on an important official occasion, you see each cannon flash and point out its smoke. But only some seconds later do you hear the gun go off. Is it true that you are hearing the gun? Or are the signals from the space capsule exploring Neptune truly the ones being heard on earth, even though the actions on the capsule had ceased to exist several hours before? Also what you immediately sense through sight appears as a comparatively flat panorama without notable distinction in the distance of its various components from your eye? Is it true, then, that you even see the cannon flashing? Do you truly see the stars, or hear the distant thunder?[25]

What one senses, as painstakingly probed in the foregoing discussions, is something real and externally existent. Through interpretation individual substances in it are located at varying distances. Through its secondary and primary qualities and the changes incessantly taking place it is cognized in terms of natures and individual existence. What is bright, what is making noise, is attained through the result of a long succession of movements extending from star or cannon to the sensory organ. The end product of stimulus and sensory reaction is what determines the percipient to become and be cognitionally the externally existent thing. In spite of distance and time lag and interpretation, what one becomes and is cognitionally in perception is the really existent shining star and the really existent flashing and roaring cannon. Through the signals received, the form of the distant thing is impressed upon the percipient and causes the percipient to be that thing cognitionally.

It is therefore true that you are perceiving the star and the cannon. In ordinary language, then, why may not one truly say that one *sees* the star or *hears* the cannon? Even though in the time interval the things had ceased to exist in reality, like stars shattered to pieces millions of years ago, you would still be literally seeing them in the epistemological signification of seeing. If you wish to be epistemologically precise, you may speak technically and say that the form received has made you be cognitionally the distant object itself. That is what is true. It is sufficient to justify the use of "see" and "hear" in ordinary language for these cases. The same considerations hold proportionally for the secondary qualities, such as color and sound. There is no evidence that these secondary qualities are present in the nerve impulses that reach the brain, and there is no need to postulate an unobservable microscopic television apparatus through which the impulses would be retranslated into colors and sounds. The end product of stimulus and sensory reaction determines the percipient to become cognitionally something really colored and something really making noise. The color or sound is not added, from some other image, to what is sensed, in the way aspects from memory and imagination are added in the percept to the original content. Rather, the color and sound and other secondary qualities are there as the really existent qualities that enable extension and substance to be sensed. The three are sensed globally, as a whole, along with their real existence. Only later in one's intellection is the analysis made into primary and secondary qualities and into essence and existence, on the ground of observed real change. The existential synthesis is in real being, and the qualities makes exist and through which the rest is known, are externally existent. In fact, it is only philosophical and psychological considerations that prompt question about the external reality of the secondary qualities. With these answered, the judgment of the ordinary person, and of the musician and artist, is seen to be true.[26]

Existence Theory. The "existence theory" of truth, then, brings out only one side of the answer. Truth is indeed concerned with stating what exists. But it has to take account of the distinction between existence as grasped by the act of judgment, and existence as represented in the judgment and cognized by reflexive simple apprehension. Only when the two objects are compared does the question of truth arise, and only through the comparison of the two can the question be answered. Existence is the measure of truth, and in that sense may be called the cause of truth and the ground or foundation of truth.[27] But truth in the sense in which epistemology is interested is not existence. It is a relation, a relation set up by reason between a mental representation and an existent on the ground that the two are seen to be equated insofar as the one represents statically the dynamic synthesis exercised by the other.

Correspondence Theory. Does the notion of a "correspondence theory" suffice for this meaning of truth as a property of the representation produced in judgment? Certainly the correspondence between subject and predicate concepts and what they represent can be very analogous and very remote. Accidents may be represented as substances, as in the proposition "Blue is a color." Matter that is unknowable in itself may be represented as a knowable subject, e.g. "Primary matter is the substrate of substantial form." Existence may be represented as a thing, e.g. "Existence is something actual." These are all true propositions. In each of them the copula may be measured against the existence it is meant to express. So, in the binary system called for by existence, the answer is affirmative. If the propositions were "Blue is a substance," or "Primary matter is intelligible in itself," the answer in the binary framework would be negative. The problem becomes acute in theological assertions, where the nature of the subject "God" remains from the conceptual viewpoint utterly unknown, and the predicates correspondingly surpass the power of the human mind to grasp, on the level on which they are now being asserted. Yet metaphysical statements of this kind are seen to be true or false respectively, when measured against the divine existence as grasped through metaphysical reasoning.

The binary system of either existence or non-existence, moreover, does not require exact correspondence even between the existence as judged and the existence as shown in the representation. The one is dynamic, the other is static. Nevertheless from the viewpoint of being and not being, the representation is either equated or not equated with the synthesizing existence in strict binary fashion. Only in that perspective is "correspondence" required for truth. The "some form of correspondence" in Russell's description[28] cannot be pushed any further.

Coherence Theory. Need a judgment cohere in a wider system in order to be true? The preceding considerations have shown how a judgment (as representation) is true. It is true if in the binary framework of being or not-being it shows itself to be equated with the existence attained in the act of judgment whose object it purports to represent. The synthesizing existence is the sole measure of its truth. No further condition of a place in a system enters into the immediate requirements for truth. Even a "wild" sense datum may in principle, though perhaps not in fact in the present state of research, be examined sufficiently to determine whether its existence is real or merely cognitional. The aching amputated leg, or lesser "phantom limb" experience, may eventually with increased psychological skill be placed in as sharp confrontation with its really existent counterpart as dream with waking state, and the definitive decision about difference or lack of difference between them be reached. The colors in migraine headaches or under electrical stimulation of the appropriate part of the cortex may at some future time be satisfactorily confronted with colors in external objects, to determine whether or not a theoretical perfect abnormal or artificial stimulation within the brain gives rise to cognition of an object that shows no existential difference from the object grasped as a result of stimulation by the normal causal chain. Philosophers are told to give great heed to the findings of experimental psychology in these areas. No better advice could be offered. But taking the findings seriously means also recognizing fully the limitations in the actual state of psychological research and refusing to draw conclusions that are not entailed by the established facts. Data on persons without previous experience of a normally functioning leg or blind from birth should have bearing on the two cases just mentioned. There are too many possibilities involved to expect at present a decision about the kind of existence these experiences immediately present in their objects. For the time being, the decision about the existence of their objects has to be given on coherence grounds as currently known, if one is following a coherence theory.

The limited use of the coherence norm, however, does not justify it as an overall measure of truth. As in number theory a formal system cannot according to Godel's theorem be proved within the system itself, so a philosophy has difficulty in establishing itself as an overall closed system. It does not seem capable of doing so in principle. Human nature, to which all other material nature is ultimately oriented, is itself endless.[29] There does not seem to be any way of showing that the universe as it exists is the best possible, and that everything is therefore required to fit into its general pattern. If it is not the best, why should not an event that is outside the pattern, say a miracle, be better than a corresponding event within the pattern and accordingly be granted a truth of its own? Rather, does not the existence or the non-existence of the miracle itself determine the truth or falsity of the statement that it has occurred? Ordinarily, then, one does not have to wait for any coherence with the whole to make a truth judgment. Where the synthesizing existence is apprehended, the truth judgment about the proposition in which it is represented is made at once.

The Pragmatic Theory. Nor does one have to wait to see whether something works or pays. Where a thing's existence is apprehended through judgment, the truth of the proposition asserting it can be determined. But what of things that do not yet exist, as in the case of projected undertakings and conduct? Can a plan not be truly good, or a moral decision truly just? The measure is the success of the enterprise, or of the moral order, that is expected to follow. While the success factor does not enter into the measure of theoretical truth, then, it has its role to play in the problem of truth in the practical and productive spheres. But truth here should lie in the agreement of action with norm or plan.

Semantic Role. The "meta" feature in truth becomes apparent enough from the reflexive character of the cognition by which it is known. The existence of external things is directly apprehended. The truth about them is attained reflexively, by seeing the accord of one's mental representation with directly grasped existence. The apprehension of the existence comes first, that of the truth comes after. In this way truth judgments are always "meta" judgments. Even when the existence concerned is grasped reflexively, as in the case of one's own self and activities, the truth judgment about the existence is subsequent. Insofar as the judgment (representation) that has truth as a relation may be regarded as a sign,[30] the truth with which epistemology is concerned has a semantic character.

Performative Role. Likewise the assertion of truth emphasizes one's original grasp of existence. The original judgment is, for instance, that snow is falling. It is expressed sufficiently in those three words. Only when you want to emphasize the fact do you bring in a truth judgment. You say that the snow is actually falling, the snow is really falling, or it is true that the snow is falling. But are you bolstering your original judgment without any new and different kind of apprehension? Have you not rather compared your own mental representation with the object originally judged, and seen that they are in accord? Is not that new apprehension of agreement the factor that grounds the emphasis contained in the truth judgment? The two judgments have recognizably different objects. The one bears immediately upon a synthesizing existence, the other upon a relation in a static representation. The relation is not something real. The existence, on the other hand, may be either real or cognitional. But since truth as a relation is a standard to be sought in cognition, it is regarded as a value and may be treated of in terms of appraisal. It is something to be striven for, thereby having a role in performance.

Truth and Knowledge. All the recognized theories of truth, accordingly, bring out one or more aspects that are important for probing its nature. Which of these aspects can explain the relation between truth and knowledge? Knowledge, in the special sense it takes on in epistemological considerations, means more than mere acquaintance. It is distinguished from perception and imagination. It is a type of intellection. The professor facing his new undergraduate class and endeavoring to shake their lethargy may ask "You see the desk in front of you, you feel it, you have had it indicated to you by others, but how do you *know* that it is there?" The judgment "It is there" is being questioned, and the answer sought is called knowledge. Can the knowledge add anything other than the express apprehension that the judgment is in accord with the reality? Similarly when the general wishes to *know* the disposition of enemy troops and armor, he does not want surmise or hearsay. He wants a report that will stand in exact equation with the existential situation. He wants a statement that is true.

These and other examples show clearly enough that knowledge in its precise epistemological sense means judgments that can be established as true. The judgments, of course, can be communicated. In this way knowledge can be shared and taught. But always with the term there is the understanding that in their source the judgments were made by persons capable of apprehending their truth, and that accordingly the judgments may be presumed to have been submitted to the measure of truth. Truth is the test of knowledge. Strictly, to *know* the truth of the judgments is to have apprehended either mediately or immediately the existence to which the judgments conform and to have seen that they are equated with it.

Relative Aspects of Truth. Since truth consists in a relation, namely in the relation of a judgment (as representation) with existence, one may say without hesitation that truth is essentially relative. How then can it be the test for knowledge, if knowledge is a type of cognition that is stable and the same for all who share it?

First, knowledge itself is something relative, even though it itself is not just a relation. It is knowledge *of* something. Like all cognition, then, it is relative to its object. Both as an activity and as a representation it bears upon the thing or things known. Its truth character bears in corresponding fashion upon the *existence* of the thing.

Further, truth is measured by existence. But all real existence directly attained by human cognition is temporal. It is continually changing from past through present into the future. To that extent the truth based upon it is contingent. What was true yesterday need not be true today, in the sphere of real existence. Abstract natures, on the other hand, are universal and accordingly atemporal as they exist in the intellect. Their existence ceases with the cessation of the intellect's activity, yet while it lasts it synthesizes subject and predicate in an atemporal way.[31] "Two and two are four" is the way the cognitional existence always synthesizes this subject and predicate in a decimally based arithmetic, and "A rose is a flower" continues to be so synthesized through the centuries just as in the time of Abelard. Yet because the existence occurs in the contingent activity of the human intellect, it may in this perspective be regarded as relative. Accordingly in the world immediately attained by human cognition "there is no necessary truth"[32] when the viewpoint is the contingent existence had by any judgment in the human mind.

Moreover, one's own viewpoint may change even while referring to the same subject. For instance, you may say that what is a small step for a man may be a giant leap for mankind. Similarly the mayor of a remote city may be an important figure in local politics but a very insignificant one on the federal scene. The opposite statements in these cases are each true in its own perspective. The statements are made from different viewpoints and accordingly in relation to different measuring rods. But the relations exist in definite fashion. By their existence the truth of the statements are perspectival. Likewise where the meanings of words change with the course of time, there should be no special difficulty. The words now stand for different concepts. The truth judgment is made according to the existence of what is represented in the new concepts.[33]

In the moral or practical order, the relativity of truth to individuals and circumstances takes on a special and even decisive role. The conformity, in which truth here consists, is with correctly habituated appetites. The common culture in which the habituation is developed, and the common knowledge used in the deliberation that precedes a moral decision, allow the moral truths to be universal in scope. This however is a universality of its own kind, enabling the moral norm to be applied flexibly in changing circumstances. The moral notions and the moral truth accordingly remain the same even though physically the actions are opposite, for instance course in maintaining a post or abandoning it as strategy requires. From the angle of truth judgments, the important point is that even though the appetitive factor is basic in moral entities, genuine rationality and universality pervade the whole moral order and raise it above a merely emotive status.

Finally, in the order of productive science the measure of truth is the plan or design in the mind of the artist or producer. If the product comes into existence in conformity with the intended design, it attains the truth appropriate to this order. In English terms such as "correct" or "exact" are ordinarily used to express this conformity. But at times "true" is found used. You may say that the marksman's aim was true if it was correctly focused on target, or that the lines of a building are true if they conform exactly to what the design requires.

From all these viewpoints, then, relativity is encountered in the truth that exists in the human mind. Yet it can hardly be the last word on truth, without becoming involved in contradiction. In the sensible world existence is incessantly changing from the past through the present into the future. But this does not impede the absolute assertion of differences between existence at different times. To be living in the twentieth century is absolutely different from living in the twelfth.[34] To make the historicity of truth mean that no truth is absolutely stable would prevent definite thought and speech. Moreover, the tenet itself would seem to imply its opposite if it is pushed far enough. If all truths had to keep changing, it itself could not remain perpetually as the overall norm. It would seem to change eventually into something non-changing, if allowed full scope for its possibilities. It would thereby imply an absolute character in truth. At the very least, it suggests that the prospect of an absolute element in truth be touched upon here. This can be done very briefly, by emphasizing the way existence as the measure of truth is absolute. Fuller discussion of the topic belongs to the problem of certitude versus scepticism, where the manner in which being contradicts non-being is examined.

Absolute Character of Truth. Insofar as existence is incompatible with non-existence at the same time in the same respects, it manifests itself as absolute. To this extent, consequently, it provides an absolute measure for truth. While rain is falling here, that rain is not synthesized existentially with "not falling." That is absolute. It is not relative to the observer. From this viewpoint the truth of the judgment has an absolute character, for it is measured by an absolute existence. Correspondingly "two and two are four" synthesizes existentially a subject and a predicate that represent the same number of units in different ways. That is the way the subject and predicate notions exist in the decimally based system, regardless of the particular individual who is doing the mathematical thinking. The truth of the judgment is accordingly absolute.

From these considerations it is readily apparent that judgments about abstract notions hold no privileged position in the question of truth, even though they have long been regarded as the model. Nor do judgments about oneself and one's activities enjoy any special privilege, as with the Cartesian "I think, therefore I am." In all cases the measure is the same, existence. Wherever the existence is apprehended through an act of judgment, it serves cogently as the measure and criterion of truth. With the cat on the mat it is just as strong a criterion as with the mathematical truths. With the externally existent world it is fully as absolute as with one's own existence and activities. The real existence of the stone or the tree that is apprehended through direct judgment is self-sufficient in its own right as a measure of truth, independently of its relation to anything else or of its place in an overall system.

Résumé. In human cognition a spontaneous urge arises to attain the truth. Truth in this way becomes the standard that is sought in the development of one's cognition. It is for epistemology a property of judgments, consisting in a relation of agreement between the existence represented statically in the judgments, and the existence apprehended dynamically as the judgments are actually made. Judgments capable of standing the test of truth form what is called knowledge. One knows a thing when one's judgment about it is in conformity with what exists in the thing itself, and one knows that the judgment is true when one sees the conformity between the judgment and the reality. Truth is thereby relative to its object, for the truth is ultimately about the object. Truth is also relative to its standard, existence, for truth is measured by existence. Truth in the human mind is relative to its own existence there, for its existence is, from that viewpoint, contingent upon the action of the human cognitive agent. But truth is absolute insofar as it contradicts falsehood, with all the absolute distinction involved in the principle of contradiction, the first principle of demonstration.

Notes to Chapter 7

1. E.g.: "It is obvious and generally admitted, that we can have knowledge only of what is true." Anthony Quinton, in Paul Edwards' *Encyclopedia of Philosophy*, IV, 345b (s.v. "Knowledge and Belief"). Cf. "There are true and there are false opinions; there is no false knowledge. This dichotomy, still reflected in ordinary language, is fundamental to Aristotelian as to Platonic thought." Marjorie Grene, *The Knower and the Known* (London, 1966) 36.

2. See above, c. 1, nn. 8-20.

3. "According to the most widely accepted definition, knowledge is justified true belief." A. Quinton, loc. cit. The first condition laid down by Aristotle for demonstrated knowledge is that it must follow from true premises--"the premises of demonstrated knowledge must be true" (*Posterior Analytics*, 1.2.71b20-21; Oxford trans.). Otherwise, the cognition is not knowledge (*episteme*)--ibid., b25-26.

4. For some medieval definitions of truth, with an account of the element brought to the fore in each, see Aquinas, *Scriptum super Lib. Sent.*, 1.19.5.1; ed. P. Mandonnet (Paris, 1929), I, 484-490. A short survey of the divine illumination theories may be found in my study "Faith, Ideas, Illumination, and Experience" in *The Cambridge History of Later Medieval Philosophy* (Cambridge, 1982), 444-455. For a bibliography on the modern theories of truth, see *Truth*, ed. George Pitcher (Englewood Cliffs, NJ, 1964), 113-118.

5. So A. N. Prior, in Paul Edwards' Encyclopedia of Philosophy, II, 224a, s.v. Correspondence Theory of Truth.

6. *Tht.*, 188D-189A. At *Cra.*, 385B, the meaning is doubtful, and may be read in the sense of the contrast between stating or not stating what exists. At any rate, the impossibility of asserting any falsehood in this framework seems upheld at *Cra.*, 429CD.

7. Above, n. 5. In the middle ages this conception of truth, with its difficulties, was known through the definition proposed by Augustine

"the true seems to me to be that which exists" (*Soliloquies*, 2.5.8).

8. *The Problems of Philosophy* (London, 1929), 190. Cf. Plato, *Sph.*, 263AB; Aristotle, *Cat.*, 12.14b14-22; Aquinas, *ST*, 1.16.2c.

9. *Cat.*, 5.4b8-10. Cf. 10.13b2-35; *Int.*, 1.16a9-18; *Metaph.*, 4.7.1011b25-28.

10. Aquinas, *De ver.*, 1.1c. Cf. *Sent.*, 1.19.5.1 Solut. (ed. Mandonnet, I, 487; *ST*, 1.16.1c; 1.2.arg. 2; 1.21.2c. In the commentary on the *Sentences* (loc. cit.) the *adequatio* is explained by *commensuratio*, in *De veritate* by *correspondentia*, in the *Summa Theologiae* (1.16.2c) by *conformitas*. The exact meaning of *intellectus*, as understood by St. Thomas in the definition, is more difficult. In the commentary on the *Sentences* it is explained as "the 'commensuration' of what is in the intellect with what is in the thing." This means that the conformity is understood as between the representation in the intellectual activity and the thing itself. *Intellectus* in this sense of a "notion" is frequent in St. Thomas (e.g., *De Ente*, 2.210-220; XLIII, 372). So taken, an *intellectus* may signify either a simple notion such as in the case of a verb or a noun, or it may signify the composite notion expressed by a sentence--*simplicem intellectum . . . intellectum compositum* (*In Periherm.*, 1.6.2; I, 29). In the *De ver.* text, *intellectus* clearly means the faculty, yet in reference to the definition of Augustine it is taken (1.1.ad 1m) as a composite *intellectus* or proposition. In the *Summa Theologiae* it is understood as the faculty. In English, there is a similar double use of "understanding" in the sense of a faculty and of the notion one has of a thing. The close relation of the two meanings allows easy passage from one to the other.

The definition attributed to Isaac has not been found in his works. On the question, see J. T. Muckle, "Isaac Israeli's Definition of Truth," *Archives d'Histoire Doctrinale et Littéraire du Moyen Age*, VIII (1933), 5-8. On the representation as the "form" of the intellect, see Aquinas, *ST*, 1.16.2c.

11. Problems of Philosophy, 190.

12. For a defense of the theory, see Brand Blanshard, *The Nature*

of Thought (London, 1939), II, 214-331. The notion of "system" is accepted against the nineteenth century Idealistic background, and the correspondence with reality is brought within the system: ". . . as soon as we attempt to say *what* is given, we find ourselves thrown back upon coherence anyhow." Ibid., 214. On coherence as "often a most important *test* of truth after a certain amount of truth has become known", see Russell, *Problems of Philosophy*, 193. On the coherence theory as meant to provide "a *test* or criterion of truth," see also Nicholas Rescher, *The Coherence Theory of Truth* (Oxford, 1973), 24. An explanation and critique of the theory may be found in Haig Khatchadourian, *The Coherence Theory of Truth* (Beirut, 1961), and shorter critiques in Russell, *The Problems of Philosophy*, 190-193, and Anthony Douglas Woozley, *Theory of Knowledge* (London, 1949), 146-164. On the coherence theory in Logical Positivism, where the coherence is with the accepted body of scientific tenets, see C. G. Hempel, "On the Logical Positivists' Theory of Truth," *Analysis*, II (1935), 49-59.

13. See William James, *Pragmatism* (London, etc., 1907), 55-81; 88-89; 122; 197-236, 299, and *The Meaning of Truth* (London, etc., 1909), v-xvi; 180-220. For critiques, see Russell, *Philosophical Essays*, revised edition, (London, 1966), 79-130; G. E. Moore, *Philosophical Studies* (London, 1922), 97-146. On the label "Transatlantic 'Truth,'" see account in Russell, *Philosophical Essays*, 112, n. 1.

14. See Alfred Tarski, "The Semantic Conception of Truth and the Foundations of Semantics," *Philosophy and Phenomenological Research*, IV (1943-44), 341-375. For a critique, see Max Black, "The Semantic Definition of Truth," *Analysis*, 8 (1948), 49-63; reprinted in *Philosophy and Analysis*, ed. Margaret Macdonald (Oxford, 1954), 245-260.

15. See P. F. Strawson, "Truth," *Analysis*, IX (1949), 83-97, reprinted in *Philosophy and Analysis* (supra, n. 14), 260-227. The background is a redundancy theory of truth, e.g. that there is "really no separate problem of truth" and that "'It is true that Caesar was murdered' means no more than that Caesar was murdered"--F. P. Ramsey, "Facts and Propositions," *Proceedings of the Aristotelian*

Society, Suppl. 7 (1927), 157; or that the "is true" is "logically superfluous"--A. J. Ayer, *Language, Truth and Logic,* 2nd ed. (London, 1946), 88. The added assertion of truth is merely for emphasis or some similar reason (Ramsey, loc. cit.) and when logically analyzed does not exhibit any real quality or real relation (Ayer, 89). On the question of an emotive theory of truth as implicit in Logical Positivism, see Barnett Savery, "The Emotive Theory of Truth," *Mind,* N.S. 64 (1955), 513-521.

A less prominent theory regards truth as an appraisal that has "two aspects, a descriptive and an evaluative"--Alan R. White, "Truth as Appraisal," *Mind,* N.S. 66 (1957), 318. For a critique, see Bernard Mayo, "Truth as Appraisal," *Mind,* N.S. 68 (1959), 80-86.

16. Above, c. 5, n. 17, and c. 6, n. 19.

17. Cf. ". . . the notion of truth consists in two factors--in the existence of the thing, and in the apprehension by the cognoscitive power proportionate to the existence of the thing." Aquinas, *Scriptum super Lib. Sent.,* 1.19.5.2. Solut.: ed. Mandonnet, I, 491. The relation is expressed as "measure" (*mensura*), ibid., ad 2m, 492-493. On the existence as either real or cognitional, see ibid., art. 1, ad 5m; I, 489. In either case the existence as an epistemological starting point is definitely there on its own feet, and precludes any epistemological need to keep justifying it by something else in infinite regress.

18. Cf.: "even in classical logic the copula does not signify by itself: it always bears upon the predicate, not in order to signify the predicate, but to signify its union with a subject." Etienne Gilson, *Being and Some Philosophers,* 2nd ed. (Toronto, 1952, 192). Accordingly, the "is" does not need to be expressed verbally. See ibid., 193.

19. This paradox goes back to Stoic times. On its status in antiquity, see Benson Mates, *Stoic Logic* (Berkeley, 1961), 5; 84. Bates notes (84) that no ancient solutions of the paradox have come down. A study of the attempted lines of solution by present-day writers may be found in R. C. Skinner, "The Paradox of the Liar," *Mind,*

68 (1959), 322-335. For Skinner the paradox "arises as the result of a mistake" (322).

20. Cf.: "Properly speaking, I perceive my own sensations or percepts; improperly speaking, I perceive an external sensible world." Denis Savage, "External Perception as Metaphor," *Proceedings of the American Catholic Philosophical Association*, 41 (1967), 83. This attitude, of course, arises from the failure to recognize the epistemological priority of the external sensible things.

21. See above, c. 2, n. 32.

22. On the "greater paradox" encountered in "replacing ordinary objects with ideas, impressions, or sense data," see Richard H. Schlagel, "The Paradox of Perception," *Proceedings of the XIVth International Congress of Philosophy* (Vienna, 1969), III, 277.

23. On the implicit assumption of one's own real existence when denying real existence to the other objects of perception, see Walter Russell Brain, *Mind, Perception and Science* (Oxford, 1951), 7-8.

24. See above, c. 3, nn. 22-23.

25. On the linguistic propriety of saying that one sees a star, "with no ambiguity whatever," see John Langshaw Austin, *Sense and Sensibilia* (Oxford, 1962), 99.

26. Cf.: ". . . if he introspects the experience it still appears as awareness of something external"--Rodney Julian Hirst, *The Problems of Perception* (London, 1959), 287. On difficulties in determining the kind of existence in cases where the external sensory organs are not excited, see Brain, 51-53.

27. "Since in the thing there is its quiddity and its being, truth is based on the being of the thing rather than on the quiddity . . . Hence I say that the being of the thing is the cause of truth, in the way truth is in the cognition of the intellect." Aquinas, *Sent.*, 1.19.5.1. Solut.; ed. Mandonnet, I, 486.

28. Above, n. 8.

29. See A. C. Pegis, "Nature and Spirit: Some Reflections on the Problem of the End of Man," *Proceedings of the American Philosophical Association*, 23 (1949), 73. On the teleology of material nature, see Aristotle, *Politics*, 1.9.1256b15-20.

30. On the way the notion "sign" (*signum*) applies to both image and concept, see John of St. Thomas, *Ars logica*, 2.22.2; ed. B. Reiser, I, 702. On knowledge as relative even though a quality, see Aristotle, *Categories*, 8.11a24-36.

31. Cf.: "For as we say of universals that they are imperishable and eternal, because they perish only in an accidental way, namely in respect of the being that they have in something else . . ." Aquinas, *Sent.*, 1.19.5.3.ad 3m; ed. Mandonnet, I, 496-497.

32. "Hence it is clear that no truth is necessary in creatures." Aquinas, *Sent.*, 1.19.5.3. Solut.; ed. Mandonnet, I, 496. The epistemological viewpoint has to regard the kind of existence upon which the truth judgment is based in the human mind. This existence can come and go. It is accidental and contingent. From the viewpoint of logic, entailment may be necessary, as in the *modus ponens*. Cf. supra, n. 31.

33. Cf.: "The first operation regards the quiddity of the thing; the second regards its being. And because the notion of truth is founded on being and not on quiddity, as has been said, truth and falsity are therefore found properly in the second operation . . ." Aquinas, *Sent.*, 1.19.5.3.ad 7m; ed. Mandonnet, I, 489. The fleeting character of temporal existence allows ample room for change in what is conceptualized, and in consequence for statements about becoming and ceasing to be true. The rapidly changing existence makes truth difficult to state correctly at a given moment--see A. N. Prior, "Fugitive Truth," *Analysis*, 29 (1968), 5-8. When new and different concepts are applied in a given context, the measure of truth will be the existence these new concepts represent. In this case ". . . it may be necessary to discard the human concepts as well as the words of those who first framed the dogma"--Avery Dulles, "Dogma is an Ecumenical

Problem," *Theological Studies*, 29 (1968), 407. But the truth or falsity of the new assertions has to rest upon what actually exists, just as did the former assertions.

34. Cf. "The doctrine of the historicity of truth . . . pretends to be a philosophical truth valid for all times and cultures. In short, total historicization is not tenable, for the doctrine of historicity cannot be formulated without denying itself." Armand Maurer, "Dewart's De-Hellenization of Belief in God," *The Ecumenist*, 5 (1967), 25a.

CHAPTER 8

Assent

Problem of Assent. With truth located in the conformity of one's judgment with what exists, a straightforward yes or no answer to the question about the judgment's truth might seem comparatively easy. You consider your judgment in the representation that stands before your reflexive gaze. You confront the representation with the actual existence that had been apprehended through your preceding act of judgment. You ask if what is represented in your proposition corresponds, in terms of being or not being, to what you have grasped in actual reality. If the two correspond, you acquiesce in the judgment as true. If they do not correspond, you reject the judgment as erroneous. The decision might be expected to turn out that clearcut. If the judgment is true, the desired knowledge is had then and there. It is measured by an absolute existence. It should therefore be final, fully satisfying, and acceptable without further question. It should command one's assent, as "assent" is commonly understood.

However, ordinary experience shows forcefully enough that the issue is usually not so transparent. One may carefully compare the judgment with the actual existence, and after the closest possible scrutiny fail for the moment to see whether or not they are equated. In that case no assent is compelled. Complicated criminal trials can go on for months in the consideration of evidence on both sides, and still not reach a verdict. Long and nerve-wracking investigation is required to find whether high government officials were involved in illegal covert activities in Iran or Nicaragua. The truth is sorely needed in such cases, for one does not like to act upon judgments that one does not regard as definitely true. What is it, then, that compels or at least allows assent to a judgment about truth?

Examples can be multiplied readily enough from one's individual experience. You are uncertain whether the car will start on this cold morning, whether there will be snow during the day, whether you will meet the person you are trying to contact. You are not sure whether you are getting the flu, whether the coffee was instant or percolated, whether the cashier made a mistake in checking the items on your tray. Or in philosophical matters you may not be certain whether Descartes was guilty of circular reasoning in his guarantee of truth, whether Hume actually meant to deny efficient causality, whether the existence of God can be rationally demonstrated, whether metaphysics and ethics are to be regarded as sciences. The continued daily necessity of making decisions, moreover, shows you that for practical purposes you often have to accept judgments of which you are not fully convinced, and you act upon them in ordinary life. Judgments, when true or not, can accordingly be accepted without having to be regarded as certain. The acceptance may be technically called assent. But whether for purposes of practical life, or for the acquisition of theoretical knowledge, one naturally seeks certainty in one's judgments. Usually people like to be sure.

Epoche. In the other extreme, however, philosophical attempts have been made deliberately to withhold assent from judgments, even when they appeared obviously true. Descartes in his philosophical method required the withholding of assent from the most evident mathematical truths as well as from all judgments about the sensible world.[1] Methodically at least, it proved possible until the truth of his own existence and thinking was faced. The ancient Greek Skeptics went the whole way. They maintained as a carefully thought out philosophical attitude that nothing could be accepted as certain on the philosophical plane. One could always find ground for doubt and therefore for withholding assent. In this framework there can be no such thing, from a philosophical viewpoint, as certainty.

This ancient Greek attitude may be called universal skepticism. In itself, "skepticism" is a good word. It means a careful consideration or examination of one's judgments.[2] In its etymology it does not imply any final suspension of assent. It was appropriated to that sense because of the position taken by the ancient Skeptics, namely that the continued examination will never result in finding truth.

But is this position philosophically defensible? The ancient Skeptics did not mean to assert as a positive tenet even the judgment that nothing can be certain. They regarded it as a position that eliminated its own certainty along with that of all other judgments.[3] They did not apply it to the judgments of ordinary living, for instance "that it is day and that we are alive, and many other apparent facts in life."[4] In practice at least, they extended this exemption to the use of words and sentences with definite meanings, as they carried on conversation and argument. How, then, can their position be refuted by claiming that it accepts implicitly the certainty of its basic tenet--"one is certain that nothing can be certain"? Or how can it be set aside on the ground that it is certain of the meanings it gives to words and sentences in its own thought and discussions? Rather, does it not seem possible, for philosophical purposes, to keep on suspending assent in the case of one judgment after another *ad infinitum*? The Skeptical position appears philosophically unassailable from its own viewpoint. It may be entirely unsatisfactory. It may be parasitical. But on its own terms it does not seem to be subject to refutation.

Closer to our own times is the view that conclusions in the experimental sciences have always to remain open to revision. Where the procedure of these sciences is regarded as the model for intellectual attainment, it will require that human knowledge strive to approximate truth without ever attaining it at any given time. Accordingly there is always occasion to withhold assent in any particular item of knowledge.

These experiences in the history of human thought show

cogently enough that it is possible, at least from the viewpoint of philosophical procedure, to suspend assent in regard to any judgment whatsoever, even the most basic. No matter how true a judgment is, that is, no matter how exactly it is equated with the actual existence that it represents, it is able to be questioned. To that extent assent to it can be allegedly withheld, if one decides with set purpose to make the attempt.

Is assent therefore an attitude of mind that rests ultimately upon the human will? Is one free to withhold assent from any judgment whatsoever? Or do some truth judgments compel assent, regardless of one's wish to dissent from them?

The answer to these questions will depend in large measure upon the nature accorded to the act of assenting. Is it in its essence a purely intellectual action? If so, it should be determined solely by its object, and not by any intervention of the human will. Further, if it is an intellectual act, is it a kind of simple apprehension or is it a judgment? On the other hand, if it is an act of the will how can it assess the truth of a judgment, unless one adopts the position that truth is what one wishes it to be? Or is there a third possibility, that assent involves in different ways the activities of both intellect and will? These considerations show that the nature of assent itself has to be examined before the problem of certainty is approached.

Nature of Assent. In what, then, does assent consist? Its object is rather easily shown to be a judgment (as representation). When you assert that rain today is certain, or probable, or possible, you are obviously not characterizing the actual falling of the rain. The actual falling will be an accident of local motion that will be synthesized or not synthesized with the raindrops in real existence as the day goes on and the weather runs its course. Nothing that could be called "certainty" or "probability" is synthesized with them in their real existence. With your judgment "It is going to rain," however, the synthesis does take place. The static representation in which that judgment consists is characterized as certain, or probable, or possible. Just as the locution "something is true" means that the basic existence judgment or proposition about the thing is true, so "something is certain" means that the truth judgment about the thing is certain. Scrutiny of the other examples will show that in every case solely a judgment existing in cognition is the object of assent. The assent does not bear immediately upon any really existent thing, no matter how much one speaks of the thing itself, such as the rain, as being certain.

These considerations establish the immediate object of assent. The object is a judgment in the static or representative sense. Whether or not the activity of the will enters into the nature of the assent, the intellectual scrutiny of a previously made judgment will in any case be required. Assent will first of all involve intellectual cognition of an already existent judgment. It has to do with an object found within intellection, even though on some occasions, like the deliberate suspension of assent, it may come under the influence of the will.

Assent, then, is concerned immediately with statically viewed judgments existent in the intellect. It is concerned with their conformity or "adequation" in regard to the existence they purport to represent. It bears on the relation of the judgment "It is going to rain today" upon the weather that will actually exist in the real world before nightfall. Is the relation one of conformity? If so, the further judgment "It is true that it is going to rain today" may be made. But one can still ask "Are you certain that it is true?" You re-examine the reasons that have led you to assert its truth, you find they are cogent in showing that no other turn is possible for the weather, and you make your reply that you are certain it is true, or simply that it is certain it will rain.

The judgment "It is certain" bears accordingly upon the relation of the mental representation to the existence it is meant to express. It seems to involve no opposition to the judgment "It is true." Both may be applied to the same judgment of existence. The weatherman, when the truth of his forecast is questioned, may review the causes and see that they necessitate his prediction. "It is certainly true that it is going to rain today," he may insist, or "It is certain that it is going to rain." On the other hand, he would hardly say "It is truly certain that it is going to rain." Like any other judgment, the certainty judgment can be questioned in regard to its conformity with the existence it is meant to represent. But in the present instance this could hardly be more than a mental exercise, just as in the case of the infinite regress in truth judgments. The pertinent concern, rather, is with the judgment "It is going to rain." The truth is regarded as presupposed in the certainty judgment, a judgment whose whole purpose is to confirm a truth that has been questioned. Assent appears as a further judgment upon a previously made truth judgment.

A judgment of certainty, then, has to include either implicitly or explicitly a truth judgment upon the same object. The truth judgment, however, does not seem to include the certainty judgment, since it regularly leaves the opening for the question "Are you certain that it is true?" The truth judgment alone and without further bolstering may be satisfactory. In that case no question about its certainty is asked. But if there is occasion for asking the question, it leads to a closer examination of the basic judgment's relation to the existence it is meant to portray. If the existence is found to require that the judgment retain its stated form, the finding is expressed in the judgment of certainty.

These considerations indicate the reason for the twofold way in which the certainty judgment may be phrased. Indifferently it may be worded "I am certain that it is going to rain," or "That it is going to rain is certain." The epistemological truth judgment, on the other hand, does not allow the personal wording. You cannot commence it by saying "I am true that . . ." The notion "true" applies only, in the present sense, to the judgment or statement. But "certain" can apply either to the judgment or to the cognitive agent, apparently without change in meaning. It implies that you have made the extra scrutiny of the grounds for the truth judgment and that you find them compelling. They compel you to make the existence judgment and the truth judgment, and they require that the existence judgment be true. In the certainty judgment the "subjective" and "objective" aspects seem to be but different sides of one coin.

The same twofold application may be noted in regard to the notions "uncertain" and "doubtful." Where the scrutiny of the reasons does not turn out to be compelling in its result, you make the judgment "I am uncertain that it is going to rain," or "That it is going to rain is uncertain." In either statement "doubtful" could be substituted for "uncertain." Again your own efforts at making the scrutiny are implied, together with the bearing of their results on your existence judgment "It is going to rain." You are doubtful about it, doubtful about its truth. Similarly it itself is doubtful, and that it is true is doubtful. If the reasons, while not compelling, incline you notably to make the judgment on one side or the other, you find it is probable that it will rain, or probable that it will not rain, or that both alternatives are probable. One may be found more probable than the other, or they may be found to be equally probable.[5] Degrees of probability become quite readily apparent. If the scrutiny, on the other hand, shows that the basic existence judgment may be true but does not offer any reasons that incline you to think that it is true, you accept its truth merely as a possibility and say "That it will rain is possible." The notions "probable" and "possible" are applied in this context only to the judgment and not to the cognitive agent. He remains "doubtful" or "uncertain" about them. Somewhat similarly he remains unconvinced, while they remain unconvincing. But in any case, language has its means of expressing the twofold aspect in judgments of assent, whether certain or probable.

Assent seems therefore to be a further judgment in which the relation of a basic judgment to the real existence is reassessed. The motives for the further judgment seem to lie in psychological conditions. A truth judgment should mean that the conformity between the basic judgment and the actual existence has been apprehended. There should be no call for a new judgment about its certainty. Once you have seen reflectively that it is true that it is going to rain, there should be no reason to ask if you are certain of it. But experience shows convincingly enough that the human cognitive processes do not always work that smoothly. Often in the past one has been sure enough about the coming rain to take umbrella and raincoat along, only to find that they were not needed. The judgment about the impending rain, to which one assented, turned out to be untrue. Similarly answers that one held to be true are marked wrong on examination papers, conclusions one held to be true are shown upon cross-examination on the witness and to be wrong, positions commonly recognized as true are found through the research of one's doctoral thesis to be untenable. After so much experience of error in what one had accepted as true, need there be any wonder at the further question "Are you certain that it is true?"

Yet in recalling one's own acknowledged errors in the past, one seems to have been certain of them even though they were not true. Wrong truth judgments were accompanied by wrong certainty judgments. Other people, moreover, claim to be certain of tenets you reject as false, for instance the superiority of communism over free enterprise. By what criterion, then, is certainty to be gauged? Granting that assent consists in a judgment, and that its object is a previously made judgment, how do you go about the task of isolating its determining factor in regard to both certainty and the various grades of probability?

Criterion for Certainty. The problem of a criterion or criteria by which truth may be known with certainty and firmness was formulated by the ancient Greek Skeptics. In various ways it was solved by them in the negative. They maintained in one way or another that there is no criterion of truth, with the result that in philosophy assent is always to be suspended and nothing is to be asserted "dogmatically."[6] Descartes faced the Skeptical problem, found that he was certain of his own thinking and existence, and saw in this instance a general norm by which the certainty of anything else could be determined: "I am certain I am a thinking being. Do I therefore know as well what is required for me to be certain of anything? Yes, for in this primary cognition there is nothing else than a clear and distinct perception of what I affirm. . . . And hence I already seem able to lay down as a general norm, that all that I perceive very clearly and distinctly is true."[7] In

Neoscholastic writings this notion of a general norm for attaining truth with certainty was taken up again under the label of "evidence" or "objective evidence," and was called the motive of certitude or the criterion of truth. The introduction of the notion "evidence" has a theological background in the traditional acceptance of the truths of reason as evident and the truths of faith as not evident. The background may be seen reflecting in the distinction between "certitude of evidence" and "certitude of authority," even in a context where evidence was being made the overall norm of certainty.

Further, a common Neoscholastic distinction was made between objective and subjective certitude, even though with some misgivings and with an effort to apply the notion of subjective to the intellective activity as the cause of certitude. Certitude was in this way regarded as primarily a state of mind. It was looked upon as "merely subjective" if it was not based upon a secondary kind of certitude, objective certitude. By objective certitude was meant the object that grounds the state of mind, or a characteristic in the object that was called objective evidence. Objective evidence in its turn was the intelligibility of the thing, manifest to the mind and causing a true judgment. The whole question was left pretty well hanging in the air. Certitude was approached as a state of mind, and objective certitude was defined as the cause of that state, while "merely subjective" certitude was the state detached from the cause.

All this hardly adds up. The notion of a "state of mind" is vague enough, and perhaps can be narrowed down to the notion of a judgment made about something that is true. Just as truth is primarily in the mind, so a judgment that is subsequent to it will also be in the mind. In this way certainty can be described as primarily a condition or state of mind. A judgment is an intellectual act, and accordingly able to give rise to either a disposition or a habit in the faculty. But to make this state of mind the starting point of the investigation, seek what causes it, and then declare it "merely subjective" if this determined cause is lacking, seems to set up the notion of certainty itself as something prior to its criterion. The procedure does not let the notion be developed in orderly fashion from the object of the intellectual act.

What, then, is the cause or criterion for certainty? In the stylized example of the cat on the mat, your friend in the next room, who doubts that the cat could have got past him without being noticed, may after hearing your assertion ask: "Are you certain that the cat is on the mat?" You look, the cat is there, you have no choice but to reply: "Yes, I am certain that the cat is on the mat." What forces you to answer that way? It is not the existence of the cat on the mat, directly apprehended through your act of judgment as you gaze on the cat in that location? The cause is the existence that is synthesizing the feline substance with the location on the mat. As long as that existence is there before the apprehending gaze of your judgment (as act), you see reflexively that the judgment (Now as representation) is true and cannot be other than true as long as the existence continues to be there. The cause and criterion of the certainty is the existence that is apprehended.

But the same existence was also the criterion and norm of truth. What is it adding when it becomes likewise the criterion for certainty? The addition just noted is that the judgment "cannot be other than true." The necessitating character of existence, already considered,[8] seems now to be coming into its own. The judgment is seen to be true because it is found equated with the existence. But this truth judgment is questioned, and another look is taken at the existent situation. The cat is there on the mat. The existence is seen to necessitate the truth character of the judgment in question. It does not allow the conflicting judgment that the cat is not on the mat. It shows that the positive assertion is certain.

This stylized example, like any other empirical fact, has to encounter many objections from possibilities of illusion and of perceptual difficulties and from the alleged impossibility of verification. The existence that is being apprehended has to be carefully scrutinized, to see if in fact it is any more than the basic actuality grasped in the judgment "something exists." But for the moment the point at issue is that actual existence is the criterion of certainty. Just what existence is apprehended can be left for later consideration in the study of the various kinds of immediate and mediate knowledge. The one conclusion drawn at present is that existence, and existence without any further support, is the criterion here. It is the necessary and sufficient cause of certainty.

Does this mean, then, that there is no "subjective cause" of certainty? Since assent consists in a judgment, it involves an act of intellection. It involves, moreover, a special effort at scrutinizing the necessitating character of the existence. Yet those activities do not contribute to the norm for certainty. They could be just as strong if the assent were withheld, or if the final judgment were that the assertion is not certain. The point at issue here is that the object of any act of cognition is always other than the cognition itself, and can be assessed without having to take into consideration the cognition by which it is grasped.

Nor is any abstract first principle required to ground certainty. The existence itself suffices. Similarly no second order study of "evidence" is required. To the extent it is apprehended the existence necessitates the certainty judgment. It does this in virtue of itself and not in virtue of any abstract principle. Philosophical training is accordingly not required for the ordinary certainties of life. As long as a person apprehends the existence at issue, he is able to swear to his certainty about it.

These considerations do away with any relevant distinction between "objective" and "subjective" certainty. From both viewpoints assent is a judgment grounded upon the necessitating character of existence. But what about the frequent occurrence of certainty judgments that later turn out to have been wrong? "I was certain that he would pay me back" was the judgment you made. To your discomfiture you find that he does not pay his debts. Is there not, then, a "merely subjective" type of certainty?

Like other judgments, a judgment of certainty may be either true or false. Just as in examining the truth of any other judgment, you look again in this case at the existential situation. Your debtor is not paying you back, though he is in a position to do so, and further inquiry shows you that this is his habitual way of acting. The closer look at the actual existence shows that your former certainty judgment was false. The problem is then thrown into the general consideration of error, and calls for careful scrutiny under this overall head.[9] How so smoothly oiled an apparatus as human intellection can function so defectively and find necessitating existence where it is not, is the actual problem here. As regards the questions of certainty, however, the criterion in both the above judgments was existence. In the first case it was the presumed existence of integrity and reliability in the debtor. In the second judgment it was the existence of the opposite disposition. The relevant problem is how the one could be confused with the other, how the first could be substituted for the second. Nothing in the objects themselves seems able to account satisfactorily for this substitution of the one existence for the other. Apparently some influence other than that of the objects known is at work, since both existences are known clearly, and not confusedly, from the standpoint of the way they are present in the mind of the person making the judgment.

Assent to Probability. In many instances, however, both in ordinary daily life and in intellectual life, the required existence is not apprehended clearly enough to ground a judgment of certainty. Future existence provides frequent cases. "It is going to rain today" is a judgment that expresses future existence. It is based not on any immediate grasp of the future existence, but upon the existence of observed weather conditions at present. Past experience testifies to the possibility of change in these conditions before the predicted event is brought about. Often the presently observed conditions allow the possibility of rain as well as the possibility of continued dry weather. The grounds in favor of one side may be stronger than the grounds against. In accord with this situation the forecast used to be called the weather "probabilities." The required criterion for assent is the future existence. This existence cannot at the present moment be grasped immediately. It can only be reasoned to from the present existent conditions. These offer grounds for concluding that it may rain, and grounds for concluding that it may not rain. Either of the two contrary judgments is able to be supported by grounds and is in that sense probable (*probabile*--able to be approved). Or just one may present grounds for approval, yet grounds that do not exclude another possibility. In that case it alone of the two would be probable. Or the one may have stronger grounds than the other, and in that case be more probable than it.

Even in regard to present existence, corresponding situations are continually met. You wonder whether or not you have picked up a virus cold. You have some symptoms to that effect, while others are lacking. You conclude that you probably have the flu, and stay home from work. The existence of the disease in your system is not at all clear from the symptoms. On their grounds you do not make a judgment of certainty, but only of probability. You assent to the conclusion that you are most likely getting the flu, with the full realization that possibly you may not be getting it. Similarly you may study whether marijuana is worse for young people than tobacco or alcohol. Your research brings to light strong reasons for the affirmative, and strong reasons for the negative. You find you cannot entirely exclude either of the two possibilities. You may finally conclude for either of the two sides, but only as a greater or lesser probability. Especially in the moral order are one's judgments continually based upon probability. Whether a particular person is reliable, whether a course of conduct is just or not, whether the Czech student did the right thing in burning himself to death in protest against the Russian invasion, and numerous other problems of like kind, keep confronting one in daily life. Grounds that allow probable judgments are usually available for both sides.

In the experimental sciences the same situation is encountered. Theories are advanced on grounds that have various degrees of probability. To the extent to which the conclusions can be supported by observation or experiment, the probability increases. To regard the results as always remaining open to revision, is to keep them in the realm of the probable, at least from the viewpoint of aspects that are considered falsifiable.

In all these instances, however, the role played by existence in determining the assent is obviously fundamental. The existence demanded is not immediately apprehended in any of them. You do not grasp immediately the future existence of the rain, or the present existence of the flu, or of the comparative harmfulness of marijuana, or of the correctness of the cases under consideration, or of the particles or gyrations concluded to by experimental science. From the immediately grasped existence of the phenomena you reason to the existence required for assent to the judgments in question. The phenomena contain grounds for reasoning to the existence you would require for a judgment of certainty. But they also contain grounds for reasoning to the opposite non-existence. After a comprehensive consideration of the whole situation, you find that the grounds exclude neither alternative. They allow as possible either the one or the other, either the existence or the non-existence that would allow a certainty judgment. To the extent the grounds are positive for either alternative, they permit a judgment of probability. Either or both alternatives may be found to be probable. But in any case, the existence that is concluded to with the possibility of its opposite is what determines the assent to the probability.

While a judgment grasping truth with certainty is called knowledge, a judgment that attains its object only with probability is called an opinion. If the probability is only slight, it is known as a conjecture or a guess. The greater the probability, the more convincing is the opinion. This should mean that assent may be given in varying degrees. Reflexively, one may be certain that one's judgment is only probable, or again one may remain uncertain about this further judgment too. Assent accordingly may be given without leaving the realm of probability.

This consideration accentuates still further the question of what brings on the assent when the object itself does not compel it. In the case of certainty the existence compels the assent. Where the assent was erroneous, the appropriate existence was not there to function as its cause. With opinion, the existence was not attained in a way that made it compel assent. It left open the possibility of its opposite. Quite apparently, then, there are instances in which the cause that ultimately determines the assent is something over and above the object known.

Suspension of Assent. In still other cases there may be no assent to either side. If asked whether there is life on any of the satellites in the galaxy Andromeda, you would have to answer that you did not know, or that you were doubtful about it. You presume there must be stellar systems with satellites in the galaxy, but whether any of them would have the conditions that give rise to life you do not know. You have no positive reasons in favor, and no positive reasons against. Your assent is not drawn to either side, because of lack of reasons. The judgment expressing this conclusion that the required reasons are lacking on both sides is called a doubt. Where reasons on either side are lacking, it is a negative doubt. If on the other hand there are equally strong reasons on both sides, assent is likewise suspended. But in this case the doubt is regarded as positive, since there are positive reasons balancing each other. You may remain doubtful for instance about the advisability of giving the vote to eighteen-year-olds, because you go along with political observers in seeing a fifty-fifty odds on each side. Finally, one may in Cartesian fashion deliberately suspend assent from one judgment after another. Again the influence of something else besides the object seems indicated.

Doubt is always included in opinion as defined above. In opinion the possibility of the opposite is acknowledged. This means that one has some doubt about the assertion to whose probability one assents in the opinion. If all doubt were excluded, there would be certainty. But if opinion means giving assent, even though in probable fashion, and doubt means suspending assent, how are opinion and doubt compatible with each other?

The answer to this query seems to lie in the restriction of the assent to one side of the pair of contradictory assertions. With regard to it there is no suspension of assent. But with regard to the other side of the pair there is suspension. One does not assent to it as true, nor as false. One suspends assent entirely in its regard. The attitude seems to be that one accepts the first side, but with the priviso that the other side may possibly be right, or possibly be wrong. In this way the opinion is not the doubt, even though an opinion is always accompanied by doubt.

Résumé. Not only truth, but also certainty about the truth, is a natural goal of human striving. But in intellectual as well as in ordinary life uncertainty is regularly encountered, and assent seems able to be withheld artificially from one truth after another. Upon examination assent is found to be a judgment that follows upon a truth judgment. It is based upon a further scrutiny of the existence upon which the truth judgment is grounded. If the existence is judged to necessitate the truth judgment, the new judgment is one of certainty. If it is judged to indicate the truth judgment but with the possibility of the opposite, the assent is one of probability. If it is judged to indicate neither side in preference to the other, no assent is intellectually induced on the basis of first-order considerations. Second-order considerations, however, may be used to break the deadlock of the equiprobable reasons.

Notes to Chapter 8

1. See references above, c. 1, nn. 8-10.

2. See Diogenes Laertius, *Lives of Eminent Philosophers*, 9.69-76; trans. R. D. Hicks (London, 1925), II, 482-489.

3. ". . . like a purge which drives the substance out and then in its turn is itself eliminated and destroyed." Diogenes Laertius, 9.76; trans. Hicks, II, 489-491.

4. See texts supra, c. 2, n. 1.

5. "Equiprobabilism" had an important part in eighteenth-century discussions on cases of conscience where the alternatives appeared to have equal probability and a decision had to be made. The background was an accepted opposition between liberty and law. This background is discussed incisively by S. Pinckaers in *Lex et libertas*, ed. L. J. Elders and K. Hedwig (Vatican City, 1987), 15-24. Epistemologically, the equiprobable would be the extreme instance in the inability to achieve assent through merely intellectual consideration of the issue. On equiprobability in a modern setting, see John Maynard Keynes, *A Treatise on Probability* (London, 1921), 41; 63.

6. See Diogenes Laertius, 9.74; trans. Hicks, 487.

7. Descartes, *Meditationes de prima philosophia*, 3.33; VII, 35.6-15 (3.34; IX, 27).

8. See above, c. 3, n. 19.

9. See above, c. 3, for errors occasioned by sense perception; and infra, c. 10, for those occasioned by faulty reasoning.

CHAPTER 9

The Ground of Certitude

Assent, as has been seen in the preceding chapter, is accorded to judgments in everyday life on grounds of either certainty or probability. Certainty, as was likewise shown, is the knowledge that a judgment already seen to be true cannot be other than it is. This certainty is based upon the necessitating character of existence, a character that has made itself manifest so sharply in the initial survey of the content in human cognition.[1] From this angle certitude is located in the intellect. It is not something brought about by the intervention of the human will. It is frankly grounded upon what is seen in the object.

Examples bear out this necessitating character of some judgments. "Something really exists," for instance, was found in the initial survey to be unshakable. No matter how thorough one's efforts, the judgment that something exists in reality cannot be overthrown when attention is focused solely upon itself. As a first-order judgment, aside from any philosophical framework, it turns out to be resistant to Skeptical shattering. It refuses to be dissipated under the rays of even the most searching direct scrutiny, in first-order knowledge.

But second-order considerations may readily be brought against it. To serve as the ground of certitude, the necessitating existence has to be *known* and *evident.* But one may ask if our cognitive faculties are reliable. Can we trust them? Though they may not be the ground of our certainty, they are at least a required condition, a *sine qua non.* Could they not, theoretically at least, be able to mislead us, or

perhaps even be meant to deceive us?[2] Does not the approach
of the Skeptics or of modern psychology and neurophysiology
throw the question of certitude into the status of a second-
order consideration, to be decided ultimately not on the basis
of the object itself but rather on the capacities and exigencies
of human cognitive faculties?   In the light of past
philosophical speculation and of present scientific facts, can
an absolute exclusion of contrary judgments ever be
guaranteed? If the possibility of an opposite judgment could
be allowed, there would be doubt.   But certainty is
incompatible with doubt.

Since the certainty judgment is the assurance that the
original existence judgment cannot be other than true, it
requires that any reasons brought forward to the contrary be
sufficiently considered and assessed in their bearing upon the
object under consideration. In the present case, the crucial
point is whether the real existence judgment is
epistemologically most basic or whether it itself is to be
gauged in the light of what is known about the human
cognitive faculties and their operations. If real existence is
grasped in cognitive priority to awareness of one's activities
and faculties, it can be judged on its own strength
independently of any second-order considerations. If, on the
other hand, knowledge of one's own mental activities comes
first from the epistemological viewpoint, this will offer the
framework in which the question is to be decided. In that
perspective, human faculties and cognitive activities turn out
to be incapable of grasping real existence. The overall
impossibility of making a real existence judgment will do
away with any truth that had been inconsiderately accorded
to the original naïve judgments. That is an outcome possible
for a philosophy based on ideas.

What have the phenomenological survey and subsequent
analysis and assessment shown in this regard? The origin of
human cognition was found to lie in really existent sensible
things. These are the first sensed, the first perceived, the first
known. The sensations and other cognitive activities by
which they are grasped are secondary from the
epistemological standpoint. One is aware of the activities

only concomitantly with and in terms of the object that is directly apprehended.[3]

This will mean that any conceptual framework will presuppose the perception and knowledge of really existent sensible things. The frameworks depend upon the real existence of the sensible objects. If the sensible things did not really exist, the frameworks could not arise in human cognition or play any role in its development. Once the epistemological priority of external sensible things has been recognized, no other natural origin for anything in human cognition can be admitted. The real existence present in sensible things is not to be assessed on independent views of human cognition and its exigencies, but solely on the strength of the real existence itself.

The consideration to be given the overall judgment that something really exists cannot, therefore, be given low profile. Rather, it has to remain dominant. There may be many philosophical difficulties raised by the workings of human cognition. Each of these has to be met in its own context. If after thorough scrutiny the difficulty still remains, it is to be regarded as yet to be solved. It remains a difficulty. But a difficulty, just as a difficulty, does not make a doubt. It can testify to the limitations of one's cognition, but not to any unrealiability on the part of the cognitive powers. Once the epistemological priority of the judgment of real existence has been satisfactorily established, the judgment itself is shown to be unassailable by philosophical frameworks that depend upon it for their own existence and functioning. In doing away with that existence judgment they would be sawing off the branch on which they themselves rest. Such, at least, is the estimate that follows upon the epistemological survey made in the opening chapters of the present study. It allows for pluralism in philosophies, but not for the use of an independent philosophical framework to refute tenets of a philosophy based upon the existence of external sensible things.

Philosophical considerations, accordingly, are subsequent in a way that does not allow them to provide any reason for doubt about real existence judgments. They can give rise only to difficulties that have to be faced and assessed to the best of one's abilities. But the difficulties do not have means of undermining the basic existence judgment. They cannot penetrate to the roots of human cognition, since they remain on a second-order level, dependent upon the first-order. They are powerless in the task of effectively challenging the spontaneous certainty of the basic judgment of real existence. The inability of Hume's speculations to prevent his return to the normal certainties experienced in backgammon and dining, bears eloquent enough witness to the persistent acquiescence in existence as real. Reasons from philosophical frameworks are unable to cast considered and examined doubt upon this certainty judgment. Upon scrutiny these frameworks are found actually presupposing the real existence they purport to deny. How this is at all possible is in itself a problem that will call for study in the theme of philosophic pluralism.[4] For present purposes, one need only note that philosophies do reason in this way. Yet philosophy cannot deny real existence without destroying itself. Concepts are taken originally from really existent sensible things. Only out of such concepts are conceptual frameworks constructed.

The certainty about real existence, then, does not have to wait till a conceptual framework has been set up. Doubts can of course be proposed by the frameworks once they have been established. But a critique of the basis of these doubts shows satisfactorily that they do not have the means of undermining the certainty of the original existence judgment. They remain to be dealt with as difficulties, but not as doubts that would militate against the certainty that is under consideration.

But is it not possible to introduce a double standard? Can one not accept the original certainty as sufficient for everyday life, while questioning a philosophically justified certainty for the judgment of real existence? May not one separate the certainty of ordinary life from what is required by the highpowered techniques of a sophisticated philosophy?

These questions bring the consideration back to the starting points of human cognition. Can philosophy have a starting point different from the sensible things with which ordinary life is concerned? The history of western philosophy provides abundant examples of thinkers who took other starting points for their speculation. The legitimacy of this procedure, along with the ways in which it is possible, will have to be discussed in the proper place in the study of philosophical pluralism. But the phenomenological survey and analysis in the preceding chapters should make sufficiently clear the fact that all the philosophical frameworks can be explained on the basis of derivation from the perception of really existent sensible things. No matter how unassailable each may be within the reasoning that takes place in its own framework, the whole framework itself cannot be used to cast doubt upon the viewpoint of one who sees it ultimately derived from really existent sensible things. The framework in itself abstracts from real existence in its starting point, and for that reason may succeed in showing that inside the framework real existence cannot be reached. But the whole procedure does not even touch the actuality from which it originally abstracted, and which it would have to affect if it were to provide grounds for doubt. Assent to the truth of the general assertion "something exists" is necessitated by clear knowledge of the existence. That knowledge antecedes philosophical frameworks.

In the sophisticated sense of a philosophical procedure that can start in abstraction from real existence, then, the radical bifurcation between philosophic tenets and ordinary life tenets is undoubtedly met within academic history. It is a pluralistic situation that will require careful investigation. For the present, the only point at issue is whether a framework that proceeds in this abstraction is capable of throwing doubt upon an existence judgment made before the abstraction is set up as a starting point. The answer is obviously that it cannot. Once the independent certainty of the everyday existence judgment is conceded, however, there need be no hesitation in granting that a philosophy may be established on another starting point. In its own framework this philosophy may reason with flawless cogency to the impossibility of proving that things really exist, or even to their express non-existence in reality. To that extent a philosopher may have this double standard. In ordinary life he may have no doubts that the things around him and the people with whom he associates really exist. But on the basis of his own philosophy he can reserve the right to doubt or deny the real existence of things, in the sense in which ordinary persons understand real existence.

A somewhat parallel situation is found with regard to the doubts suggested by the findings of experimental science. The neurophysiologist knows that the stimulation of the cerebral cortex is a necessary condition for any sensation, and he is quite strongly inclined to think that it is a sufficient one. He knows that patients report seeing colors as a result of electrical stimulation of the nerves, or hearing music in a room across the street when none is actually being played there. He may conclude that what is called the really existent world is but the result of mental activity and, at least immediately, can be given no further status. But he will probably have a sufficient sense of humor to see that he is making one exception. In the framework in which he thinks, all the phenomena are produced by a brain. There must be at least one brain that does the producing. It cannot itself be a mere phenomenon. If it were, it would be produced by another brain. In any case, therefore, there is a brain with more than phenomenal status. Naturally enough, that brain is his own. He is immediately aware of its activities, and his scientific findings, on their own level, do not lead him to any insurmountable doubt regarding its existence in the sense that is ordinarily meant by real existence.

From all angles, then, the reasons brought forward to cause doubt concerning the overall judgment that something really exists turn out to be second-order considerations. Upon close examination they are shown to presuppose in one way or another some real existence, even though they may be set in a conceptual framework whose internal starting points do not ground philosophically any justification for it as real. Epistemologically the real existence is prior to the conceptual frameworks and is immune to the sweep of their attacks. The reasons that they offer for doubts do not descend to the deep level of the original judgment of real existence.

In this way the reasons offered do not set up an effective doubt bearing upon the opposite of the judgment that something really exists. The opposite, namely that nothing at all exists in reality, is definitely excluded. There is no doubt whatever in its regard. The condition that would make the assent merely opinionative is lacking, for there is no room here for allowing possibility to a contrary judgment. The judgment that something really exists turns out to be absolutely certain when one carefully and exhaustively re-examines the ground upon which its truth is based.

A further noticeable characteristic about this basic judgment of real existence is its immediacy. It is made wholly in virtue of the real existence of which one is aware. It is not made in virtue of the trustworthiness of one's faculties, or on the strength of some other judgment of existence or of nature. It is made before one knows anything about faculties, and is not reasoned to from any premise that would be a judgment concerning them. It does not presuppose a judgment about anything else. In a word, there is in this case no other judgment that would play a mediating role. The real existence is apprehended in virtue of its own self, and not on the strength of any other object. The judgment of real existence may accordingly be called an immediate judgment. In that sense it is an instance of immediate knowledge.

Existence of Self. From the really existent object directly grasped, the concomitantly apprehended self is gradually distinguished with clarity. The sensible body in which it functions is likewise gradually distinguished from the ambient. This was made apparent in phenomological survey, and is borne out by psychological findings. The self and its body were apprehended as really existent. Can any effective doubts be raised against the real existence of one's own self and one's own body? The notion "effective" in this question will continue to have the force accorded it in the preceding discussion. It would designate a doubt that would remain after thorough scrutiny of the reasons upon which it is based. It would mean that the reasons for the doubt still leave in suspense any absolute assent in regard to the truth. It would reduce to the status of opinion the original existence judgment.

About the existence of one's own self, doubt seems impossible to establish on the first-order level. "I think, therefore I am," as Descartes maintained, cannot be shaken by any consideration brought against it on its own level in one's waking state. Aside from the Cartesian implications of epistemological independence of the body, the judgment persists as the basis of an anti-skeptical argument that had been used centuries earlier by Augustine.[5] One's own real existence stands continually before one's awareness, concomitantly in every sensation, perception, and thought, and expressly in every act of reflexive consciousness. In this way it proves much harder to attack with second-order considerations than any other instance. Where speculations like those of Hume virtually do away with it on their own grounds, the need of a return to backgammon and good cheer makes itself all the more sharply felt. Arguments of that kind are met upon examination with the same assessment that they receive when brought against the overall judgment of real existence. They are on a level that keeps them from penetrating to the deeper plane on which the original judgment of one's own real existence arises. They cannot impugn or weaken the grounds that necessitate this judgment, for they cannot touch them. Nor can they provide contrary grounds on the same plane. They leave untouched the judgment of the real existence not only of the flowing stream of one's thoughts and feelings, but likewise of oneself. The conceptual framework in which the objections arise is seen to be in fact dependent upon the prior existence exercised in the one who does the thinking and conceiving. Philosophically the real existence of self may be shown to be doubtful, or to be an entirely illegitimate conclusion. But no matter how often the self is philosophically made to die, there is always a real self that has committed the murder and that continues to preside at the funeral rites.

At least, that is one's own experience when one reasons philosophically to one's non-existence in reality. Facing you starkly is the real and lived experience that is of concern at the present moment of the epistemological inquiry. The judgment that one really exists in one's own self in some way apart from the real existence of any directly perceived object, remains unaffected on its own level by arguments brought against it. That level, however, is basic and is presupposed by the whole philosophical framework in which the arguments against one's own real existence are cast. On that level no reasons appear for causing suspension of assent because of some possibility of truth in the opposite judgment, the judgment that one's own self does not exist in the real world. Rather, this opposite judgment is definitively excluded by the necessitating character in the existence of which one is aware in oneself.

This knowledge of self-existence, in the sense that one really exists in distinction from the real existence of the directly known object, may likewise be called immediate. Time and effort may be required to bring it into express contrast with directly known existence and to formulate the difference. But the directly known existence never was the means for any reasoning to the concomitantly grasped existence of self. Existence of self was always apprehended with the directly grasped existence. It was never mediated. In that important and relevant sense, the judgment that one really exists as oneself, is an immediate judgment. Its dependence upon a directly apprehended object is limited to concomitance, and does not imply derivation or source. It has to accompany another judgment, but it is not mediated by that judgment. Nothing can function here as a syllogistic middle term.

Multiplicity of Existents. One has certainty, then, in one's judgment about two real existents. They are the directly apprehended object, on the one hand, and oneself on the other. But what about one's judgments of many individual existents in that directly apprehended object, and especially of other selves? Do these judgments that individuals have separate existence each in itself enjoy the same type of certainty as the two existence judgments already considered?

Or can reasons to the contrary effectively persist in regard to them, reducing them to the status of opinion or of doubt?

The phenomenological survey showed that the object directly perceived does not appear immediately as a multiplicity of substances. It appears immediately as multiple in quantities and qualities. It appears immediately as substance, but not as multiple in substance.[6] Hence there is no immediate absurdity in a monistic conception of the sensible universe. Is this consideration sufficient to cast doubt upon the truth of one's spontaneous judgments that each piece of metal, each stone, each tree, each animal, each man has his own individual real existence?

The judgment that each has its own existence, one may recall, is based upon the unity recognizable in groups of activities that indicate a common source, or in the way in which the patients undergo the results of these activities. Actually, what is immediately observable here consists in the changes in quantity and quality and subsequent categories. On the basis of these changes one infers different and multiplicity in substantial existence. But one has no immediate perception or knowledge of differences in them on the substantial level.[7]

Viewed in this perspective, the question narrows down to differences in substantial existence. Anything else that exists presupposes the existence of substance, as is clear from the phenomenological survey. But if one cannot apprehend the differences in the substance immediately, but only infer them from observed groupings and changes, how can one expect certainty in judgments about individual existence? The robot may perform faultlessly on the stage, allowing the audience to judge him a human being. Vice versa, a figure in the puppet show may go through all his motions stiffly to the delight of the spectators, only to leave them with a feeling of foolishness at being so easily duped when he breaks into a genial living smile and graceful bow at the end of the performance. Observed groupings of changes can lead to wrong judgments about the human existence or non-human existence of the substantial agent. Illusions, hallucinations, sleight of hand, suggestion, poor conditions of observability, haste in inference, all unite in stressing the possibility of error in regard to the individual substantial existence. May not one generalize and say that no judgment regarding the existence of directly known individual substances can be absolutely certain? Oneself is known only reflexively, not directly.

No second-order consideration can readily brush aside this reasoning. The fact that one does not immediately apprehend the individual differences remains unchallengeable. As far as one's immediate knowledge is concerned, the directly known object does not manifest separate substantial existences. True, it does not manifest anything against this tenet. But why could not what is immediately observable be in some theoretical way reconciled with unitary substantial existence, at least as a possibility, in the sense of a single substantial existence for the whole?

There are, however, second-order considerations that bring the likelihood of the opposite judgment to the zero mark. The total absence of any indications that the whole universe is acting like a single living organism, the satisfactory explanation of it as a vast complexity of millions of different bodies joined together on mechanical and physical principles, the difficulties in accounting for a moral order if all human bodies were but phenomenal manifestations of one and the same substantial reality, combine to eliminate any probability from the judgment of single unitary substance for the whole corporeal world. Not enough likelihood remains to cause any real doubt. The first-order judgment that metals, plants, animals and men are a multiplicity of real different individual existents continues to be accepted with certainty in ordinary life, even after the searchlight of philosophical scrutiny has shown that it is an inference and not an item of immediate knowledge. The metaphysical possibility of a unitary substantial existence for the material world may be admitted, as far as purely epistemological reasons play their role. But the total lack of any positive indications that such is the case, and the practically absurd consequences for moral and social life, eliminate all effective force from this theoretical possibility. In fact it does not cause a doubt. The separate existence of individual substances in the material universe maintains its status as a judgment not merely of the highest probability, but of certainty. Yet after philosophical scrutiny it has to be recognized not as immediate knowledge but as inference, and in a particular instance one has to be sure one has exhausted all the relevant possibilities concerning the thing's individuality. Even if that has been done, the type of certitude will be practical or moral. It will not be theoretically absolute, unless miraculous intervention can be precluded. The normal course of nature or morals is regarded as morally or practically certain, and not just as highly probable.

Determination of Individuals. How far, then, does the certainty in regard to separate individual existences extend? In particular and not at all infrequent cases, first-order reasons may cause doubt, and finally the certainty that an error was made. Illusions have occasioned erroneous judgments that particular things exist, things that after normal consideration are shown not to have existed at the time of the judgment was made. Psychological study can establish how the illusion took place, and leave one without the least doubt that the judgment was mistaken. On physical grounds a mirage can be explained, doing away with all doubt about the erroneous character of the judgment that what existed before one's gaze was water. The jewelry that one accepted as aquamarine turns out after chemical tests to be but a clever imitation. Hardly a day passes, perhaps, without the making of an erroneous judgment about the existence of some particular thing. That is a first-order consideration. The second-order knowledge that the existence as particular is not the object of an immediate judgment but is an inference, suggests that in an inference error is possible. This possibility is exemplified in fact in the instances just noted.

The reasons why the errors have been made can be established by scientific investigation in cases like the foregoing. The result is certainty that the formerly accepted judgment was erroneous. One is left with certainty, not with either doubt or error, in regard to the matter in question. Overall confidence in the certainty of one's cognition is not impugned. Rather, greater care is inculcated in paying closer attention to what one actually apprehends, implying full confidence in one's considered judgments. The end result is certainty.

Quite different is the result in cases about the extent of the material synthesized by an individual existence. In inanimate things is the conglomerate stone or piece of metal the individual existent, or is it the molecule, or the atom, or the fundamental particle? In colloidal solutions are the components individual existents, or is there the one substantial existence synthesizing the whole? In animals, to what extent have hair, horns, hoofs and blood any such individual existence apart from the existence of the whole organism? Is a transplanted heart a separate individual existent to be accepted or rejected by the host, or is it assumed into the one substantial existence of the latter?

In instances like these greater or loss probability may be reached for one or the other side, or the whole question may remain in doubt. Again, there can be no serious thought of impugning in Skeptical fashion the overall certainty of one's judgments. The limitation of the means of human investigation can be judged with certainty, the areas it penetrates can be distinguished with certainty from those of which it is aware but into whose nature it cannot enter. The intellect shows itself capable of controlling its range with certainty, even though the certainty may be that in this particular matter its results consist in probability or doubt.

Finally, a believer in transubstantiation has to face a situation in which, by all natural and scientific tests without exception, the inferred existence should be that of bread or wine but is not. Could he extend that particular situation to cast doubt on the normally inferred existence in all other material things? Here one need only recall the Skeptical philosophy of William of Ockham.

As far as this problem can be the concern of philosophy, the answer is straightforward. It is based upon the same second-order considerations that were applicable to the possibility of a unitary substantial existence for the totality of the material world. No positive reasons appear for doubt about the individual existence indicated by each thing's grouping of activities and other accidents, and moral life requires in general the correspondence of activities and substantial existence. The exception admitted on the grounds of religious faith is expressly regarded as an exception, as miraculous. It has its positive religious grounds, but is far too restricted to have any detrimental effect on the morally necessary correspondence of activity and substantial existence in ordinary circumstances. In a word, it is a type of belief that does not allow extension beyond its own very restricted ambit, and does not require any change in the second-order considerations that apply in the questions of distinguishing an individual existence from other existence possibly substituting for it.

Externality. May one be certain, though, that the directly known existence is actually outside one's cognition? Is the existence of an external world incontrovertibly certain? Can one be without doubt that the sensible universe exists objectively, in the sense in which objectivity is opposed to a merely subjective production? In other words, are there sufficient grounds for certainty that one's cognition reaches beyond itself?

Serious difficulties arise and persist when the questions are framed in this way. They presuppose, in accord with the Cartesian background, that one's cognition has its starting point within itself and has to proceed outwards. The problem how anything beyond thought could at all be within thought will, in this setting, play a troublesome role. The approach is in terms of nature rather than of existence. The exterior thing is regarded from the viewpoint of its having a definite nature, and cognition as another nature. The problem is how the first nature can get inside the second, or how the second can get outside its own self. The difficulties encountered when the questions are posed from this viewpoint seem insurmountable.

But is it the naturally indicated way of placing the questions? The real existence of the directly sensed object, as the phenomenological survey established, is an epistemological starting point. From the epistemological standpoint it is not dependent on anything else, and markedly not dependent on the cognitive agent or any of his activities. The directly perceived object is grasped as existent in itself. It is not apprehended as existent in the percipient, even though the existence of the percipient is concomitantly attained. Neither existence is apprehended as dependent on the other, from the epistemological viewpoint in which knowledge of the one would allow inference to the knowledge of the other.

The basic synthesizing actuality in the object sensed or perceived, then, is its own existence. It is not something brought about by the percipient. It confronts the percipient as an independent starting point, not as something that results from the percipient's presence or activity. Epistemologically it is not to be approached in terms of the percipient but in terms of itself.

Accordingly the correct approach to the questions at the opening of this section is not from the side of the cognitive agent. The initial query should not ask whether the directly perceived object exists outside the percipient, but whether it exists in its own self. The notion of externality should not for the moment be introduced. Rather, the directly perceived existence should be scrutinized from the viewpoint of what it brings about in the thing it is actuating. There is as yet no need to ask whether cognition is extending beyond itself. The existence grasped is existence of the object in its own self, not existence in the percipient.

Concomitantly, of course, the percipient's existence is also apprehended. But it is an independent existence, from the epistemological viewpoint. Epistemologically it is not reducible to the existence of the directly grasped object, just as the latter is not reducible to it. Each is irreducible to the other as an epistemological starting point. In contrast, the cognitional existence of the object within the percipient's activity is apprehended as dependent upon the percipient and in this way reducible to him as to its efficient cause, the cause that has brought about the cognitional existence in the particular case.

In contrast to the object's cognitional existence *within* the percipient's activity, the object's existence in its own self may be labeled external. But that is just an afterthought, a subsequent reflection. The real existence as originally grasped is existence in the object itself, not existence under the aspect of external. Only when the concomitantly grasped percipient is made the explicit object of an act of reflection, and the object's cognitional existence confronted with its existence in itself, is the notion of externality in the existence introduced to explain the contrast.

The difficulties, accordingly, are obviated when the questions are correctly posed. What is crucial is that the directly perceived object exists in itself, just as much as the percipient exists in herself or himself. Irreducible to the existence of the percipient, the object's real existence cannot be located within the percipient, as is the object's cognitional existence. Only in this entirely subsequent way do considerations about externality enter into the problem. They are therefore unable to affect the certainty of the original judgment of real existence, once their provenance has been carefully analyzed. The judgment that the object really exists in itself is exactly on a par with the judgment that the percipient really exists in himself, the only difference being that the former judgment is direct, while the latter is concomitant upon it.[8] Both judgments bear upon existence in reality, in contrast to a judgment of cognitional existence.

External Qualities. Once the problem of external existence has been seen in its proper perspective and incidence, it ceases to be a factor that could undermine certainty in regard to the real existence of corporeal substances and their primary qualities. The immediately known substances are bodies, and the extension each has is grasped as existing in the body itself, and not in the percipient's cognition. But in regard to the secondary qualities, the problem is not so easily set aside.

The special difficulty here arises from the neurologically based view that brain activity may be not only a necessary but also a sufficient cause for sensation. In the examples already noted, electrical stimulation may make a patient see colors that are not located outside the brain, or hear music from across the street that is not being played there. If these colors and sounds are grasped by the patient as really existing, they provide instances of erroneously apprehended existence in immediate judgments. The existence in this case is not inferred. It is sensed and known immediately. If apprehended as real, it would give rise to a plain contradiction. The percipient would become and be cognitionally a real existent that was not really existent.

This problem is serious, and has to be approached with great care. First of all, the radical difference between the existence of a color perceived in a really existent object and the color imagined in a phantasy or daydream, is sharp enough. The colors of the desk and wall in front of you appear existent in a different way from that of purely imaginary colors. The sound of the wind you are actually hearing presents a different kind of existence from the imagined sounds you conjure up in a novel you are writing. The difference is clear. Is it possible to confuse irremediably the one with the other?

The results of much more perfect means of stimulation and of sharper confrontation with cognition effected by the normal causal chain will be required before adequate consideration can be given to this problem. Will cochlear and retinal stimulation be found necessary for causing the impressed species that determines the percipient to become aware of the real existence of secondary qualities? Have certain kinesthetic factors also a role to play in causing this species?

In the present state of research no definite answer can be given to these questions. The difficulties remain as difficulties. But are they sufficient to cause any effective doubt in regard to the real existence of the secondary qualities in the external object?

Under normal conditions the difference between colors perceived as really existing and colors apprehended as having merely cognitional existence is clear enough. The one type of existence is grasped as dependent upon the substantial existence of the object, the other and cognitional type as dependent upon the activity of the cognitive agent. But exactly where is the really existent color sensed? There is no evidence of the sensed color or sound in the cortex. It cannot be located there. There is color on the retina, and in the distant object. There is no evidence of its presence in the light rays between object and retina. It is not perceived in these intervening waves. The only two places where the color can be located are the retina and distant object. The color is perceived initially and directly as existent in the latter only. To perceive it as existent on the retina a further act of perception is necessary, in which the retina itself is made the direct object.

Yet the color is not immediately grasped as distant. What can happen to it in the media between the distant object and the retina establish this beyond question. Is it the color on the retina that is sensed? The production of sensations of color without any stimulation of the retina would militate against this. In any case, the location of the color's real existence as in the distant object is a matter of interpretation. It is sensed as a really existent accident. It is sensed as existing in a directly perceived object, and not as existing in the percipient's activity. The distant location of that object, insofar as the color exists in it, is the result of the interpretation made in perception. If, in distinction from association through memory and imagination, the artificial stimulation of the cortex determined the percipient to sense a really existent color, a contradiction would be encountered. There would be sensed a really existent color that was not really existent. If on the other hand the artificial stimulation is merely recalling colors, or imagining colors, and associating them with an externally existing object as its colors, the problems hardly go beyond those encountered in the interpretative process that regularly takes place in perception.

There are undoubtedly a great many difficulties in regard to knowledge about the existence of the secondary qualities. But to the extent these difficulties are understood at present, they can hardly make one effectively doubt the real existence of the qualities themselves. The differences between a really existent green and an imaginary green remains just as sharp as the difference between a real apple and an imaginary apple. The problem of the location of the really existent color as sensed still bristles with unsolved difficulties. But its existence in reality as an accident of an external thing does not stay subject to doubt. It continues to manifest itself as existence that is dependent upon the existence of the directly perceived object, and not as dependent upon the existence and activity of the percipient.

The approach to the secondary qualities from the standpoint of their existence rather than of their location does not even commence to remove the difficulties. But it does prevent the difficulties from causing effective doubt. It leads to the knowledge that the real existence of the secondary qualities stands in its own right regardless of location. It shows how the difficulties urged in the foregoing considerations are problems of interpretation, problems of the kind usually met with in perception. It allows the real existence of the qualities to remain as an immediate object of knowledge, and not as a spontaneous inference. It emphasizes the important consideration that external existence means existence outside the cognitive activity of the percipient or knower, and not necessarily existence outside his or her real self or body.

The Criterion. In the judgments of existence so far considered, immediate knowledge of existence in contrast to inference has emerged as the criterion of certainty. Where the existence is immediately known, there is no possibility of anything getting in between the subject and predicate of the judgment to occasion doubt or error. Where the existence is known by reasoning, the existential synthesis in each subsumed premise has to be examined and known immediately in itself. If the thing so known is something really existent, the knower is at once, cognitionally, that really existent thing, with the full necessity that existence requires. The same holds proportionally where the existence of the object is cognitional. The judgment of certainty is thereby intellectually necessitated, with immediate knowledge of existence everywhere the criterion.

The process leading up to the certainty judgment, then, consists in carefully scrutinizing the alleged reasons for doubt. If the reasons dissipate and vanish under the exposure to the scrutiny's discerning rays, the necessitating force of the existence makes itself expressly felt because of the new concentration of attention upon it. It was there from the start, determining the existence judgment and the truth judgment to be what they were. But now, on account of the doubts that had been raised, the attention is focused on its necessitating character. It is now seen expressly as necessitating the judgment, something which it did all along but to which express attention had not been drawn. In being reexamined on the occasion of the suggested doubts, it shows that on its own strength it necessitates the truth judgment already made. It expressly manifests the necessitating character, not only from the viewpoint of defense against the particular difficulties brought forward, but much more positively as necessitating the judgment regardless of whatever other difficulties that might possibly be alleged. It allows one to make the certainty judgment without having to wait till all possible difficulties have been set aside. Its necessitating character lies in its own actuality as existence, and does not require any cumulative consideration of all possible objections before it can close in with its overpowering force.

This has been the case in the immediate judgments considered so far in the present chapter. The real existence of the directly known object of perception or sensation turned out to be necessitating just on its own strength. It compelled a certainty judgment. The concomitantly grasped existence of self, as real existence, did the same. The cognitional existence of things in the percipient's activity, likewise, allowed no doubt. In confrontation with the cognitional existence within the percipient's activity, the existence of the directly known object immediately appeared as external when as existence in the thing itself it was expressly contrasted with the internal existence. The distinct existence of the accidents in the directly known object, and in particular that of the secondary qualities, is seen to exercise its necessitating strength in determining judgments of certainty. From these instances a criterion can be tentatively formulated. If an existence is immediately grasped, and continues on close scrutiny in reexamination to manifest the immediacy, it necessitates a judgment of certainty.

In contrast, what has happened when the judgment did not turn out to be immediate? The instance encountered was the determination of individual existence, in the sense of the separate existence of each corporeal substance. Here the close scrutiny showed that since the immediate judgments concerned activities or other accidents, and not the distinct substantial existence, the latter existence was not known in a way that at once compelled a certainty judgment. The alleged reasons brought forward to show that each tree, each animal, each man is an individual thing with distinct individual existence, can be dissipated. Other reasons for accepting the judgment as certain can be brought in. But in this case the necessitating reason is not the individual existence itself, for here the individual existence is not grasped in the way that would allow it to exercise its necessitating force.

Apparently, then, existence that has been known through an inference does not in itself compel a certainty judgment. Immediacy seems required for this. In particular judgments of existence there is the possibility of doubt and error, of illusion and hallucination. Certainty in these judgments will have to be attained through other considerations than that of just the immediately grasped existence in each case.

Principle of Contradiction. The certainty judgments so far considered have all been abut the existence of concrete corporeal things. Even the real existence of oneself is grasped as the existence of a concrete corporeal agent. But one wishes also to be certain about the abstract principles and truths that come within the object of one's intellectual gaze. Is their certainty or probability or doubtfulness to be gauged in the same way as in the instances of concrete existence?

Since truth is always based upon existence, and the judgment of certainty bears upon truth, one may expect that in this sphere also the question of certainty will focus upon existence. But the existence now will not be real existence, because abstract principles do not have their existence in the real world. They belong to an order that abstracts from the individual, and for that reason they can be universal. What kind of existence do they have, then, and how can that existence be probed in view of attaining certainty?

Each instance of real existence judged certain in the foregoing discussion excluded the corresponding non-existence. The directly perceived existence would not have been necessitating the truth judgment, except for that exclusion. It could not have made one certain, had one held that the directly perceived object could be non-existent. In every instance, existence is found to do away with the opposite situation. When scrutinized in an abstract concept, this necessitating role appears with full vigor in the relevant existence. It is manifest immediately. Existence contradicts non-existence. One and one *are* two. They are not three. Black in the universal is not white in the universal. The abstract object is what it is, and cannot be what it is not, in the same respects. Existence absolutely excludes its opposite.

One may test this truth in as many instances as one wishes. In every case the existence is found to make the corresponding non-existence contradictory. But more than that, the very concept of a thing existing is based upon a judgment that would have been incompatible universally with any judgment that the same thing did not exist, in the same respects. The subject of the existential actuality may in this way be universalized, yet retain the predicate of existence. The assertion then will be: "A thing cannot exist and not exist at the same time in the same respects."[9] For Aristotle and the Scholastics this was the first principle of demonstration.[10] As it was meant that only one side of a pair of contradictories could be true, it later acquired the title of the principle of contradiction. It was presented in this way by Leibniz, but with the understanding that it was a principle of essences.[11] Since an essence could not have an internal contradiction, many modern writers have looked upon it as expressing the essence's non-contradiction, and have accordingly changed the name to the "principle of non-contradiction." Being a *truth*, however, it should be viewed as based upon existence rather than upon essence. Regarded from this standpoint, it will express the contradiction that existence gives to non-existence. No apologies, therefore, need be made for continuing to call it the principle of contradiction.

But what kind of existence does the principle, in its status as a principle, enjoy? It obviously does not have real existence. Its subject is a universal, standing for every possible instance of "thing." The predicate is existence taken universally, with its necessitating characteristic expressed. The principle is not asserting that anything does in fact exist, but is bearing upon "thing" and "exist" in general. The act of making the judgment, of course, really exists in the intellect. It is individual. But what kind of existence does the object represented in the act possess?

When a nature is universalized in the intellect, the existence it enjoys there is cognitional, not real. This cognitional existence synthesizes the nature with its specific and generic traits, in a synthesis that holds universally, no matter where the nature may be. Man, for instance, is a sentient, living, corporeal substance, regardless of where human nature is found. Existence gives rise to difficulties as a predicate, but in the principle of contradiction the way it actuates its subject is being expressed. It actuates its subject in a way that necessarily excludes the opposite, and prevents the opposite from being predicated of the subject at the same time and in the same respects. The subject is thing in general. When "thing" as a supergeneric nature receives existential actuation in the intellect, it receives the actuation in such a way that the opposite cannot be true of it. The nature of anything as a "thing" requires existential actuation of this kind, in the way any essence demands existence. This is at once apparent in the general nature of a thing, when it is viewed in relation to its existence. Universally it is a potentiality for existence in a way that does not permit it to be non-existent in respect of the existential actuation it possesses. In a word, it presents itself as a potency that is not open to both existence and non-existence at the same time in the same respects. It either exists or does not exist. Its very nature as a thing universally renders these two opposite predicates incompatible in it in exactly the same respects.

Whether the principle is expressed as "a thing does not both exist and not exist at the same time," or as "a thing cannot exist and not exist at the same time," the meaning is therefore the same. The modal form merely makes explicit what is already there in the character of existence. Existence contradicts non-existence in a way that necessitates. That aspect of necessity goes with the existence, and is expressed in the modal wording. Upon that aspect the judgment of certainty in its regard is based. When asked if one is certain that this principle in its universality and super-universality is true, one sees that the nature of the subject necessitates the predicate. That is the way a thing is necessarily related to its existence.

When the notion of a thing, then, is given cognitional existence in the intellect, the composite of thing and existence involves universally the necessity that excludes the opposite non-existence. This is what is expressed in universal form in the principle of contradiction. The principle is instantiated in every individual thing that exists, and in every universal notion that has cognitional existence in the intellect. It is all-embracing in extent. Since it expresses the character of the most fundamental actuality in the thing, the existence, it is likewise the most basic of all judgments. For that reason it was called the first principle of demonstration. The reason will become clearer in a moment when other principles are considered. Its basic role, however, does not at all imply any other origin than sensible things. It is not an eternal truth that would have an epistemological origin outside real things or in an apriori of the intellect. Rather, it is the universalizing of what is first seen in individual sensible things, just as any universal nature is the conceptualization of something that is perceived in the sensible world.[12]

Abstract Truths. Do these considerations in regard to certainty apply to abstract truths in general? Does certainty in them rest upon the existence that synthesizes universal subject and predicate in the intellect?

In a principle like "The whole is greater than the part," the subject includes the total comprehension. The predicate has relatively a lesser comprehension. The very nature of the whole demands accordingly that when synthesized in cognitional existence with this predicate, the judgment expressing the synthesis be necessarily true. No possibility of the opposite is recognized, no matter when an individual situation may be. The nature of the subject is such that it allows itself to be synthesized only with this predicate and not with its opposite. The universal notion "whole" is a potency to cognitional existence in the intellect only in a way that shows it to be greater than any one of its parts. This is immediately seen when one looks at the nature of a whole in the universal status. The existence that synthesizes subject and predicate in the intellectual cognition consequently necessitates the judgment. It leaves no room for doubt or for mere probability.

The same can be seen in considering other abstract truths. Where the cognitional existence in the intellect immediately synthesizes the universal subject with the predicate, it necessitates the judgment of certainty. Equals added to equals give equals, five is more than four, a triangle is a plane figure--all exhibit subjects whose nature cannot be given existence as a universal without immediately involving the predicate. There is no inference to the predicate. The nature of the subject, rather, shows immediately that it necessarily involves the predicate in existential synthesis. The judgment expressing that synthesis accordingly has to be true. It is a judgment of certainty.

In a logical context this is expressed by saying that the notion of the predicate is contained within the notion of the subject. Epistemology spells out what is meant by being contained in a notion. The meaning is that the existence given the notion as a universal in the intellect necessarily synthesizes the predicated notions with it, so that the subject universally is what the predicate expresses. The all-pervading force of the first principle of demonstration is seen in each of these truths. The existential synthesis, now expressed in English by "is" instead of "exists," contradicts its opposite. If the whole by its nature is greater than the part, it does not allow even a single instance of a part greater than a whole. The existence is necessitating in respect of this predicate for the subject as a universal. Where the existence that synthesizes subject and predicate is immediately apprehended, it renders certain the truth of abstract principles in their universality.

In abstract truths just as in judgments about concrete individual things, then, existence immediately grasped gives rise to certainty. It is a sufficient cause. Trustworthiness of faculties or of abstracting processes does not enter the question. The principle of contradiction as the absolutely first demonstrative principle makes itself clear in the very character of existence, so much so that its denial would be its affirmation since the denial would have to be understood as, in its nature, not being the affirmation. The other truths rest upon the immediately grasped synthesis of subject with predicate.

On account of the immediately known existential synthesis, expressions of these judgments may be ranked as "basic statements" or "protocol sentences." But this does not give them a monopoly on the notion of first or basic principles of scientific reasoning. On account of their universality they keep recurring in the course of rational procedure. From that viewpoint they have their privileged status. But as the basis for certainty they have no predominant role over particular judgments of fact. Judgments such as sugar is white or water flows downwards are just as compelling as far as certainty is at issue. Any reexamined existence constitutes a sufficient basis for certainty. Immediate judgments of fact function therefore as first principles in our reasoning processes. Their certainty is not derivative from prior knowledge of the abstract principles. It stands on the strength of the particular existence that is involved. The recognition of protocol sentences, in consequence, does not imply the acceptance of any "principle-philosophy." Any immediate judgment, whether universal or particular, stands squarely on its own feet as far as the certainty factor is concerned.[13]

The study of certitude has inevitably occasioned considerable repetition of topics previously discussed. That is endemic to the theme of certitude, since it means a return to the existence upon which a truth is based and a reexamination of the way that existence was grasped. Much easier might seem the claim that evidence grounds certitude, and that one need merely look and see what the evidence in a particular case is. With that claim, however, the Pandora's box of the traditional Skeptical arguments springs open. These objections call for answer in terms of the factor that has to be evident. Upon this factor the whole inquiry needs to be focused. It turns out to be the existence to which truth in each case has to conform. The problem is thereby thrown back into the existential considerations that have been found so laborious. The problem of the criterion or criteria of certitude is deep, and the Skeptical objections through the centuries cannot be neatly dismissed by the mere mention of the notion "evidence."

Résumé. In every case where existence is immediately grasped, it allows one, upon close reexamination of this immediacy, to be *certain* of a judgment. In renewed focus, the real existence of the directly sensed object is sustained as immediately apprehended. Likewise the real existence of the cognitive self is upheld as immediately perceived and known. The existence of these objects in themselves, and in that sense externally from the viewpoint of existence in cognitional activity, is thereby found known with certainty. Individual existences in what is directly known are not immediately discernible on the substantial level. In their regard certainty has to be sought in other considerations, and in numerous cases cannot be attained. The existence of distinct primary qualities is apprehended immediately, therefore with certainty. The existence of secondary qualities is grasped as real, immediately, in the sense of existing in the real world in contrast to cognitional existence. But the problem of their location as really existent qualities raises difficulties that have not as yet been solved. In abstract truths, the existential synthesis that joins subject with predicate in universal fashion is in many cases grasped immediately. In that event it necessitates a certainty judgment. This occurs in regard to the principle of contradiction, and in numerous other abstract principles in which the nature of the subject makes manifest immediately that it could not have existence in the intellect without thereby synthesizing the predicate notion. Accordingly existence immediately apprehended gives rise to certainty when it is definitely recognized and inevitably established as such. In this way existence is shown to be the ground of certitude, and immediate knowledge of it is the criterion. Whether it is possible for beliefs to be certain in some other way remains to be discussed.

Notes to Chapter 9

1. See supra, c. 3, n. 19.

2. Cf.:". . . we have heard that there exists a God who is all-powerful and by whom we have been created. We do not know whether he has perhaps willed to create us such that we are always deceived, even those thing which appear to us most evident; . . . And, if we imagine that we have our existence not from the all-powerful God, but from ourselves or someone else, then it will be all the more credible that we should be so imperfect as to be always deceived, to the extent we assign a less powerful author for our existence"--Descartes, *Principia philosophiae*, 1.5; A-T, VIII, 6.14-24 (IX^2, 27). Other references to the *Dieu trompeur* may be found in the Index, s.v., A-T, XII, 77. On the role of the Skeptical thinking in the background of modern philosophical development, see Richard H. Popkin, "The Sceptical Crisis and the Rise of Modern Philosophy," *The Review of Metaphysics*, VII (1953-1954), 132-151; 307-322; 499-510. A short survey of the modern situation may be found in Bertrand Russell, *Human Knowledge: Its Scope and Limits* (London, 1948), 398-417.

3. See Aristotle, *De anima*, 2.4.415a14-22. Cf. supra, c.2, n. 29.

4. See infra, c. 12.

5. "Si enim fallor, sum. Nam qui non est, utique nec falli potest: ac per hoc sum, si fallor." Augustine, *De civitate Dei*, ed. Emmanuel Hoffman (Vienna, 1899), I, 551.6-7. On the sources in Augustine and the use made of them for the Cartesian *cogito*, see discussion in Etienne Gilson's edition of Descartes' *Discours de la méthode* (Paris, 1930), 295-298.

6. See supra, c. 3, nn. 23-25.

7. For a discussion of this doctrine in Aquinas, see R. B. Gehring, "The Knowledge of Material Essences according to St. Thomas Aquinas," *The Modern Schoolman*, 33 (1956), 153-181. With this may be compared the formulation that the real essences of bodies remain unknown, as in Locke's *Essay concerning Human Understanding*,

3.3.18; ed. Peter Nidditch (Oxford, 1975), 418-419.

8. From this viewpoint the brain itself is an external existent. The basic notion of an external object of cognition has to be kept carefully distinct from the notion of what is outside one's body. The difficult "projection" to the exterior world holds equally well for the real existence of mind and its corporeal organ, when the starting point is located in human ideas. For discussion, see Walter Russell Brain, *Mind, Perception and Science* (Oxford, 1951), 7-8. It is quite possible to regard the cognitive agent himself as a fleeting mixture that appears temporally in the reality of being, as in Parmenides, *Fr.* 16 (DK), if one starts from cognitional existence alone.

9. See Aristotle, *Metaphysics*, 4.3.1005b19-22. Cf. Plato, *Theaetetus*, 183AB.

10. Cf.: ". . . for this is naturally the starting-point even for all the other axioms." Aristotle, *Metaphysics*, 4.3.1005b33-34; Oxford trans. ". . . it is the first philosopher who is chiefly concerned with the first principle of demonstration." Aquinas, *Commentary on the Metaphysics of Aristotle*, 4.6.596, trans. John P. Rowan (Chicago, 1961), I, 241.

11. ". . . the other great principle of our reasonings, viz., that of essences; that is, the principle of identity or contradiction: for, what is absolutely necessary, is the only possible way, and its contrary implies a contradiction--*The Leibniz-Clarke Correspondence*, ed. H. G. Alexander (New York, 1956), 57. Cf. ibid., 15. These passages are from Leibniz' Fifth Paper, no. 10, and Second paper, no. 1. Against that background the notion of the principle as "the Law of Non-contradiction" was introduced by Sir William Hamilton, *Lectures on Metaphysics and Logic*, ed. Henry L. Mansel and John Veitch (New York, 1883), II, 58-59.

12. This means that in the Aristotelian approach the basis of all natural certainty, including that of the first principle of demonstration, remains located in sensible things. Cf.: "And on this account the Philosopher at the end of the *Posterior Analytics* shows that the cognition of the principles comes to us from sensation."

Aquinas, *Summa theologiae*, 1-2, 51, 1c. In becoming cognitionally the really existent sensible thing, the percipient is immediately aware of the necessity involved in existence. Only when the starting point of our cognition has been systematically located in human ideas, is there room for a second-order undermining of the origin of abstract principles in sensible objects. For Ockham the divine power could produce sense cognition apart from the real existence of the sensible thing: "Every effect which God can produce by means of a secondary cause He can produce directly on His own account. God can produce intuitive sense cognition by means of an object; hence He can produce it directly on His own account." Ockham, *Ordinatio*, Prol., 2; trans. Philotheus Boehner, in *Ockham, Philosophical Writings* (Edinburgh, 1957), 25-26. Ockham himself may be defended against Skepticism on the ground that "in his teaching there is no room for a deceiving God"--Boehner, "The Notitia Intuitive of Non-Existents according to William of Ockham," *Traditio*, 1 (1943), 232. Nevertheless the tenet that sense cognition can be produced independently of the object's real existence would undermine the status of external sensible things as epistemologically the primary existents. Ockham's further teaching that it is possible to see (literally) a substance whose proper accidents are not visible to the percipient would reinforce this situation. On Ockham's views here, see Gabriel Buescher, *The Eucharistic Teaching of William of Ockham* (St. Bonaventure, NY, 1950), 95-104. On the crucial importance of remembering that the cognitive subject in this regard is the sensible human composite, see Etienne Gilson, *Réalisme thomiste et critique de la connaissance* (Paris, 1939), 184-212.

13. A doctrine of three, and only three, fundamental truths attained some prominence in Neoscholastic writings. They were one's own existence as the primary fact, the law of contradiction as the primary principle, and the aptitude of the mind to know. See Peter Coffey, *Epistemology* (London, 1917), I. 128; Paul Gény, *Critica* (Rome, 1927), 108. They were meant not as chronologically the first items known, but as the basic criteria in the reflexive judgment of certainty--Gény, 109-111. The background was the fundamental role given to certainty in the philosophical thinking of James Balmes--see Balmes, *Fundamental Philosophy*, trans. Henry F. Brownson (New York, 1880), I, 3-246. The norm was "before raising the edifice,

CHAPTER 10

Grounds of Error, Opinion, and Belief

Will. The immediate knowledge considered in the preceding chapter seems to have as good a title to "knowledge by acquaintance" as any knowledge of things.[1] Whether the existence upon which the certainty is based is that of a concrete sensible individual or that of the union between two abstract natures in the mind, it immediately necessitates the judgment. It leaves no room for dualism in regard to truth or falsehood.[2] It is an actuality with which one is immediately acquainted, not a subsequent synthesis imposed by the mind upon the terms as a result of inference or manipulation. It is known, not fabricated.

Immediate judgments, whether of concrete fact or of abstract universality, are accordingly the result solely of acquaintance with objects. The immediate acquaintance with sensible existents always takes place through the twofold activity of simple apprehension and judgment. One never occurs without the other. Both are equally immediate, from the epistemological standpoint. The result is that here the judgment of fact is the immediate apprehension of real existence. In the perspective of logic, the two terms may be regarded as separate and as prior to the copula. But in the actual apprehension neither term is attained apart from the existence that is expressed in the judgment. "The cat is black" is grasped as a single synthetic whole. The immediate judgment "Something exists" represents an absolutely primitive acquaintance with the actuality expressed by the verb. Similarly "The object is extended" asserts an immediate acquaintance with the actuality that synthesizes the two terms. Analysis into subject and predicate, substance and accident, essence and existence, is epistemologically subsequent.

Likewise in abstract truths the copula asserts the cognitional existence that synthesizes the natures in the intellect in accordance with their universal exigencies. With that synthesizing actuality one is immediately acquainted. It is not superadded by the mind to already fully constituted terms. In the universal judgment "Two and two are four" the subject notion cannot be brought into existence in the mind without involving universally the predicate notion. The subject here is by its nature four units. That is the only way its nature will allow it to exist abstractly in the intellect. The existence is not inferred or subsequently added. It is apprehended from the start. The judgment is literally knowledge by acquaintance, when "acquaintance" is philosophically understood.

These immediate judgments determine the mind to assent, whether one wishes or not. One may deny them in words, but not in thought while one is considering their objects.[3] On the strength of philosophical tenets one may deny that the external world exists. But to have any doubt about its real existence while one is actually seeing its glow in a sunset, feeling the thrill of its wind and waves as one speeds over a river's surface on waterskis, or enjoying the wine and steaks of a candlelight dinner, is literally impossible. You have no doubt yourself, and at the time you would consider a denial of the real existence on the part of someone else as merely a different way of using words and concepts in order to fit them into a philosophical framework. In the perspective of immediately grasped objects, the real existence of the sensed things or the involvement of predicate notion in subject is epistemologically primitive. When known it compels assent. In that way the assent is spontaneous.

In these ways, then, the necessitating character of existence is seen to be the cause, and its immediate grasp the criterion, of certainty. Wherever the existence is immediately apprehended, it exercises this necessitating influence on the intellect. One cannot be apprehending the existence immediately and at the same time be doubting about it. It shuts off all possibility of doubt while it is under immediate consideration. In regard to mediate cognition, however, it need not be exercising this function. Reasons for certainty may have to be sought elsewhere, or the mediate judgment may be left in the probability or doubt.[4]

In opinion, one does in fact give assent to a judgment apart from the necessitating influence of immediately apprehended existence. There is doubt that the opposite judgment is excluded, nevertheless assent is given. The giving of the assent is not caused ultimately by the existence apprehended, since in this case it does not necessitate. What then is the further cause that ultimately determines the assent?

If, as has been urged, "probability is the very guide of life,"[5] the judgments necessary for leading ordinary, everyday life will in great part be opinions. You wait for your electric alarm clock to go off in the morning till you being to suspect a power shutoff, you turn the tap as usual even though you have been through times when the water had unexpectedly been turned off, you wait till the last minute before leaving the house in spite of past experience of the car's failure to start. The probability is sufficient for you to act on these judgments. It is something you want to do, something you freely decide to do. You could have taken the opposite attitude, you could have been fidgety and scrupulous. But in the long run you know that attitude would not pay off.

You assent to these judgments, then, because you want to. You have objectives in life, and to attain the objectives you have to act. Since probability is the best you can attain in so many of the judgments that are geared to action, you accept it regularly. It is far better than complete lack of assent to any judgments, and consequent lack of action. The worst thing would be to do nothing at all.

The point brought out by these considerations is that the human will can bring about assent. It can be the ultimate determining factor. This is continually experienced in daily life. One knows what it is to deliberate carefully and finally make up one's mind. The decision to accept or reject a judgment to which one is not necessitated by the existence of the object, remains within one's free choice. The choice will be prudent only if it follows the greater probability or at least solid probability. Nevertheless it is always a choice, always a free decision.

Assent can accordingly be determined by the human will, where it is not necessitated by the object's existence. How the will acts upon the intellect is a study for natural philosophy, not for epistemology. Similarly the problem how the will can be free is the concern of metaphysics. In its own sphere epistemology is content with the observed fact that one can cause assent by one's own decision in cases where the assent is not caused by the existence as apprehended in the object.

The assent caused in this way by free decision is of course changeable and reformable by free decision. One may have firmly assented to the judgment that the Expos would not win, on the basis of personal impressions and of the odds given by the bookmakers. As the World Series progresses and the Expos lead three to one, the judgment may be freely changed to its opposite, or may be clung to with an eye on the possibility of a three-straight winning streak. The probability increases with the exact calculations required to send men on a lunar voyage, which have to keep within the margin of error that could be corrected by the spaceship, or by the lunar module as it lands. It may leave an extremely wide margin in the area of data collected by the social sciences. But in all these cases the possibility of the opposite is not removed. Calculations may be mathematically exact, but the use of a measuring rod in applying them brings its problems. The result is the frequently stressed provisory character of the intricate findings of experimental science, and their openness to ever more exact measurements. But in most cases an exact margin of error seems able to be determined, and within that margin the findings may be accepted as certain. In some cases only a statistical certainty can be attained, which does not warrant application to any definite individual instance. All this is a far cry from the way certainty is necessitated by immediately apprehended existence.

What, then, is the problem at issue here? Where the

existence as apprehended does not necessitate assent, the human will can enter and cause the assent given to judgments based on probability. But there is a price. The assent caused by the free decision of the will can be erroneous, as in the opinion that the Expos would not win. It brings to the fore the problem of error.

Error. Error is a ubiquitous fact. One is aware of one's own mistakes, one sees every day mistakes made by others. As an undeniable fact, error has to be explained in an epistemology. An epistemology that fails to explain it, or that turns out to be incompatible with its presence, cannot hope to be successful.[6] Yet error is something that is wrong. It goes against the criterion of existence. It rests ultimately upon a lack of the existence affirmed in a judgment. It cannot expect, therefore, an explanation of the same caliber as that given to truth and certainty. These rest upon existence, error upon non-existence. To give error the same rational status as truth would seem to involve equal status for being and not-being, in Democritean fashion.

Two extremes are accordingly to be avoided in the objectives envisaged in an epistemological study of error. One would be to deny error, or to ignore it, or to avoid showing how it actually takes place. The other extreme would be to legitimize it, to claim that it follows just as necessarily as does truth from the nature of things. The facts, of course, have to be examined carefully without a preconceived framework into which they would be forced. They have to dictate their own conclusions. The most one can say in advance is that if either of the above extremes should turn out to be the case, epistemology would be in trouble. Failure to account for error, if the history of the discipline tells anything, will wreck it as a philosophical procedure. Giving error a status equal to that of truth would, in the other extreme, involve a positive status for non-being. Nevertheless, the approach to the facts has to be with an entirely open mind.

What happens, then, when one makes an erroneous judgment? In filling the sugar bowl with salt, one judged that the white granular substance in the large sack *was* sugar. On tasting it on one's cereal, one becomes aware of the mistake. Actually, the immediate judgment was "This *is* a white, granular substance." In that there was no error. The judgment in that generic form was necessitated by the percept. The generic notion was synthesized with the subject in the perceived real existence. The real existence, accordingly, is guaranteed. But in the circumstances the generic nature was far as the percept went. The specific nature was not sensed. Nor was there any compelling reason for adding it. A closer scrutiny would have shown that there was not sufficient ground for adding it to the percept. Yet it was synthesized by the mind as included in the object that was actualized by the originally perceived existence.

This consideration brings out forcefully the active role of judgment. It shows that the nature of judgment is not just passive in the way any act of cognition is passive insofar as cognition is reception into a cognitional power. Here the object is not only received into the activity of the cognitive agent. The object is elaborated. It is worked upon in a manner that extends it beyond what was immediately sensed. In the present example the object was sensed in a way that necessitated a judgment in terms of its generic nature. But the synthesizing activity of the intellect went further and added the specific nature of sugar. Subsequent sensation showed that this addition was erroneous. The judgment was made about a percept that contained an added specific nature over and above the generic object originally sensed.

Numerous other examples would readily bear out the point that the human intellect can add to the synthesis originally apprehended other features stored in the memory or worked out by one's imagination and thought. In the present case the notion of sugar was uppermost in the mind because sugar was what was being sought. The notion was inadvertently joined into the existential synthesis. Why? The further synthesis was not necessitated by the white granular object perceived. For practical purposes, sugar for the cereal was on one's mind. In haste and inadvertence one added the specific nature to the percept. Clearly enough the cause of the erroneous judgment is the interference of the human will. The percipient in this case wishes the substance to be sugar, and precipitously impels the intellect to make this judgment.

Analysis of any error will bear out this conclusion. Something that was not apprehended in the original existential synthesis or syntheses has been inserted in a judgment. When the original syntheses are closely examined they are found to lack the superadded notion. The real existence is there, in the originally grasped object. But in the manipulation by the cognitive agent it is made to synthesize wrongly in the representation a predicative notion taken from elsewhere. Why the agent acts so hastily and inconsiderately is a problem for psychology and ethics. The concern of epistemology is with the fact that the agent does so. This is a condition that goes with human freedom of choice. The problem of freedom in its turn is a problem of metaphysics, not of epistemology. Epistemology is content to observe the fact that freedom is there and at work. The problem of error is in this way brought back to an existential, in contrast to an essential, source. The reason is shown why error need not have any necessary cause in the nature of things.

Also the reason becomes apparent why error cannot be classed simply as not-being, or as bearing fundamentally on something that is non-existent. Basically, in error, there is existence that is apprehended. In the above example it was the real existence of a white granular substance. That real existence was represented by the active manipulation of the intellect as synthesizing also the specific nature of sugar. In actual reality the existence synthesized the nature of salt, not that of sugar, with the subject. But it is the real existence that continues to be basic in the representation, even though it is wrongly extended to synthesize a different specific nature from that which it synthesizes in reality.

Corresponding considerations apply in the cases where the originally grasped existence is cognitional. Errors frequently occur in the abstract order in which mathematical objects have their existence.[7] An immigrant accountant may carry over as a one an uncrossed seven. His books will be out of balance by six in the column in which the error occurred. But the existence that synthesized the preceding numbers into a single sum persists and is now made to synthesize wrongly a one instead of a seven. Likewise in regard to things that exist only in imagination errors may be made in having the original existence synthesize wrong predicate notions. To think that Swift's Lilliputians were of huge size in comparison with normal Englishmen would be mistaking them for Brobdingnagians. The original existence generically of characters in Swift's writing is preserved for the notion of Lilliputian, and on a rereading of Swift's description of them they are recognized as small enough to keep running over Gulliver. In every error, in a word, some originally grasped existence is encountered.

Error, then, is satisfactorily accounted for by an epistemology that proceeds in terms of existence. It is assured of an existent object, and it is not maneuvered into a position where it would be required to follow logically from an antecedent situation. It is given its ultimate determination by a free cause, a cause that is to be explained in existential and not essential terms. For the same reason it is continually open to correction. The original existential synthesis can always be scrutinized again, and its actual embrace can be ascertained. In this way the cause that allows error provides for its correction. Error does not indicate an irremediable defect in human cognition.

Strictly, the problem of error is a problem of judgment, as outlined above. Nevertheless one speaks of error in regard to instinct, on the merely sensory level. A bird caught in a room will fly repeatedly against a window, knocking itself out. Its instinct and experience prompts it to fly ahead where no obstacle is visible. Because no obstacle is visible it proceeds as though no obstacle were there. In the present cause it is mistaken. This is to be explained through the limited range of instinct, and the ways in which animal life instinctively adapts itself to patterns. The application of the notion of error to lower orders than the sensory can hardly be more than a metaphor, for instance in saying that nature made a mistake in producing the lungfish, or the grain a mistake in sprouting during the early warm spell that was quickly followed by a frost.

Inference. In its strict sense as a judgment, the foregoing considerations make clear, error is a mediate tenet. An erroneous judgment is of its nature a mediate judgment. In it there is always presupposed, at least ultimately, an immediate judgment of existence. A further notion intervenes and is wrongly synthesized. In the example just used the process was from the original immediate judgment necessitated by the real existence to a judgment that was not necessitated by it. "This is a white granular substance" led to "This is sugar" through the intermediary "Sugar is a white granular substance." The rules of logic show how the inference here is not justified. The intermediary or middle term is not properly distributed. Epistemologically the mediating process allows a wrong predicate notion to come into the synthesizing embrace of the originally apprehended existence. Consequently error, though impossible in an immediate judgment, is shown to be a possible in a mediate one.

As has just been seen, however, it is also possible to correct errors. Mediate judgments, accordingly, are able to be certain. The mediating process can result in truth as well as error. Each step in the process has to be carefully scrutinized, in order to be certain that none of the judgments assert what is beyond the object apprehended at each particular stage. In extending knowledge, the reasoning process takes premises each of which asserts a truth and which in confrontation with each other make manifest a truth that neither contained separately. If the premises are both true and the existential synthesis of one is seen on confrontation to include the synthesis expressed in the second, the combined synthesis is seen to be true.

Besides the careful checking of each step in the reasoning process, there is also in the experimental sciences the convincing double check of verification. Exact reasoning concluded to the existence of the planet Neptune. This was then verified by telescope. The existence of molecules, inferred from Brownian movements and transference of odors and diffusion of gases, has been verified with the electron microscope. Through their methods these sciences have reached sufficient certainty in their conclusions to make possible space travel, lunar landings and cosmic exploration. In some cases only high probability can be reached, and verification may be lacking. The shift to the red in the spectrum means that the object is receding at high speed, but just how this applied at the tremendous distances of the outer galaxies remains obscure enough to leave some doubt about the fact that these galaxies are actually receding at the calculated speed. In consequence these sciences allow many of their conclusions to remain probable until verification has taken place. Strict certitude in the conclusion, before observational or experimental verification, would require that each of the premises in the long reasoning be certain, and that thereby the connection of each with the one preceding it be immediately apprehended. To be certain of each premise is to be certain upon their confrontation that the existential synthesis of at least one of them extends also to the middle term as introduced in the other. Severally at each link the connection is immediate and the certitude is spontaneous. But in the long chain of reasoning, to keep all the premises simultaneously before one's gaze is difficult if not impossible. One may remember clearly the conclusion of a geometrical theorem worked out carefully years ago, while not being able at the moment to recall the steps by which it was reached. For this reason Descartes required the divine guarantee in order to accept the correctness of reasoning already made, when each link was no longer in view.[8] Trust in memory, however, is regularly found sufficient. Yet memory can play tricks at times, and a new checking may be found necessary. The assent here, therefore, cannot be spontaneous. It is influenced by the will, though on the basis of solid experience. But the length of the reasoning does not essentially affect the certainty. Any dependence on the human will is only for saving the time that would be required for explicit manifestation of all the premises. Untouched is the essential process of reasoning from premises to conclusion.

So, where one premise is that the liquid in this pitcher is water, and the other premise that water contains two parts of hydrogen, one knows that the liquid in the pitcher contains that amount of hydrogen. The first premise is accepted through simultaneous perception of sight and feeling. There could be error in it, but the possibility of error is considered negligible in the circumstances in which the only colorless liquid around is that which comes out of the tap. Definitely the judgment is not made on any chemical analysis of the water into its elements. The truth of the second premise is accepted from chemical experiment. If one accepts the first premise as true and certain, and the second similarly as true and certain, one is correspondingly certain that the third is true. The existence that makes this liquid be water necessarily makes it be two parts hydrogen. This is not seen in either of the premises separately, but when seen on their confrontation with each other acquires the same kind of certainty as the premises possess. Their certainty is shared by the conclusion.

In this way, by careful scrutiny of each step, one can attain certainty in the conclusions of the long and complicated reasoning of mathematics or metaphysics. The original premises have to be immediately known, and the rules of logic have to be observed in using only those forms of reasoning that extend the existence grasped in the first premise to what is synthesized in the second. Each step in this way is an immediate apprehension of existence. The certainty of the concluding judgment is accordingly based upon the certainty of the premises, even though the conclusion is a mediate judgment.

Science. Through reasoning from immediate judgments to conclusions, and where possible applying the methods of verification, the many sciences have been gradually built up. Scientific results are accordingly mediate tenets. The notion of mediate judgments was essential to the traditional concept of science. Science was a knowledge of conclusions.[9] As knowledge, it required certainty.[10] Since there are many ways in which immediate judgments could be grouped as principles of scientific reasoning, various divisions of the sciences have appeared in the history of western culture.[11] During the past century, however, the term "science," which before had been used for the philosophical, mathematical, moral, theological and experimental sciences, came to be restricted largely to the experimental field. Mathematical disciplines, such as geometry or trigonometry, continued to be called sciences in a less emphatic way. The philosophical and theological sciences never completely gave up their traditional claim to the title, and some writers continued to regard ethics as a science in the traditional Aristotelian understanding of the term. In more recent years the emerging and rapidly developing social sciences have been strongly vindicating their right to be recognized as sciences, and have practically everywhere succeeded in these efforts.

At the present moment the situation may be summed up by saying that "science" without further qualification still refers to the experimental sciences. To use the term in any other sense requires added designation, for example mathematical sciences, philosophical sciences, social sciences. Epistemologically, the one point at issue is that all these disciplines proceed from principles to conclusions. They provide mediate cognition. They are systematically developed bodies of knowledge in which reasoning, that is, drawing conclusions from premises, plays the characteristic role. In many a great part of the time may be taken in collecting data. But mere collection is not enough to raise the process to the level of science. Explanation has to enter. This will consist in gathering more general principles from particular data, and in using the more general principles to account for the more particular phenomena or to reach new knowledge. The twofold procedure will involve both demonstrative and probable reasoning.[12]

The experimental and social sciences keep evolving in a more or less fluid state, with boundaries often overlapping. Optics, mechanics, and harmonics were recognized along with astronomy as separate sciences in Aristotle's time.[13] Physics and chemistry and biology became solidly established in modern times, and new sciences such as radio astronomy continue to appear. They develop their own techniques, but usually no attempt is made to draw their exact boundaries. A similar situation is found with the social sciences.[14] With the philosophical sciences this is even more accentuated. Logic, natural philosophy, metaphysics, and ethics, have been recognized with varying consistency since Greek times. But a number of others have been marked off as philosophical procedures that are applied to designated objects, such as epistemology, theodicy, esthetics, philosophy of science, philosophy of history, philosophy of language, philosophy of religion. There seems in fact little reason why any special subject that is sufficiently deserving of philosophical investigation should not be able to give its name to a new discipline as interest concentrates upon it in the course of cultural history.[15]

Opinion. The type of inference that science aims to achieve is demonstration. It wishes to prove its conclusions and in this way establish them firmly as truths. Where each premise in the reasoning can be established as certainly true, and the reasoning itself is logically correct, demonstration is achieved.[16] But in a great part of the material dealt with in both philosophy and the other sciences, demonstrative certainty does not seem attainable. In other instances it has been attained only slowly through the centuries, or within a definite margin of error. The result is that merely probable conclusions abound. Accordingly one speaks unhesitatingly about the opinions of philosophers or of scientists in their own fields. Probable conclusions are found copiously in the organized bodies of knowledge that go under the name of sciences. The notion of opinion, however, is used most frequently in regard to the tenets held in ordinary everyday life. Most of the judgments necessary for practical living have to be made as inferences. Judgments regarding the measures for conserving health, for succeeding in business deals, for predicting the weather conditions, are not immediate. Nor in the ordinary person at least, are they formally scientific conclusions. They are conclusions that are not necessitated by the premises, and accordingly can be erroneous.

An opinion is therefore always an inference. It is a mediate tenet. There can be no such thing as an immediate opinion. Of its nature it has to presuppose premises, of which at least one will give it definite existence to reason from, while the other or others provide notions that can be brought into this existence only with probability.

Belief. The mediate tenets so far considered in the realms of error, science, and opinion have been regarded as based upon one's own cognition. The basic premises were immediate judgments made by oneself. The inferences likewise were looked upon as drawn entirely by oneself. But there is another type of tenets, that plays an overwhelming part in daily life. These are based not solely on one's own cognition, but also upon the intermediating cognition of others. What is happening at the moment in Russia or in China is not immediately known by people located in America. It becomes known to them through the write-ups in the newspapers and the voices and pictures that come over the radio and television networks. In every such case someone else is perceiving the events and narrating them over the mass media. Though one does not perceive them oneself or infer them from what one has perceived, one does not hesitate in accepting this news in the main as true and certain. An occasional item, perhaps, will bring the quick reaction "I don't believe that." But for the most part, people believe what they learn through the mass media. They consider as worthy of credence the tenets that are mediated in this way.

The use of the term "belief" for a tenet so acquired is common in ordinary language and has good sanction in philosophical tradition.[17] However, since "belief" in present philosophical parlance can mean any tenet whatsoever, a more precise word for the acceptance of a tenet through the mediation of someone else's cognition might be "faith." In ordinary language one speaks of taking something on faith when someone else has said it. Likewise the term "faith" has solid backing in philosophical tradition for its use as a synonym of belief in the present sense.[18] So when dependence on the word of another needs special emphasis, the mention of "faith" will be in order.

What, then, is meant by accepting a tenet on faith? First of all, it is concerned with something that you cannot see or hear for yourself. You know from listening to a reporter night after night that he can be depended upon to give accounts of things that later are verified as correct. You are satisfied that he is at present in Africa to report the fighting. When he appears on the television screen you are satisfied that he is communicating to you what he himself is perceiving. You give your assent to what he says. Why? You consider that he has obtained at first hand through actual perception the news he is communicating. You consider that he is trustworthy in reporting it correctly. These two conditions, the knowledge and the trustworthiness of the narrator, are called in this perspective his authority. The authority consists in the knowledge of what is being communicated and the disposition to communicate it truthfully. When this authority is accepted, all that is required is the fact of the communication, which you yourself are now observing on the television, to complete the conditions for assenting to the tenets.

Technically, this assent can at its best be only probable. There is always the possibility of error on the part of the narrator, and the possibility of a failure to communicate correctly and truthfully. Even the fact of the communication on the television screen is not entirely above suspicion, since there is the remote possibility of a tampering with tapes and a substitution of words or pictures. In building up the authority here a great many steps, many of them based themselves on other authority, are involved. But from past experience one gets accustomed to relying upon the mass media in various degrees, from slight credence in events to which no particular care is presumed attached, to events of great moment in which any carelessness or deceit would bring intolerable discredit upon the news agency. In these really important matters, the high degree of probability accorded the matters communicated may be called moral certainty.[19] It is certainty sufficient for acting without hesitation in practical matters, even though technically from the epistemological viewpoint it may be only probability of the highest type.

In the sciences, the term "authority" in this sense is of frequent use. A person who is competent in a science and is able to communicate his knowledge correctly, is called an authority in the field. His statements and his writings in the area may be accepted without much hesitation. By way of such authority the findings of scientific investigation seep through the everyday world, and are woven into the fabric of ordinary life. In that way, too, the knowledge acquired in one discipline is communicated for use in other disciplines, even though the experts who make scientific use of it in their own work have accepted it only on faith. Most of the knowledge learned in school is taken on faith in the teacher's competence. In some branches, such as arithmetic, the objective may be to make the pupil see for himself under the guidance of the teacher, even though for practical purposes formulae and tables may be accepted on faith. In other branches, such as history, geography, hygiene and all sciences where books substitute for direct observation, faith is the means of learning.

The widespread role played throughout one's life by this type of mediate tenets is obvious. Education, social intercourse, business dealings, all depend greatly upon what others say. Court cases involving this most serious issues, even the life of a defendant, are decided on the testimony of witnesses and experts. The information obtained by intelligence agents is required for mapping the strategy of battle. The epistemological understanding of the way these tenets are acquired and the multiple possibilities of error involved by it, gives the overall reason why life guided so extensively by this type of cognition can culminate in frequent tragedies. Finally, in religious belief, where the term "faith" is regularly used, the general analysis of the mediate nature of the tenets correspondingly applies. The authority here is that of the divine truth, and accordingly is an authority that cannot be deficient either in its knowledge or in its veracity. The difficulty lies rather in establishing the fact of the communication. That fact is beyond the reach of philosophy to investigate, since it is a supernatural intervention that is not perceived nor deducible from anything perceived. It is matter for theological scrutiny. Epistemology therefore can show only that even religious faith consists in the acceptance of a tenet on the authority of someone else, and is accordingly a type of mediate cognition. The one difference that epistemology can point out between this and all other cases of authority, is that here the credentials, namely the knowledge and veracity, are not open to defect and in consequence will, as far as they are concerned, give rise to full technical certainty and not just to probability. But about the remaining link, the fact of the communication, epistemology has nothing to say. It shows, though, that in any case the tenets will be accepted on authority, and therefore will remain faith. Absolute certainty here will not make them knowledge.

Common Sense. A notable assemblage of tenets are regularly grouped together under the designation "common sense." The assemblage is often taken as the collection of tenets held prior to scientific or philosophic investigation. It would consist of pre-scientific views that are frequently dispelled upon serious examination. It is also understood as the body of principles used by well-balanced people for guiding their everyday life, in contrast to a philosophically developed ethics. Are the tenets that makeup this assemblage mediate, or immediate, or a mixture of both?

Originally, the notion "common sense" seems to have included two different factors.[20] It had the meaning of tenets commonly accepted by a group, and also of tenets spontaneously held on the impulse of human nature itself. Taken in the first meaning, it would be cognition based upon authority, in this case the general authority of the group. It would be as unreliably as the group's own cognition, for instance in matters that are the concern of astronomy or chemistry. It would likewise change with the general progress of information through the centuries, as in the case of the flatness of the earth or its location at the center of the universe. Likewise as a guide to practical conduct it would vary with the cultural changes of the group. Understood in this meaning, common sense would be clearly a species of faith. It would consist in the acceptance of tenets on the group's authority.

In reaction to eighteenth and nineteenth century Idealisms, however, the notion of a spontaneously necessitated knowledge made common sense a candidate for the function of a criterion of certainty. In this role it meant judgments that were not based upon any antecedent ones.[21] It accordingly consisted of immediate judgments commonly made by men. In this understanding of it, it is undoubtedly knowledge that is incontrovertibly certain, and the source to which much mediate knowledge is to be reduced. But in this sense it has nothing specially focused on pre-philosophic or pre-scientific views. It is rather the common origin of both scientific and pre-scientific cognition, as far as mediate tenets are in question. Restricted to the immediate tenets, it would not basically coincide with what is usually understood by "common sense," insofar as the notion expresses group views that are subject to change with the course of times. It would at best be a vaguely recognizable part of the conglomeration, and would be functioning as a criterion not so much in virtue of the necessitating character of existence in each individual case, but rather in virtue of the *common* presence of these judgments in mankind.

As a combination of both mediate and immediate judgments, then, common sense as ordinarily understood can hardly function as a criterion of truth or certainty in theoretical matters. In practical matters, it has its role to play, since the common estimation of moral situations, at least within the limits of a given culture, usually turns out to be the correct one and can often serve to engender the moral certainty that suffices for human conduct. But in either case, as far as the notion of "common" is stressed, common sense is appealing to the authority of the group. Whatever non-authoritative side it may be regarded as possessing, does not seem to allow it any special epistemological role.

Résumé. Mediate tenets may be errors, scientific conclusions, opinions, or beliefs in the sense of tenets held on faith. Errors are found in every case to be caused by the intervention of the will that impels the intellect to synthesize wrongly an additional notion in the embrace of an existence already legitimately apprehended. They can be corrected by closer examination of the original existential syntheses. Scientific conclusions are reached with full certainty by drawing the conclusions allowed by the premises, thereby synthesizing with the originally apprehended existence the predicates made manifest by each new premise. Where the premises do not allow full certainty, the conclusions are incorporated into the science with their varying degrees of probability. Opinion is a mediate tenet whose premises as understood at the time allow only probability, and not certainty. Faith is the acceptance of tenets not through one's own cognition alone but on the authority of someone else. It is accordingly a tenet mediated by the knowledge and communication given by the other person, and varies in probability with the estimate of the person's reliability in regard to both knowledge and truthfulness. In human authority these can never be absolute and accordingly cannot give technical certainty, though they may often give practical certainty. Finally common sense, insofar as it is understood as a group of tenets accepted on the authority of the general public, is subject to the same considerations. It cannot give the theoretical certainty required for speculative science and philosophy, but only, and within limits, the practical certainty desired for moral action. Divine authority remains accordingly the only kind of authority that can ground absolute certainty. But acceptance of the fact of a divine revelation as absolutely certain transcends natural capacities and depends upon supernaturally infused grace. However, that is a matter for consideration in sacred theology, and not in philosophy.

Notes to Chapter 10

1. On "knowledge by acquaintance," see Bertrand Russell, *The Problems of Philosophy* (London, 1929), 186.

2. ". . . we may draw wrong inferences from our acquaintance, but acquaintance itself cannot be deceptive. Thus there is no dualism as regards acquaintance." Russell, ibid.

3. So, in regard to the first principle of demonstration: "For it is impossible for any one to believe the same thing to be and not to be, as some think Heraclitus says. For what a man says, he does not necessarily believe"--Aristotle, *Metaphysics*, 4.3.1005b23-26; Oxford trans.

4. See supra, Chapter 8, nn. 6-11.

5. "But to us, probability is the very guide of life." Joseph Butler, *The Analogy of Religion*, ed. W. E. Gladstone (Oxford, 1897), 5. In this regard, the "fear of the opposite" was traditionally noted. Even in entirely speculative matters or in inconsequential affairs, one has little hesitation in saying "I'm afraid I may be wrong." But the more exact formulation should make the doubt bear upon the opposite side, in the meaning that "I assent to the one side, while suspending my assent to the contrary judgment." In this way assent can be genuinely given to the proposition, even though fingers are kept crossed in regard to what the future is going to show.

6. E.g., epistemological monism, which allows no representation to mediate between knower and object known. References on this topic may be found in A. Ryan, "Two Essays on American Critical Realism," *Revue de l'Université d'Ottawa*, 6 (1936), Section spéciale (5) 109*, n. 22.

7. On the way the mathematical entities remain *real* quantities even though they are being studied in abstraction, see T. C. Anderson, "Intelligible Matter and the Objects of Mathematics in Aristotle," *The New Scholasticism*, 43 (1969), 2-5, and "Intelligible Matter and the Objects of Mathematics in Aquinas," ibid., 557-565.

8. See Descartes, *Principia philosophiae*, 1.13; A-T, VIII, 9.14-10.4 (IX, 30-31). Cf. H. G. Wolz, "The Double Guarantee of Descartes' Ideas," *The Review of Metaphysics*, 3 (1950), 473-489.

9. E.g.: "Nam scientia est per decursum a principiis ad conclusiones." Aquinas, *In primum librum Posteriorum analyticorum Aristotelis expositio*, 36.11 (Spiazzi no. 318); ed. Leonine (Rome, 1882), I, 287b.

10. E.g: "Sicut enim scientia importat certitudinem cognitionis per demonstrationem acquisitam . . ." Aquinas, ibid., 44.3 (Spiazzi no. 397); I, 320a. On the certainty in the moral sciences, see *In II Post. analyt.*, 12.5 (Spiazzi no. 525).

11. See references infra, c. 11, n. 20. A short but panoramic view of the contemporary situation may be found in Tadieusz Kotarbinski, *Gnosiology* , trans. G. Bidwell and C. Pindar (Oxford, 1966), 311-385.

12. In the Aristotelian tradition, demonstrative reasoning gave conclusions that are certain: "By demonstration I mean a syllogism productive of scientific knowledge, . . . the premisses of demonstrated knowledge must be true, primary, immediate, better known than and prior to the conclusion, which is further related to them as effect to cause." Aristotle, *Posterior Analytics*, 1.2.71b17-22; Oxford trans. The condition "better known" could be taken from the standpoint either of the human knower or of the intelligibility of the object just in itself--ibid., 71b33-72a5. Consequently there can be demonstration of causes from effects, and demonstration of effects from causes. Where the latter type was based on the proximate cause, it was called *dioti* (Latin *propter quid*) demonstration. Where in negative demonstration it was based on a remote cause, it was known as *hoti* (Latin *quia*) demonstration. The designation *hoti* was given also to the demonstration of causes from effects. See Aristotle, *Posterior Analytics*, 1.13.78a22 ff. In this connection, the Oxford translation renders *hoti* by "the fact," and *dioti* by "the reasoned fact." Both these classes of demonstration, however, give a reason. Both are meant to explain with certainty. The Greek and Latin designations *hoti* and *quia* offer no difficulty or inconvenience in carrying the notion of "because."

13. See Aristotle, *Physics*, 2.2.194a8; *Posterior Analytics*, 1.13.78b34-40.

14. On the situation in the social sciences, see William P. McEwen, *The Problem of the Social-Scientific Knowledge* (Totowa, NJ, 1963), with bibliography 549-575. See also the Unesco volume on the main trends, *The Social Sciences* (The Hague, 1968).

15. In this perspective the designation "philosophical sciences" can serve a useful purpose. It is able to mark off the area common to each of the many diverse philosophies without bringing in the radical differences in the philosophies themselves as they treat the respective topics. For instance, metaphysics means a considerably different enterprise respectively in Aristotle, Aquinas, Scotus, Hegel, Collingwood or Heidegger. Yet in all these philosophies the subject matter can come under "metaphysics" as the common designation of a single philosophical science. In the Scholastic tradition there need be no hesitation in using the expression "philosophical sciences," since in Aristotle (*Metaphysics*, 6.1.1025b18-1026a31; 11.7.1063b36-1064b13) natural philosophy and primary philosophy (metaphysics) were recognized as sciences along with the mathematical and practical and the productive sciences. Logic, though not classified by Aristotle with the sciences, is mentioned (*Metaphysics*, 11.1.1059b14-19; *Rhetoric*, 1.4.1359b10; *Eudemian Ethics*, 1.8.1217b19) as a science. Against that background these disciplines are accordingly classed under the title "The Philosophical Sciences" in the *Christian Culture and Philosophy Series*; see William E. Carlo, *Philosophy, Science, and Knowledge* (Milwaukee, 1967), 61 ff. See also its use as the chapter heading in Kotarbinski's *Gnosiology*, 384-385. But also outside Scholastic circles the designation "philosophical sciences" may be seen, e.g. *Encyclopaedia of the Philosophical Sciences*, ed. Henry Jones (London, 1913).

16. See supra, nn. 10 and 12.

17. See *O.E.D.*, s.v. *Belief*, 1 and 2. Cf. James F. Ross, "Testimonial Evidence," in *Analysis and Metaphysics*, ed. Keith Lehrer (Dordrecht, 1975), 36 ff.; Henry Bars, *The Assent of Faith*, trans. Ronald Halstead

(London, 1959), 15-24. On the wider acceptance of the term "belief" in current philosophical writing, see David Malet Armstrong, *Belief, Truth and Knowledge* (Cambridge, 1973), 3-5.

18. In James Mark Baldwin's *Dictionary of Philosophy and Psychology* (New York, 1911), s.v. *Faith*, faith is considered as practically identical with belief, and as meaning "acceptance of something as true . . . on grounds that, in whole or in part, are different from those of theoretical certitude," and requiring "the moment of will . . . in the form of some subjective interest or consideration of value." John Hicks, in Paul Edwards' *Encyclopedia of Philosophy*, s.v., notes: "The view that faith operates not only in religion but also in many other spheres has an extensive literature." On the "common use" of the term in Scholastic tradition to signify "a cognition obscure and based upon the testimony of the one who is speaking," see Suarez, *De fide*, 1.1.11, in *Opera Omnia*, ed. Vivès (Paris, 1856-1877), XII, 12a. Cf. "belief, or a habit by which one assents to the things he does not see, on account of the authority of the one who is speaking" --Salmanticenses, *Cursus theologicus*, 17.Proem.6 (ed. Paris, 1870-1873), XI, 2b. The notions to be safeguarded in this tradition were the lack of evidence in the object and the intervention of the will to cause assent. The Salmanticenses add that this is the most characteristic (*propriissima*--ibid.) acceptation of the term "faith."

19. On the designation "moral certitude," as used for the probability sufficient to make a firm moral judgment, see Joseph Gredt, *Elementa philosophiae aristotelico-thomisticae*, ed. 7a (Freiburg i. Breisgau, 1937), II, 55 (no. 669). It is a somewhat different notion from the type of truth and exactitude that for Aristotle (*Nicomachean Ethics*, 1.3.1094b19-25) is appropriate for practical philosophy, namely the truth of judgments that hold "roughly" and "for the most part" (b20-21). The Aristotelian notion would mean certainty within a given margin of error, which is not exactly the same notion as grounds for acting prudently in a definite set of circumstances.

20. On this point, see Etienne Gilson, *Réalisme thomiste et critique de la connaissance* (Paris, 1939), 15. Gilson (ibid.) notes that

the passage from one factor to another is easy and natural.

21. E.g.: "I believe the expression *common sense* to denote a law of our mind . . . consisting in a natural inclination of our mind to give its assent to some truths not attested by consciousness nor demonstrated by reason, necessary to all men in order to satisfy the wants of sensitive, intellectual, and moral life." James Balmes, *Fundamental Philosophy*, 1.32.316, trans. Henry F. Brownson (New York, 1858), I, 221.

PART THREE . . . .ORGANIZED KNOWLEDGE

CHAPTER 11

The Sciences

Bodies of Knowledge. From the days of the ancient Greeks the results of intellectual investigation have been assembled into distinct units under the designation of "sciences" (*epistemai*; Latin *scientiae*). Close attention has been given to the classification and coordination of these organized bodies of knowledge. As was noted in the preceding chapter, the term "science" was traditionally used for the mental activity that consisted in deducing conclusions from premises.[1] Its transfer to the knowledge attained by deduction from principles is readily understandable. But first and foremost the notion it emphasized was that of actually knowing. It denoted primarily the intellectual activity. Only from this angle did it name the achievements of the activity as "sciences" after they had been organized into appropriate bodies.

There has, however, been a considerable lack of uniformity in the ways in which the sciences have been divided and classified in the long history of western thought. The way that has endured the longest and that still has basic value for understanding the nature of the various sciences, is that of Aristotle. It is a division that springs from the fundamentally different types of starting points in which the sciences originate. On the one hand there are starting points or first principles in the things themselves that confront the human mind. They are present in the things independently of participation by the knower. Principles such as "things cannot be and not be at the same time in the same respects," "being in reality is different from being in cognition," "bodies are extended in three dimensions," "four is the square root of sixteen," "a middle term has to be properly distributed," face the knower independently of any input from his side in regard to their natures. The roles of the knower is here that of a spectator. He looks at these starting points, and sees they are that way. He plays no part in shaping their nature. His intellectual activity is speculative (Latin *speculativa*) in the meaning that he is a spectator, or theoretical (Greek *theoretike*) in the sense of contemplating what lies before his gaze.[2]

Other types of reasoning find their starting points not already existent in the things that confront the knower, but rather in his own engagement with them. The knower is conscious of his own freedom to act or refrain from acting according as he sees fit. He sees that he should act with wisdom, courage, temperance and justice. These are principles or starting points that are not existent in what confronts his speculative gaze. He has to find them in his own moral habituation. From them he reasons to the way he should act in his daily conduct. His thinking here is practical, in the sense of bearing upon what he should do, in contrast to what already exists. This type of thinking was accordingly called practical on account of its specification by conduct (Greek *praxis*).

Finally, there is the type of knowledge that bears upon the making or production of things. Rhetoric is meant for speech-making, architecture for building, horticulture for gardening. This type included both the crafts and the fine arts. Again, the starting points were found in the knower. They were the plans or designs or blueprints or directives according to which the work had to be carried out. The starting points were not things already existent in reality, but ideas in the mind of the producer. For that reason the knowledge was called "productive" (Greek *poietike*), in the sense that it bore upon the production of something not already existent, such as a poem, a piece of music, a house or a ship.[3]

At times Aristotle was content with a twofold division, though always with the theoretical sciences on the one side of the dividing line and the rest on the other. That partition emphasizes the basic cleavage between sciences whose starting points are in the things, and those whose starting points are not in the things but in the knower. Distinction between the terms "practical" and "productive" in this regard, as a study of Plato's use of the two terms will show, was none too clearcut in the immediate background of Aristotle's writing. The distinction did not have to be evoked on every occasion. However, Aristotle's tripartite division is formal and firm. It is indispensable for a thorough grasp of the respective natures of each of these types of science.

Since the overall Aristotelian specification of the sciences is grounded upon the types of starting points or principles from which each proceeds, a preliminary word about these principles is in order. They are of two kinds, at first sight visibly opposed to each other in direction. They can be effects, as starting points for reasoning to causes, or causes, as starting points for reasoning to effects. Where the nature of the causes is immediately known, as in the case of numbers or of basic geometrical figures, the causes can function as first principles. Units are the causes of all other numbers. Points, lines and surfaces are the causes of geometrical entities. When the cause exactly matches the effect, it gives *the* reason why (Greek *dioti*, Latin *propter quid*) in complete and thorough explanation. This type of starting point is available for mathematics. Where the effects are known in priority to the causes, however, the situation is the reverse. Here the effects have to be the starting points or first principles for reasoning to the cause. The usual darkness during the day is the starting point for reasoning to its cause, which turns out to be the eclipse of the sun. At least *a* reason why (Greek *hoti*, Latin *quia*) is given.[4] So in the philosophy of nature the starting points are extension and change, which are the effects of corporeal nature in its composition of matter and form. From those effects the reasoning to the substantial nature of bodies takes place. In metaphysics the beings of the sensible universe are the starting points. From them one reasons to the causes of their being, namely to immaterial substance. In a word, the constitutive principles of the things themselves are not always the starting points or first principles from which our scientific reasoning about them begins.

Yet one does not go very far before realizing that both types of principle are compatible in the same science, and both may have to be used. Aristotle cites with approval the way this problem had been introduced by Plato, under the simile of a race in the stadium. The question was whether the direction of the race was from the judges to the far end of the stadium, or the reverse. The obvious answer is that it had to be first in the one direction, and then on the return be in the opposite direction. Correspondingly in a science such as metaphysics, or the philosophy of nature, or ethics, the starting points or first principles are the effects. From them one reasons to their causes, through *hoti* or *quia* demonstration. But once the causes are reached, these causes become the principles or starting points for the *dioti* or *propter quid* explanation. So in ethics the individual acts performed as the result of correct training are the first principles (*archai*) for ethical reasoning. But complete happiness (*eudaimonia*) is the first principle (*arche*) for understanding why one should act morally.[5] Similarly in metaphysics and in the philosophy of nature, immaterial substance and matter plus form function respectively as the starting points for understanding the effects from which the scientific reasoning originally proceeded. Both directions are required.

Theoretical Sciences. In its reasoning from principles to conclusions, each science in the Aristotelian perspective seeks to understand things in terms of their causes.[6] Metaphysics is concerned with their absolutely first or highest causes. For this reason it was, for Aristotle, science in the highest degree. In the framework of focal meaning this implied that metaphysics is the primary instance of science and thereby the model that all other instances strive to imitate as best they can. Against that background his own name for it was the primary philosophy. He also described it as "theological science," with the divine as its specifying object. In the focal reference setting, this made it the science of the primary instance of being, and thereby the science that dealt universally with all things under the aspect of being, for the nature that specified it was the very nature (*physis*) of being.[7] That is the way it was unhesitatingly viewed by the Greek commentators. With Christians, Moslems and Jews this conception of the science caused difficulties. But with Thomas Aquinas the distinction between essence and existence allowed common being to function as the specifying object of the science. The primary being was not ranged under common being. It had the role, rather, of the cause of common being. This has suggested a recent description of the Thomistic conception of metaphysics as, in Heideggerian terminology, "onto-theo-logical."[8] However, with Francis Bacon the unitary Aristotelian metaphysics was broken up into several sciences, and finally, in the wake of Christian Wolff, a more or less generally accepted interpretation split it into ontology and natural theology.[9] Ontology was regarded as a general metaphysics treating universally of beings as beings. Natural theology was special metaphysics dealing with a particular object, God. Ontology was in this way regarded as a science of being *qua* being that was not specified by the primary instance of being. With Descartes mathematics had become the model science. Yet from Aristotle's viewpoint metaphysics was the "most exact" of all the sciences, even though the Stagirite himself was accustomed to apply the notion "exact" to the procedure of the mathematical sciences.[10]

Next in the scale of the theoretical sciences was the philosophy of nature. From observed effects in the sensible world it reasoned to matter and form, in the category of substance, as the first principles of nature. In their light it explained motion and change.

Finally, another type of theoretical science for Aristotle was located in the mathematical realm. The specifying object for these sciences was seen in abstract quantity, namely in quantitative substances taken in abstraction from their sensible qualities. The Stagirite himself ranged astronomy, optics, harmonics and mechanics under "the more physical of the mathematical sciences." Their procedure was mathematical, even though they were engaged in definite areas of nature. Their type of demonstration was *dioti* or *propter quid*, in contrast to the *hoti* or *quia* procedure used in parallel treatments of those same areas from qualitative starting points.[11] The qualitative phenomena did not make manifest the specific natures of the material things, and in consequence did not open the way for *dioti* procedure in natural philosophy beyond the generic treatment of them as bodies.

Logic, though designated by Aristotle as "the science which is concerned with demonstration and scientific knowledge,"[12] was regarded in Peripatetic tradition as a preparation for the sciences rather than as a science in itself. Consequently it does not appear in the Aristotelian classification of the sciences, although in other ancient classifications, of Megarian and Stoic provenance, it occupied a leading place.

Practical Sciences. Radically different from theoretical science in starting points was the Aristotelian conception of practical science. Its starting points were not in nature but in free choice. Each free decision meant a new beginning that was not determined by any antecedent natural causes. This required starting points that were not set in any inflexibly stable fashion but were open to variation in accord with the incessantly changing circumstances that faced the free agent. The starting points of the practical sciences, then, were established by the free decisions of the individual. Yet as the choices of a rational agent they were under the obligation of being made according to right reason. They had to respect the natures of things and had to spring from correct habituation. These conditions gave rise to a type of universality that held "roughly and for the most part," thereby providing the kind of stability appropriate to this type of science. They allowed absolute decisions about right and wrong. By them the free men (*eleutheroi*) were bound by omnipresent moral regulations, in contrast to the random activity of slave or beast, for, under the aspect of the *kalon*, moral goodness carried its own intrinsic attraction and obligation.[13]

Any science regulating free human conduct, whether on the

plane of civil government or household management or individual behavior, would in principle come under the cover of practical science. Important for epistemology is the impossibility of reducing practical science to any theoretical source. Practical science uses freely the results of theoretical science, and draws upon them abundantly. But it is built solely upon its own independent starting points. It cannot be looked upon in any way as a branch or offshoot of theoretical science in this Aristotelian conception of its nature.

From a contemporary viewpoint, perhaps the strongest objection to this Aristotelian conception of practical science is its alleged circularity. Its starting points depend upon correct upbringing of the individuals from their earliest years. Yet that upbringing presupposes correct moral notions already dominating the ambient. Aristotle gives no indication of being bothered by this objection. Against his background of eternal cosmic successions it could hardly have had any force. Before every generation there was a preceding one to hand down the correct moral habituation.[14] Likewise for Christian or Islamic or Jewish philosophy there could be no special difficulty here, for the moral commandments are accepted as given in one way or another by divine revelation. But in a purely naturalistic acceptation of the development of human culture there would seem to be insuperable difficulty facing acceptance of the Aristotelian notion of practical science. Sociobiology, for instance, wishes "to explain ethics and ethical philosophers, if not epistemology and epistemologists, at all depths."[15] This and any other attempt to explain ethical principles by theoretical demonstration runs counter to the radically different origin of the two types of science in the Aristotelian conception. Practical science cannot be derived from theoretical principles. This holds likewise for any Neoscholastic effort to subalternate ethics to rational psychology.[16] But as regards the present objection, the charge of circularity looms large before the mind of anyone who approaches the Aristotelian practical philosophy today without an already accepted supernatural explanation for the factual origin of morality. Aristotle may just have been lucky in having at hand the

Greek notion of eternal cosmic recurrences to forestall the circularity objection to his conception of practical science. But that does not at all diminish the worth of his immediate positive insight into the nature of moral principles. Those principles were actually at work in the civilization of the Greek city state. As starting points for a distinct scientific procedure they stood on their own feet. From the viewpoint of practical science itself they did not call for any theoretical explanation or justification. Their actual presence in Greek conduct enabled them to serve as independent starting points. Any theoretical account of their origin was a task for a different type of science.

Productive Science. The third type of science for Aristotle was the productive kind. Different from the practical type, its starting points were naturally fixed and stable. But in common with practical science they were located within the knower. They consisted in ideas or plans or designs to which the projected work had to conform as though to a blueprint. They were accordingly definite and set in their nature, like the design of a house or a table. They were not incessantly changing with the ongoing turmoil of circumstances, as was the case with free choice and right reason. Aristotle's own work in this region was in rhetoric and in literary criticism. But the examples he repeatedly used were spread across the general panorama of arts and crafts such as carpentry, shipbuilding, bridle-making, harness-making, music, painting and drama. Some arts, however, such as military strategy, horsemanship, navigation, household science, and medicine, had objects with considerable variation and required adaptation at the moment to changing circumstances. Arts of that nature could be used by Aristotle to illustrate the way practical science kept adapting itself to its own incessantly varying object. His use of such examples to illustrate the procedure of practical science, coupled with the interchangeable use of the terms "practical" and "productive" in preceding Greek thought, tended to obscure the dividing line between the practical and the productive. As a result, this distinction failed to play any really notable part in the tradition that passed through the middle ages into early modern times.

Medieval Tradition. The patristic and medieval thinkers handed down faithfully enough the ancient Greek tradition on the sciences. From the time of Boethius (ca. 480-425) the general Aristotelian cast was quite visible, though it was interlarded with Stoic and Neoplatonic influences. But the most notable innovation in the middle ages was that sacred theology came to be given the highest rank among the sciences. It was regarded as the summit towards which all the others could converge.[17] It was introduced into the Aristotelian schema through location alongside the philosophical theology that had occupied the top niche in the theoretical sciences, which themselves were the highest type of science for the Stagirite. There were inconveniences in this tactic. Sacred theology directed human conduct and in consequence had to be conceived as a practical as well as a theoretical science. Further, the fact that it proceeded from premises not intrinsically evident to the theologian had to be faced. This objection was met by the stand that the origin of sacred theology was in the divine knowledge, where the truths were indeed evident. The theologian was thereby sharing in genuine knowledge accepted on faith, in a way that was paralleled with the acceptation of mathematical knowledge on faith by optics and music.[18] From both angles sacred theology not only was a science but also held the highest place among the sciences.

Seventeenth-Twentieth Centuries. In the wake of the Renaissance and with the sway of the Enlightenment, the attitude towards the status of sacred theology as a science changed radically. For Descartes, the mysteries of faith were indeed to be believed, but they had to be excluded from the domain of rational inquiry.[19] They could not come under the clear understanding that was demanded. Then with the Enlightenment the obscurity of religious belief became diametrically opposed to the liberating vision of science. The result was that religious belief, where accepted by a scientist, had to be kept in a mental compartment sealed off from scientific discourse. Communication between the two was not permitted. Sacred theology could in no way be regarded as a science.

In the course of the twentieth century, however, this hermetically sealed division became more difficult to sustain. The work of theologians such as Karl Barth, Paul Tillich, Rudolf Bultmann, Karl Rahner, Bernard Lonergan and Jaroslav Pelikan could hardly be given an inferior intellectual rating. Theologians used auxiliary sciences with an expertise to which the scholarly world could not be blind. The prestige of *The Harvard Theological Review* and the standards of some outstanding theological schools could not be ignored. Sacred theology became accepted by and large as a respectable field in which to work. But the question of its status as a science tended to be left in abeyance. Absolute certainty for its starting points would presuppose an infallibility that many theologians seemingly wished to avoid at all costs, in the interests of scholarly freedom. Lack of that infallibility, others claimed, would reduce sacred theology to the level of a social science governed by statistics. The question is still subject to scholarly debate, and with it the propriety of regarding sacred theology as a science in the truest sense of the term.

Contemporary Attitude. All in all, however, the broad outlines of the ancient Greek classifications of the sciences filtered through the medieval variations and adaptations, and continued to serve as a substrate for earlier modern versions.[20] But are those outlines flexible enough to welcome into their embrace the vast expansion and proliferation of the current natural and life and social and engineering and medical sciences? At first sight the present-day developments throw the traditional schema of classification strikingly out of balance. The bulk of what today is conjured up by the mention of "science" lies outside the philosophical areas that predominated in the traditional structure. It may be even regarded as lying outside the purely mathematical, as seems presumed when someone is said to be a mathematician rather than a scientist. The term "scientist," first coined in 1834, was originally meant to cover the whole traditional field of the sciences.[21] But almost immediately it became restricted to persons engaged in the natural and life sciences. There has since been a gradual broadening of the term to allow the designation "social scientist." But no philosopher or theologian today would call himself a "scientist," no matter how scientific he claims his work to be. The nuancing of these terms seems to reflect an evolving mentality, though with the basic notion of science focused upon the natural and life sciences that have developed so marvelously during the last three centuries and still set the tone even when one speaks today of library science or of the philosophical and theological sciences.

Yet in spite of the overwhelming concentration of personnel and effort and financial resources on areas outside the philosophical and theological and purely mathematical orbits, it is hard to see how the contemporary viewpoints break through the traditional outlines. There is notably more research and cataloguing, with the computers able to handle it. But Aristotle's own massive research on animal life shows clearly enough that the ancient mentality was not at all unaware of its necessity or insensitive to its value. Aristotle likewise required a corresponding breadth of investigation in regard to practical science.[22] The present emphasis on copious research and organized experimentation fits perfectly into the traditional schema. Moreover, the genial mentality of the present-day scientist is not that of the book-burning advocated by Hume. Today's scientist may be anxious to get for his own area whatever is available from government and private funding. But he does not deny the claims of other fields. He has plotted off his own particular territory. He feels perfectly at home in it, and can converse freely enough with his immediate neighbors. As they get more distant from his borders he begins to find their language a bit hard to understand, and as they get more remote he throws up his hands with incomprehension and lets them go their own way in peace. He extends that same attitude towards philosophy and theology. He realizes that people are at work in those fields, and he leaves the tasks to them. He has very little concern with making everything fit into a single overall view. Epistemologically his attitude is correct, for as seen above,[23] each science starts from its own principles. There is no question here of a universal tree upon which the particular sciences depend for life and nourishment.[24]

With all this in mind the present-day outlook begins to seem remarkably similar to the traditional way of classifying the sciences. If the 1988 "Critical Bibliography" in *Isis* may be taken as an overview of the current distribution from the cultural viewpoint, the place listed first in order is given to philosophy, with philosophy including traditional logic. The one heading "philosophy" covers everything that today would be listed academically under philosophy, in the way in which philosophy nearly everywhere today is rated as one department among others. Next in the *Isis* listing comes mathematics, including mathematical logic. Then come the "physical sciences," spelled out as astronomy, physics and chemistry. So far the resemblance to the traditional classification is startling. But soon the modern expansion and different balance make themselves felt. The earth sciences follow, spelled out in considerably greater detail, as is also the case with the "biological sciences" and the "social sciences" and "medicine and the medical sciences." "Technology," covering the area of the ancient productive science, namely the "arts and crafts" as well as all engineering, is then accorded considerably more space than any of the other divisions. Finally, "pseudo-sciences" and "ancillary disciplines" rate a few entries. Sacred theology is not listed.[25]

Except for the non-appearance of any radical distinction between practical philosophy (ethics) and theoretical philosophy, and the overwhelming weight of the sciences that have burgeoned during the last three centuries, the historical development of the traditional classification is not hard to see. There is hostility towards the pseudo-sciences, for they are pretending to be what they are not. But there is no hostility to other disciplines, disciplines authentically engaged in their own proper fields.[26]   A science like astronomy is proud of its ancient history, while another such as chemistry may not be too ready to claim ancestry in people like alchemists.   But not only for the historical understanding of the division of the sciences is this study of the traditional classification important.   Also for a doctrinal understanding there is much to be learned from the foundations given the classification by Aristotle. Epistemologically the differences between theoretical, practical and productive science can hardly hope to be understood without the help afforded by the Starigite's penetrating insights, which in this case have been long forgotten or neglected. For instance, the reason why practical science cannot be reduced to theoretical starting points is made very clear by his reasoning. Yet people keep wanting to base moral conduct on psychological and other theoretical grounds, as in sociobiology.   Stoics and Epicureans, both holding like Aristotle necessitarian conceptions of nature, were still in sufficient solidarity with the tradition to resist any temptation to reduce their ethics to natural principles. But to be aware of the reasons for this, the aid of Aristotle is indispensable.

Sacred Theology. The item that has disappeared entirely from the foregoing *Isis* survey, an item added by the medievals to the classification, is sacred theology. For the medievals, sacred theology was distinguished from "philosophical theology"[27] through its starting points or principles.   Its principles were accepted as divinely revealed, and because the divine authority was all-knowing and infallible, those principles were held as absolutely certain even though not intrinsically evident. Conclusions drawn from them were in this way held to conform with the Aristotelian requirement of scientific certainty, though it was a certainty of faith and not of knowledge.   But infallibility, as already noted, is a sensitive point in current theological discussion. If it be required for recognition of sacred theology as a science, numerous theologians will prefer to have the formal scientific status rejected. In Neoscholastic circles, moreover, even where the origin of Scholastic philosophy within sacred theology is enthusiastically recognized, the prospects of a dreaded "management" by theology from the vantage point of rank as a supreme science have been sharply felt.[28] In the present situation, then, the question of sacred theology as a science is easily sidestepped. A cultural bibliographical survey such as that of *Isis* feels no obligation to list the considerable yearly output in sacred theology under a title characteristic of it as theology.

Epistemology itself has no means for judging the truth or the certainty of the starting points for sacred theology, in either positive or negative tone. The most it can conclude is that if definite divine revelation is accepted, the authority it would involve gives rise to certainty. The principles and conclusions may then be denominated knowledge through focal reference to the divine knowledge in which they have their source. Sacred theology would then be reinstated as culturally recognized science.

Pure and Applied Science. There is a distinction met frequently in modern classifications that is not found in the older tradition. It is the division into pure and applied science. This is not at all parallel to the traditional distinction between theoretical science on the one hand and practical and productive science on the other. The general notion of the modern distinction is that pure science develops knowledge just in itself, while applied science puts that knowledge to use. This is by no means the same as the Aristotelian notion of theoretical knowledge as contemplation of things, while practical or productive science is performative in character. For Aristotle practical and productive sciences do make copious use of theoretical knowledge. But that is not what constitutes them as sciences. They are constituted as distinctive sciences by their radically different starting points. They are fullfledged sciences in their own right, and not merely applications of theoretical knowledge. To know how to build a house is a different type of knowledge from the arithmetical and geometrical knowledge of the measurements used. The contrast cannot be developed in any clearer lines, for the alleged distinction between pure and applied science has never been satisfactorily explained, and never clarified in a way that would allow it to stand up for comparison with the traditional distinction between theoretical knowledge and practical or productive knowledge.[29] But at least one may say that the attempted descriptions of it show clearly enough that it does not coincide with the traditional Aristotelian distinctions.

Agreement and Disagreement. In the sciences, as the foregoing considerations bring out, human intellection reaches its full-blown natural maturity. Through the sciences people are carried outside their immediate selves and share everywhere in the same beneficent achievement. Computers function in the same way in America, Asia, Australia and Europe. Books are printed and circulated, radio is heard, and television screens are watched. Milk is pasteurized, food is conserved and transported in hermetically sealed containers, techniques are interchanged and developed in common. In all these spheres human thought and activity are brought into relative agreement by the sciences. Through them, all humanity is melded vitally into a single organic world.

On the other hand, disagreement is found to spring from the deeper intellectual involvement. Carefully thought out world views have pitted masses of humanity against one another, as the titanic conflicts of the present century between communism and fascism and democracy make manifest. The differences in thinking are widespread and profound. The students demonstrating in Tiananmen Square at Beijing, some with their lives on the line in hunger strike, exemplified one way of thinking. But facing it loomed the grim communist tradition with a readiness to sacrifice personal initiative and human lives on the grill of a Marxist ideology. Disagreement could hardly be more profound and more terrifying.

How does this situation come about? In the mathematical sciences there is not too much trouble in attaining common agreement. That two and two are four is spontaneously accepted, and translation from one system to another can readily be made. In the qualitative order tastes may differ, but they allow sufficient agreement for common statistical conclusions. Likewise in the productive sciences common techniques are pursued with success. But in the sciences that have as their objects being and corporeal nature and human conduct, the case is very different. These sciences are metaphysics, philosophy of nature, and ethics. They are philosophical sciences. In them disagreement is deep and all-pervading, and seems to increase with their advancement. In answer to Kant's three questions, what people can know is definite and satisfactory in some sciences. But in the philosophical sciences, even about what knowledge itself is, as in epistemology, there is found radical and omnipresent disagreement. In regard to Kant's other two questions, namely about what people should do and what they may hope for, there is not sufficient agreement about the nature of science or about eschatological matters to work out an acceptable answer.

One need not be surprised, then, at the willingness today to sidestep the question whether sacred theology is a science, or at the failure to provide a satisfactory explanation of the difference between pure and applied science. But the situation does raise the question of the extent to which philosophies are radically pluralistic. The thoroughgoing disagreement about the overall meaning of the universe and of the ultimate destiny of man is present as a fact. An epistemology that has shown how scientific knowledge is the means for unifying human thought faces the question of why and how philosophy diversifies it. The epistemology should terminate in making manifest how philosophy, while diversifying, provides on its own level the means for assuring intercommunication and dialogue and reciprocal help. Epistemology will thereby show how philosophy is a common enterprise, carried on in a single global village.

Résumé. The sciences are bodies of organized knowledge that have undergone systematic development since ancient times. In Aristotle they were divided into theoretical, practical and productive sciences. Acquaintance with the Aristotelian basis facilitates understanding of the history of their classification and of the way they are to be interrelated in today's tremendous expansion of their range. They bring human knowledge from its humble origins in everyday sensible things to its present commanding view of the universe. The sciences thereby exercise a unifying effect on human affairs and human life in general. Yet they do not bring about a unified view on the meaning of the universe as a whole and on human destiny. Underneath the unifying efforts lies a radical pluralism of philosophical outlooks. To investigate that philosophical pluralism and its import for human culture will be the culminating task of an epistemology.

Notes to Chapter 11

1. See Chapter 10, n. 9; also ibid., n. 12. The etymology of the Latin *scientia* is uncertain; see Ernout-Meillet, *Dictionnaire étymologique de la langue latine* (Paris, 1932), s.v. *scio*. On the gradual transition of words like "art," "culture" and "science" from the meaning of a mental activity to the resultant bodies of achievement, during the last decades of the eighteenth century and the first part of the nineteenth, see Raymond Williams, *Culture and Society 1780-1950* (London, 1958), xiii-xvii. A complete shift may be seen in the word "business."

2. A story handed down about Pythagoras relates that "he compared life to the Great Games, where some went to compete for the prize and others went with wares to sell, but the best as spectators; . . ." Diogenes Laertius, *Lives of Eminent Philosophers*, trans. R. D. Hicks (London and Cambridge, Mass., 1958), 8.8; II, 327-329. The original anecdote was meant to illustrate the superiority of philosophic *life* over the other types. This was rather different from the question of superior status *within* philosophy itself, but the same kind of reasoning could be extended to the ranking of speculative philosophy over the practical and the productive.

3. "Now physical science, too, happens to be concerned with some genus of being (for it is concerned with such a substance which has in itself a principle of motion and of rest), and it is clear that this science is neither practical nor productive. For in productive sciences the principle of a thing produced is in that which produces, whether this is intellect or art or some power, and in practical sciences the principle of *action* is in the doer, and this is *choice*; for that which is done and that which is *chosen* are the same thing." Aristotle, *Metaphysics*, 6.1.1025b18-24; Apostle trans. The tripartite division is also given at *Metaph.*, 11.7.1064a10-19, and at *Topics* 6.6.145a14-18 and 8.1.157a10-11. Where the division is bipartite, theoretical science is always a member, with the other member practical science at *Metaph.*, 2.1.993b19-23, *De anima*, 1.3.407a23-25 and 3.10.433a14-18, and *Politics*, 7.14.1333a16-25, and productive science at *Metaph.*, 1.2.982b11-28 and 12.9.1075a1-3, *De caelo*, 3.7.306a16-17, and *Eudemian Ethics*, 1.5.1216b10-19.

4. See Aristotle, *Posterior Analytics*, 1.13.78a22-79a16. Cf. *Metaph.*, 8.4.1044b13-15, on the cause of the eclipse.

5. Aristotle, *Nicomachean Ethics*, 1.4.1095a30-b8; 1.12.1102a2-4.

6. Aristotle, *Metaph.*, 1.1.980b27-981b17.

7. Aristotle, *Metaph.*, 4.2.1003a34;4.3.1005a33-b2; 6.1.1026a18-32; 11.7.1064a33-b14.

8. Hermann Weidemann, *Metaphysik und Sprach* (Munich, 1975), 32-38; 176.

9. For documentation on these tenets in Bacon and Wolff, see J. Owens, "Theodicy, Natural Theology, and Metaphysics," *The Modern Schoolman*, 28 (1950-1951), 126-137; and "Is There Any Ontology in Aristotle?' *Dialogue*, 25 (1986), 697-707.

10. Aristotle, *Metaph.*, 1.2.982a12-28. Cf. 2.3.995a8-16. Something was "exact" to the extent it was free from complication. This could be understood in a good or bad way. Its Platonic background may be seen in Plato's *Philebus*, 56B-58D.

11. Aristotle, *Physics*, 2.2.194a7-12; *Posterior Analytics*, 1.13.78b37-79a2. Aquinas notes that this lack of penetration into substantial differentiae holds even for "rational" in the definition of man: "Since, according to the Philosopher, we do not know the substantial differences of things, those who make definitions sometimes use accidental differences because they indicate or afford knowledge of the essence as the proper effects afford knowledge of a cause. . . . The same is true of rational . . ." *Truth*, 10.1.ad6; trans. J. V. McGlynn (Chicago, 1953), II, 8.

12. Aristotle, *Metaph.*, 11.1.1059b18-19; Apostle trans.

13. See Aristotle, *Metaph.*, 12.10.1075a19-23. The obligation arising from the *kalon*, or the morally right thing, is regularly expressed in Aristotle by the impersonal verb *dei* (ought). Aristotle

(*Nicomachean Ethics*, 3.1.1110b9-11) carefully distinguished this moral obligation from natural compulsion. It is the recognized obligation to follow right reason in free acts of a rational agent. On the nature of Aristotelian practical science, see Henry Veatch, "Concerning the Distinction between Descriptive and Normative Sciences," *Philosophy and Phenomenological Research*, 6 (1945), 284-306; Mortimer Adler, "Aristotle's Conception of Practical Truth and the Consequences of that Conception," *Paideia*, Second Special Issue, ed. George C. Simmons (Brockport, NY, 1978), 158.

14.   Motion and time were eternal for Aristotle--*Metaph.*, 12.6.1071b6-10. The succession of changes accordingly never had a beginning.   On the succession of civilizations, see *Metaph.*, 12.8.1074b10-12; *Politics*, 7.10.1329b25-31; *De caelo*, 1.3.270b19-20; *Meteorologica*, 1.3.339b27-30.

15.   Edward O. Wilson, *Sociobiology. The New Synthesis* (Cambridge, Mass.: Harvard University Press, 1975), 3.

16.   "Ex dictis deducitur Ethicam subalternari tertiae Philosophiae naturalis specialis parti, quae est de anima. Cum enim obiectum (partiale) tertiae partis Philosophiae naturalis specialis sit actus humanus, Ethica huic obiecto superaddit differentiam accidentalem, quae est moralitas, de qua agit per se." Joseph Gredt, *Elementa philosophiae Aristotelico-Thomisticae*, 7a ed. (Freiburg, 1937), no. 879; II, 303.

17.   A sketch of the development of this innovation may be found in James A. Weisheipl, "The Structure of the Arts Faculty in the Medieval University," *British Journal of Educational Studies*, 19 (1971), 263-264.   "The study of theology thus always remained primary throughout the Middle Ages" (264).

18.   "Et hoc modo sacra doctrina est scientia, quia procedit ex principiis notis lumine superioris scientiae, quae scilicet est scientia Dei et beatorum. Unde sicut musica credit principia tradita sibi ab arithmetico, ita doctrina sacra credit principia revelata sibi a Deo." Aquinas, *Summa theologiae*, 1.1.2,c.

19. "Ita si forte nobis Deus de se ipso vel aliis aliquid revelet, quod naturales ingenii nostri vires excedat, qualia jam sunt mysteria Incarnationis & Trinitatis, non recusabimus illa credere, quamvis non clare intelligamus." Descartes, *Principia philosophiae*, 1.25; ed. Adam & Tannery, VIII, 14.19-23 (IX², 36). In Bacon, sacred theology had been mentioned as a science but without further attention to it in his classification. "We shall, therefore, divide sciences into theology and philosophy. In the former we do not include natural theology . . . but restrict ourselves to inspired divinity . . ." Bacon, *On the Dignity and Advancement of Learning*, 3.1; Colonial Press rev. ed. (London, 1900), 76. The Leibnizian notion of "theodicy," however, was deliberately meant to draw upon both philosophy and sacred theology. See Leibniz, *Essais de théodicée*, 1.1 (Amsterdam, 1710), 105-106.

20. See Joseph Mariétan, *Probléme de la classification des sciences d'Aristote à St. Thomas* (Paris, 1901; J. A. Weisheipl, "Classification of the Sciences in Medieval Thought," *Mediaeval Studies*, 27 (1965), 54-90; Robert McRae, *The Problem of the Unity of the Sciences: Bacon to Kant* (Toronto, 1961); Robert Flint, *Philosophy as Scientia Scientiarum* and *A History of Classifications of the Sciences* (reprint, New York, 1975). Flint misses completely the nature of Aristotle's distinction between practical and productive knowledge: "The narrow, the really untenable distinction between Productive and Practical Sciences was dropped, and philosophy came to be divided simply into two great branches, the Theoretical and Practical" (84).

21. See references in *A Supplement to the Oxford English Dictionary*, ed. R. W. Burchfield (Oxford, 1982), III, 1542, s.v.

22. See *Nicomachean Ethics*, 10.9.1181b15-23.

23. Cf. supra, nn. 2-3.

24. This was the conception in Bacon: ". . . like the branches of trees that join in one trunk," *On the Dignity and Advancement of Learning*, 3.1; 76-77, and in Descartes: "Ainsi toute la Philosophie est comme un arbre, dont les racines sont la Metaphysique . . .",

Principes, Preface, no. 26; IX², 23-25. "Branches" misses the autonomy given by the object of each science.

25. See "One Hundred Thirteenth Critical Bibliography of the History of Science and its Cultural Influences," *Isis*, 79 (1988), 33-63. The section is on the "Histories of the Special Sciences," with philosophy listed as the first of these sciences. Likewise at the beginning of the bibliographies for the different chronological periods, philosophy is listed first along with general histories (65). This listing of philosophy as a science has been the regular practice of *Isis* in recent years. The perspective is cultural. Generally speaking, however, it is hardly standard usage today to refer to philosophy as a whole under the designation of "a science," though its different parts may readily be called "philosophical sciences." Philosophy, moreover, is not longer distinguished from the arts and sciences as though it constituted a separate school. Everywhere it is a department, along with the other departments, through CUA at Washington and USC at Los Angeles still preserve the etiquette "School of Philosophy." Its present organization as a department seems reflected in the *Isis* classification of it as "a science."

26. On the functioning of the natural sciences in today's world see J. W. Grove, *In Defense of Science: Science technology, and politics in modern society* (Toronto, 1989), especially in relation to technology (25-47), sociobiology (111-119), and religion (154-168). An overview of the situation from the viewpoint of "metascience" may be found in David Oldroyd, *The Arch of Knowledge* (New York, 1986). On pseudo-science, see Grove, 120-150. Hume's (*Enquiries*, 12.3.132) book-burning attitude has quite apparently become outdated.

27. "Theologica ergo philosophica"--Aquinas, *In Boeth. De. Trin.*, 5.4.Resp; ed. Decker, 195.22. Cf. "Accordingly, there are two kinds of theology or divine science. There is one that treats of divine things, not as the subject of the science but as the principles of the subject. This is the kind of theology pursued by the philosophers and that is also called metaphysics." Aquinas, *The Division and Methods of the Sciences*, trans. Armand Maurer, 4th ed. (Toronto, 1986), 52. On the topic, see M.-D. Chenu, *La théologie comme science au XIIIᵉ siècle*, 3rd ed. (Paris, 1957), and "Is Theology a Science?" trans. A. A. N.

Green-Armytage (New York, 1959). Also A. Hayen, "La théologie au XII⁰, XIII⁰ et XX⁰ siècles," *Nouvelle revue théologique*, 79 (1957), 1009-1028.

Contemporary theologians, however, show no burning desire to have sacred theology labeled as a science, even though in the post-modern mentality the natural sciences are not necessarily the model for the notion. Today the theologians shun a rigid deductive procedure from infallible and all-embracing first principles. They wish to lean rather on the lived experience of religious believers. Yet the traditional notion of sacred theology as a science took ample account of the practical beliefs of the faithful for the role of first principles, and used judgments of connaturality based on the affectivity of grace in the individual believers. On the development of doctrine, attention was given to the blossoming of dogmas in religious experience as well as to the basic dogmas themselves. From an epistemological viewpoint sacred theology may well be regarded as a science in the fashion of the medieval theologians, for sacred theology is an organized body of knowledge and as such calls for location and ranking among the sciences in general. But how this question is to be handled in any particular epoch is a matter for the theologians of the time, on the one side, and the cultural connaisseurs on the other.

28. ". . . a theologically managed philosophy--philosophy used and shaped by the theologian in his world and for his purposes--is not philosophy." Anton C. Pegis, *St. Thomas and Philosophy* (Milwaukee, 1964), 39-40. Cf. 88.

29. "The nineteenth century invented the terms 'pure' and 'applied' mathematics . . . a terminology which is far from being adequate and satisfactory." Cornelius Lanczos, *Applied Analysis* (Englewood Cliffs, N.J., 3rd printing, 1964), 1. In this context the term "pure science" is understood to mean a discipline pursued on account of its own intrinsic appeal, while "applied" characterizes one pursued for utility or some other extrinsic purpose. Yet all have intrinsic appeal, and all can be pursued for other purposes. Theoretical physics and theoretical mechanics are applied mathematics in their special areas, and themselves can be applied in applied physics, applied

psychology, applied cybernetics, applied radiology, applied geography, and so on. But, as Lanczos notes, the terms "pure" and "applied" will continue to be used, "even if they have been coined wrongly by conjuring up associations that are not warranted philosophically (1-2). On mathematics in today's life sciences, see J. G. Defares and I. N. Sneddon, *An Introduction to the Mathematics of Medicine and Biology* (Amsterdam, 1964); and for the social sciences, John W. Bishir/Donald W. Drewes, *Mathematics in the Behavioral and Social Sciences* (New York, 1970).

CHAPTER 12

Philosophies

Pluralism. Although superficially the panorama of philosophy may appear marked off into neatly etched philosophical sciences, such as metaphysics, ethics, philosophy of nature, philosophy of law, philosophy of sport, and so on, a little experience of it in any of its systematic partitions will show that the really basic divisions in philosophical thought are much deeper and transcend the schematic lines. The character of each of the above named disciplines will differ profoundly in accord with the many varied types of philosophical thinking. Specification by the objects of the various philosophical sciences is a relatively minor factor in their philosophical differentiation. For instance, if you ask Aristotle what metaphysics is, he will answer, if you explain the term to him, that it is a philosophical theology with the primary instance of being as its specifying object. If by way of seeking a second opinion your inquiry is addressed to Aquinas, you will be told that metaphysics is the science of common being without specification by divine being. If you then go to a Neoscholastic, you may get the answer that it is a study of things in the third degree of abstraction. For Bonaventure and Francis Bacon it was a subdivision of natural philosophy, contrasting rather sharply with the strong Aristotelian distinction between the two disciplines.[1] For Collingwood it was a positive science that catalogued historically the absolute presuppositions of people. In the heyday of hard-core logical positivism it was nonsense, literally non-sense, because it tried to bear on a non-sensible object. These were all given as professional answers. They were meant as serious replies to people asking professional advice.

This situation in regard to each particular systematic division is, however, fully in accord with the nature of philosophy as a whole. The traditional notion of it was handed down, in Cicero's celebrated definition, as knowledge of things human and divine and of their causes. But in the Cartesian conception, philosophy is a study built on clear and distinct ideas, or built on sensations for the Empiricists. For the nineteenth century ideals it was a building of grandiose intellectual systems of thought. For the Pragmatists it was a directing of theory to action. For the Phenomenologists it was a study of vivid appearances intuited as essences in their own right. For the Structuralists it was a study based on the symbolic orders or types upon which our knowledge is held to bear directly. For the linguistic analysts it was a clarification of concepts or a study of the behavior of words. The general spectrum seems to be indefinitely wide and to vary in great depth.

It is these profound differences in the nature of philosophy itself, rather than any systematic partition on the basis of specifying objects, that give rise to the uncontrollable variety of philosophies that parade across its history. Atomism, Platonism, Aristotelianism, Augustinianism, Thomism, Scotism, Ockhamism, Cartesianism, Phenominalism, Kantianism, Hegelianism, Phenomenology, Existentialism, Linguistic Analysis, and many other distinct types of thinking have been engaged in its enterprise. When traced to their ultimate sources these ways of philosophizing all turn out to be radically diverse. They commence from different starting points, and each proceeds in its own characteristic manner. Often each of them uses a terminology it can call its own. But even where the same words and the same expressions are used, as was to a large extent the case in Scholastic philosophy, the meaning and implications can be profoundly different. The result is that the reasoning in each may be formalized without revealing any flaw in the logical sequence of the thought, and yet they lead to widely divergent conclusions.

This phenomenon of a radical pluralism is readily observable in even a glance over the history of western philosophy. It cannot help but be a sensitive area in the study of human thought. In it, in fact, may be expected to lie the culminating interest of epistemology. Epistemology itself is a philosophical study, and after explaining the different kinds of cognition that come under its purview, it may be expected to have a special interest in concentrating upon the generic type of knowledge to which it itself belongs, namely philosophy. If generically philosophy is radically pluralistic, epistemology itself will be radically pluralistic by that very token, and will have to present its conclusions as being those that stem from a particular type of philosophizing. An epistemology will thereby show why its conclusions do not hold in other philosophies, and yet make clear that it is not maintaining a conception of general relativity in philosophy except in the historical perspective that each genuine philosopher thinks in his own characteristic way, differently from others.

In consequence, no philosophy will be able to refute any other. Each is on a different wave length. But that fact allows them to be broadcast simultaneously, without interfering with one another. Further, it enables the listeners to benefit by each of them. The ensuing communication and dialogue bring about the one global philosophic enterprise. Each philosophy may claim and prove, but always on the strength of its own starting points, that its conclusions are the true ones. That is the historical perspective. Epistemology shows which starting points are correct and how other philosophies are to be gauged in their light. But epistemology can do this only in the framework of a particular philosophy. That is the paradox of philosophical thought. To explain it is epistemology's final task.

How then, in detail, does philosophical pluralism come into being?

Things, Concepts, Language. The preceding inquiry has shown definitely enough that an object and the cognition of it are two epistemologically irreducible starting points. At the origin of human cognition the thing sensed and the human percipient are each apprehended as existents, with the sensible thing as existent in itself and also in the percipient. Neither existence is derived from the other. Each is of independent status. This is the way they are originally grasped in human cognition. In that existentially independent way the object and the percipient play their roles as epistemological origins. The percipient gives existence to the activities of sensible cognition and perception, in which no new object is produced but new cognitional existence is given to an already really existent thing. In intellection the natures of the things are abstracted and given cognitional existence by the knower. They can be considered just as they are in their separate cognitional existence and made the primitive starting points for philosophical thinking. In this way things and thought offer themselves each as independent origins for philosophical procedures.

There is a still further complication. Human cognition and what it grasps about its objects are communicated from person to person and handed down from age to age through language. Language is a medium that contains all that is communicated. It has its own existence, separate from the existence of the things or of the thought. Why can it too not be made an independent starting point for philosophical thinking? There is no apparent reason why it cannot play this role. Through the middle decades of the present century it has in fact done just that. It has the great advantage of offering as the starting point an interpersonal and therefore an acknowledge public milieu. With language the medium is in fact the message, as far as content is concerned.[2]

There can hardly be question of excluding any of these three facets in a particular philosophical procedure. A philosophy that regards sensible things as basic will not dispense with thoughts about them, nor fail to consider the language through which thoughts and things are discussed. In various questions, without at all disregarding its radical approach from sensible things, it may choose to enter upon the discussion from the standpoint of the word used to express the topic. Aristotle and Aquinas, even though adhering unswervingly to the fundamental approach from really existent sensible things, often commence the treatment of a particular theme with the examination of the various meanings of the relevant word.[3] Philosophies that start from thought, in the wake of Descartes, can be very interested in the things of the external world.[4] The linguistic approach is crucially concerned with the elucidation of concepts, and even of facts, and can look towards positive, not merely therapeutic results.[5] One may expect that the three dimensions will be present in any philosophical discussion. Language will be communicating thought, and the thought will be about things. The epistemological problem, rather, is to inquire about the reciprocal relations of the three as independent philosophical starting points, and to understand what happens when any one of the three is chosen as the basis upon which the respective roles of the two other existentially independent origins are to be assessed. Likewise it includes the consideration of techniques for isolating as basic some feature common to two or even all three of the different types of starting points. This is the case with the common nature in Avicenna and Duns Scotus, or in the symbolic orders of the modern Structuralists.

In the opening chapter of *On Interpretation*, Aristotle sketches succinctly but in easily recognizable fashion the relations of each of the three orders to the other two: "Spoken words are the symbols of mental experience and written words are the symbols of spoken words. Just as all men have not the same writing, so all men have not the same speech sounds, but the mental experiences, which these directly symbolize, are the same for all, as also are those things of which our experiences are the images."[6] Language expresses thought, thought presents things. The epistemological investigation just undertaken bears out this analysis of the reciprocal relations of the three kinds of existentially independent starting points. Sensible things in their own real existence are epistemologically basic, since they are the first objects of which one is directly aware. Upon them human cognition is originally focused. Only in terms of them can anything be represented in one's cognition and discussed in language. Equally immediate, though not equally basic in the sense just mentioned, is the concomitant cognition of the awareness itself and of the cognitive agent. Because equally immediate this can be regarded in reflex cognition as an independent starting point for all one's philosophy. On the intellectual level it blossoms into a marvelous and finely articulated array of concepts. But even in these concepts, what is directly represented is the object. The concept itself is known only concomitantly or through reflexion. The object other than the concept remains basic. It is what the concept expresses. It is what gives the concept its content. It thereby provides even the terms in which the concept itself is represented.

Correspondingly, language is an independent approach to philosophy. When you wish to become acquainted with the thought of Plato or of Aristotle, you start with their written words, or at least with the spoken words of the instructor. The written or the spoken words have their own independent existence on the printed page or in the sounds uttered. In general, philosophy is learned in this way. Yet here again the content is what the words express. It is the thought, the thought that in turn presents the things. Apart from the thought, the words would be of no help. A Hungarian or Japanese translation of Aristotle could not serve as a starting point to the Stagirite's thought on being or on morals for one who did not understand the language. Even though existentially independent, then, language becomes language only through expressing thought, while thought can be represented only in terms of objects other than itself.

These considerations should be of service in the inquiry into the radically pluralistic condition of philosophy. Broadly, there are three kinds of independent starting points. The starting points can be found in things existent in themselves, in concepts existent in human cognition, and in language existent on the printed page or in spoken sounds. Existentially, these starting points are independent of one another. All three offer themselves as they stand. Yet they are related to each other in a way that makes things basic, thought a presenting of things, and language an expression of thought. Does it make any difference where one begins? Or will the reciprocal relations of the three have decisive influence upon the choice of a starting point for one's philosophy?

Perhaps the best way, or even the only feasible way, to answer this question is to take a look at the various types of philosophy in action. A complete coverage, needless to say, would mean a study of the whole history of philosophy. But a glance at some typical instances of philosophies that commence in each of the three areas of independent starting pints would be sufficient for the present epistemological purposes. They should show convincingly enough the manner in which each kind of starting point functions and how it is able to take care of the considerations that arise from the other two facets that it has in some way to involve.

Approach From Things. Historically, the approach from the side of things was the first to make its appearance in western philosophy. It continued in various forms till the time of Descartes. Thales and the other Presocratics were directly concerned with the sensible universe itself, rather than with human thought about it. Even Parmenides was regarded in Greek tradition as a physicist, and his poem as a treatise on nature. No matter how closely thought was identified with being, as was everything else, the approach in the poem seems definitely from the side of being, not from the side of thought. In the doxastic conception of the sensible universe that seems to stem from the last part of his poem, the multiple and changing cosmos may well be regarded as a production by cognitive processes.[7] Nevertheless the philosophizing starts from this cosmos as a thing or group of things. There seems to be utterly no question of opposing one's representation of it to the cosmos itself, and starting from the representation.

With Plato, the picture assumes clearer lines. Through sensation ever changing things were perceived, through *anamnesis* unchangeable things beheld in a different world were recalled.[8] In whatever way one may explain *anamnesis*, the twofold origin for human cognition seems to be mandatory.[9] It consisted in changeable things in the sensible world, and of unchangeable things, above the limitations of space and time, in an intellectual world. But in either perspective the starting point lay in things that had their existence independently of human thought. There was no question of starting from the thought or representations by which either class of things was grasped. The twofold origin gave rise to a distinct type of philosophizing that has exercised during influence down the ages under the name of Platonism, in all its multiple forms.

In Aristotle both types of object have their origin in one and the same type of objects, namely the things of the sensible world.[10] In Aristotle, too, the epistemological relations of object and cognition are brought sharply into focus. In every act of cognition an object other than the act is expressly known or perceived, and the cognition itself only concomitantly.[11] Cognition is accordingly explained as the union of the two in such a way that in the act of cognition the percipient or knower is the object perceived or known.[12] The starting point of the procedure is clearly enough located in things, with the acknowledgment of the concomitant awareness of the cognition. In this way Aristotle was able to explain cognition as expressing things, the language as expressing cognition.[13]

For Aquinas, in turn, the twofold way in which a sensible thing presents itself to human intellection gives rise to a surprisingly new epistemological starting point in things. From the viewpoint of its nature, a sensible thing is known through conceptualization. From the viewpoint of its existence, it is apprehended through judgment. The articulation of this double grasp and its implications makes Thomistic philosophizing radically different from the original Aristotelian procedure. For the epistemological inquiry it results in a much more profound and satisfactory explanation of the reciprocal bearing of object and cognition on each other. Every finite nature is shown to abstract from existence in such a way that of itself the nature is totally devoid of being, while open to both real and cognitional existence. The starting point, in consequence, remains in sensible things. But the explanation in terms of real existence and cognitional existence accounts for the twofold being of the one and the same object. It shows how the thing that is really existent outside the cognition is the thing that has cognitional existence within the awareness and is thereby the thing that is perceived or known.

Other starting points in sensible things have been fruitfully exploited in the course of western thought. With Duns Scotus, for instance, the first object of human cognition is the common nature regarded as formally distinct from the individuating characteristics.[14] In other dominant tradition both essence and existence were regarded as basic realities, each having its own type of being.[15] Reality, as might be expected, proves rich enough to offer numerous other such starting points, each able to set in motion a new and distinct way of philosophical thinking.

May this approach from the side of things, prevalent throughout western thought before the time of Descartes, be called "Realism"? If "Realism" is defined as the type of philosophy that allows to things an existence independent of human thinking, it would bring Pre-Cartesian thinking under its range.[16] But does not the designation then become misleading? It introduces real existence in terms of contrast with existence in cognition. Implicitly it takes for granted that the starting point of philosophy is the presence of things in cognition, and that the question then is whether they continue to exist in any way after the act of cognition ceases. This falsifies the whole approach of the Pre-Cartesian philosophies, for it subsumes their approach under the approach from human cognition. Consequently it tends to make them a species of the Cartesian type of philosophizing, and to impose upon them the requirement of proving the real existence of things from starting points in human thought. It cannot be expected to reach any other kind of existence than that which can be explained through the notion of cognitional existence. Real existence will in consequence be some kind of existence outside cognition. In this way it will be represented only negatively, in relation to cognitional existence. The basic positive status of real existence will thereby be lost, and will never be recovered. Instead of a primitively apprehended existence of a thing in itself, definite and unchallengeably basic, real existence will be an appendage that has to be reached and explained philosophically through cognitional existence.

In regard to medieval thought, moreover, there can also be another sort of confusion. In explaining the controversy on universals that runs through medieval philosophy, historians use the term "realism" to describe the tenets of those who placed the universals *in re*, that is, regarded them as existent somehow in reality. Opposed were those who placed them *in voce*. In this contrast of realists with nominalists, realism means giving either to universals, or to common natures as common, an existence of some kind in the real world. It is not concerned with the problem whether the object of cognition in general, and of sensible cognition in particular, has existence outside the cognition. In point of fact, none of the medieval thinkers who are opposed to the "realism" of the universals would seem to have had any doubt about the existence of an abiding external world, in independence of human cognitive activity.

The label "Realism," however, is currently given to the ways of thinking that preceded Descartes. No matter how inept one considers it, one has to learn to live with it in this context. A supplementary query then comes to the fore. If the Pre-Cartesian philosophies are to be classed as realisms, what kind of realism do they exhibit? Are they to be dismissed summarily as types of "Naïve Realism"? A little reflection on the elaborate and penetrating examination of cognition in Aristotle and Aquinas should be enough to make this suggestion seem ridiculous. In other thinkers, such as Parmenides and Plotinus, there is evidence of a sophisticated study of sensation. But in the light of what has been seen in the foregoing epistemological survey, is there anything naive in accepting the real existence of sensible things as the foundation of all other human knowledge? Nothing can be more certain than the tenet of their real existence. Their real existence, rather, is what supports the whole superstructure of knowledge, truth and certainty. Does not the actual naïvité consist in accepting uncritically the notion that like a material thing cognition must have its own self as the thing most present to it? More obvious, even, is the naïvité in concluding that other persons and other things are, as known, products of one's cognition while at the same time dealing with them continually in actual life as independent existents.

Approach From Concepts. Since through reflexion one's own concepts are immediately known, they offer themselves as an independent starting point for philosophical procedure. This method was exploited by Descartes. It has proved exceptionally fruitful in the large number of philosophies which it has since inspired, and has been successful in the exploration of countless individual problems. Yet it has found itself helpless in face of the recent deconstructionist attacks on the way it privileges the epistemic life. As the concept is the thing in cognitional existence in the intellect,[17] the Cartesian mentality allowed the implications of the concept to be drawn unimpeded to their ultimate conclusions. By presenting the various aspects of the known thing separately and in clearly distinct and articulated fashion, the Cartesian approach offers tempting foundations for philosophical edifices. In fact, it enables one to proceed, as in mathematics, unencumbered by particular existence and free from the confusion engendered by sensible tone clusters and amalgamations, as well as by language, history and tradition.

But this approach gives rise to serious difficulties. It meets a projected dualism of thought and reality, or of mind and matter, or of phenomenon and thing, or of the abstract versus the concrete or lived world. Bringing only the one type of existence, namely the cognitional, into its immediate grasp, it has to journey in some way from cognitional existence to real existence. This has invariably proved an impossible undertaking. The way of causality remains closed, since it assumes without warrant the externality of the cause.[18] Even the real existence of self, as Hume's speculations showed, cannot be reached from this starting point.[19] Real existence of self and of an external world has either to be postulated, or required on grounds of practical living or on the authority of common sense, or else the problems are dismissed as nonsensical or as so many different ways of looking for a ghost in a machine.

Linguistic Approach. Like the novelty of the Cartesian approach from thought, so in its turn the present-century approach from language may appear to its advocates as the coming of philosophy into mature status.[20] Language contains all that philosophy need investigate. Things can be left to science. Semiotics in this way assimilates the whole of philosophy.

In its present-century origins, the new way of philosophizing first advocated concentration of attention on the questions asked rather than on the answers sought. Through analysis of ordinary language, concepts are elucidated and philosophical problems are solved. In this way concepts are approached through language. Can one go further in the process and arrive at things? In point of fact, the analysts can hardly help but eventually encounter things, for "thing" is a word that calls for explanation. Accordingly "information about the nature of things"[21] may emerge, but it will not concern philosophy in its own characteristic activity. The linguistic approach is entirely tolerant, therefore, of a real thinking subject and of real sensible or external things. It does not require either as a focal point. Yet it can deal extensively with both. There need be no surprise, in consequence, to find some thinkers using the linguistic approach and becoming deeply immersed in problems of reality such as freedom, other selves, or the existence and attributes of God.

In taking a linguistic unit as its point of departure, this approach has the advantage of being able to delimit a particular philosophical issue and discuss it within manageable boundaries. It has the corresponding disadvantage of not viewing each particular problem against the background of the totality, and of not integrating it into a common fabric. Needless to say, it offers apparently unlimited possibilities of different philosophical developments. In recent hermeneutics the linguistic approach has been deepened to include the history and tradition handed down in language and thereby shaping each individual's way of thinking. Every philosophic tenet accordingly requires interpretation through the historic situations that influenced it, in unending regress. Philosophic understanding consists in giving that interpretation.[22]

To a thinker in the Aristotelian tradition, the linguistic approach may seem line starting to build with the third floor and working downward. Yet that comparison is too drastic. For Aristotle, philosophy does not mean building, but understanding in terms of causes. Theoretical philosophies have their objects already there for study, while practical and productive disciplines, though bearing on things yet to be done or made, work through relations or materials already attained. Things, though, and language have been long familiar to a person before philosophy commences. He or she is confronted by all three together, and is able to make the choice. Sooner or later, however, the problem of how to get from one to the other has to be faced.

Other Designations. There are also numerous trends in philosophy that may not fit any too neatly under the three broad divisions just listed. Some stretch in one way or another across the boundaries. Idealism, for instance, reaches from ways of thinking like that of Parmenides or of Plato or of Plotinus in the first division, to the systems of Berkeley and Hegel and Bradley in the second. Pragmatism and Personalism can be shown to cover ground in each. In Husserl, phenomenology may seem a clear case of starting from the Cartesian *cogito* through bracketing existence, yet later phenomenology may seem from the start to be immersed in a real *Lebenswelt*. Similarly existentialism in Sartre may seem also to have the Cartesian starting point, and yet elsewhere to be commencing from real vivid existence. Each philosophy has to explain its own internal consistency. For the present epistemological interests, the issue to be emphasized is the seemingly unlimited number of starting points that are offered for philosophical development, thereby making philosophy radically pluralistic in nature.

Further, the motivation of the individual thinker exercises great influence in the selection of the starting points for his or her philosophy. A person deeply moved by the miserable economic conditions of much of the third world is easily led to Marxist principles, as is illustrated by the development of recent liberation philosophies. Interest in languages and philology was back of the movement towards linguistic analysis. Concern with tragedy prompted developments in existentialism. Correspondingly the motivation in Christian philosophy or Islamic philosophy or Jewish philosophy leads to the choice of starting points from which distinctive philosophies develop.

This consideration is particularly relevant in regard to the long debate whether there is such a thing as genuine Christian philosophy.[23] If by Christian philosophy any reasoning from divinely revealed premises were included in its procedure, the notion would be self-contradictory. Its content would be intrinsically evident and not intrinsically evident in the same respect, for a chain is no stronger than its weakest link. But Christian philosophy, as contrasted with sacred theology in its history through the centuries, demands as its basis naturally known premises only. It has indeed as its object the universe as known through both reason and revelation. But that is the object with which it deals, while the starting points from which it reasons are entirely of natural origin. Quite as philosophy of religion can deal with divinely revealed doctrines as objects, so a Christian philosophy, while holistic in scope, can deal with the integrated universe though it is reasoning solely from naturally known principles. Christian philosophy is a general philosophy, and not the study of a particular human activity as is the philosophy of religion. But it is the religious interest that leads it to select its starting points.

These, then, are the data in regard to philosophic pluralism. How are these data to be evaluated?

Authentic Diversity. The presence of myriad possible starting points in the overall object of philosophical investigation guarantees the authenticity of philosophic pluralism. Unlike mathematics and the experimental sciences, philosophy does not mark off a special area in which definite and commonly acceptable starting points emerge. Rather, it faces the totality as a totality, and seeks to enter by some one of the many doors that it encounters. Pluralism is not an accident or an error in philosophy. It is a phenomenon that arises from the all-embracing character of the philosophical object.

This will mean that the direction and course and achievement of any philosophy will in principle be determined by its starting point. Plato quoted a Greek proverb that the starting point is half the work. He added his own comment that to him it seemed more than half.[24] Aristotle repeated this observation in respect of ethics.[25] These seem to be understatements. If philosophical pluralism is genuine, the starting point should inevitably determine the whole future of each philosophy, and render it irreducible to any other. Philosophies may be grouped broadly in terms of their starting points in things, thought, and language, and then in ever narrowing classifications on the basis of other affinities within these fundamental divisions. Finally they may open out into the individual peculiarities in the thought of every person who philosophizes. These differences and resemblances require penetrating investigation and sensitive appreciation. But the possibility that in the end the myriad philosophies may be reduced to a unity modeled on mathematics or experimental science, seems excluded irrevocably by the character of the philosophical object. People are built differently, and their fingerprints, physiognomies and philosophies vary indefinitely.

Translation. Is it possible, in this radical pluralism, for one philosophy to understand any other? Can each one express, in its own terms, what the other means to say? Is translation achievable.

Since the overall knowable object is the same for each philosophy, it offers phases that are attained by some as starting points, and by others as problems to be explained through other starting points. All immediately observable phases, accordingly, are accessible to every philosophy. The differences lie in the priority given them, respectively, for philosophical reasoning. No cause, therefore, emerges why everything that is immediately observable may not be translated from one philosophic language into another. The terms are present in each. Where starting points, however, restrict the language in regard to mediately known areas, inability to translate will occur. If the starting point allows reasoning only to sensible things, the philosophy will have no means of expressing authentic notions of the supersensible. Where the starting points are exclusively theoretical, they will not permit the expression of genuinely practical principles and conclusions. Where "relevance," on the other hand, is the basic criterion, the inherent worth of theoretical knowledge will be missed.

These considerations are enough to show that different philosophies, no matter how authentic each is, have greater or lesser powers of penetration and range, determined in every case by the virtualities of their respective starting points. It is part of an epistemological investigation, consequently, to assess their respective capabilities, at least in descriptive terms. An evaluation, of course, can be made only on the principles of some definite philosophy. It will differ widely, even radically, in accord with the different starting points. One cannot philosophize in a vacuum. The clearly articulated first principles have to support all the rest, wherever conclusions have to be drawn. Dialectical surveys and examinations may be used extensively, as with Aristotle,[26] to bring one's mind to bear upon those starting points, and dialogue with others may keep one reexamining and reassessing them. But ultimately it is in the light of those basic and indemonstrable principles that one passes philosophical judgment on anyone else's thinking.

The radical differences of viewpoint become sharply accentuated when the varying estimates of the distinct philosophical sciences are reviewed. Metaphysics and ethics, especially, have been presented in an amazing variety of colors. The estimates of metaphysics range from dynastic supremacy as queen of the sciences to dyslogistic scorn as an abyss of sheer nonsense. Ethics has been given roles from that of the practical science for guidance of human conduct and for making people good, to that of a merely descriptive study of human behavior. These marked differences in assessment of the various philosophical disciplines indicate a radical cleavage in viewpoint. The ultimate task of epistemology is to examine the fundamental diversities encountered when one reaches the philosophical level, and to explain them in terms of their causes.

Certainly pluralism has persisted throughout the whole history of philosophy. Studied efforts to overcome it, and to establish unity in philosophic thought, invariably result in the addition of one more philosophy to the already existent multiplicity. Today, just as in the time of Francis Bacon and René Descartes,[27] the philosophical panorama presents to the observer a seemingly universal disagreement among the professionals in the philosophic enterprise. "Philosophers never agree on anything" is a common conclusion. Often it is enough to turn away with contempt minds attracted by the neat unanimity of other high school and college disciplines at any given epoch. But the pluralism is a fact. Epistemology has to explain why philosophers cannot achieve the unity that is found so admirable in mathematics and experimental science at each particular stage of their respective development.

A question, then, may be asked against this background. Is there anything in the nature of the philosophical enterprise that makes a radical pluralism unavoidable? Is it necessary for philosophy, or can it be overcome? How far does it extend? Does it mean that ultimately every individual person should have his own philosophy, different from that of everyone else? If so, how can philosophical chaos be avoided? The answers should emerge clearly enough from the foregoing considerations. Things, thought and language offer a myriad choice of starting points. Each thinker can choose independently and differently. His choice will determine the course of his philosophizing. The choice will in practice depend in large part of temperament and upbringing. One philosophy cannot be used to correct another, since it proceeds from starting points different from those of the other philosophy. One may become appalled at the results to which one's philosophy is leading, say to totalitarianism or to moral anarchy. One may then abandon the philosophy and start another from different principles. But as long as one remains within the framework of a genuine philosophy, one is thinking in a radically different way from other philosophers.

No matter how much may be learned from the study of other types, then, attempts to establish the basis of any one philosophy by the procedure of some other is doomed to failure. That technique would do away with genuine pluralism, for it would allow all philosophical thought to be derived ultimately from a single source. Perhaps the most significant instance of that procedure has been the trend called "Transcendental Thomism."[28] In it the categories or requirements of human thinking are made the basis of reasoning to the real existence of external things, thereby claiming to establish or at least confirm the ground on which Aquinas built his philosophical thinking. The circularity in that way of reasoning is apparent. If all natural human knowledge for Aquinas originates in real sensible things, one's knowledge of thought structure must have its ultimate epistemological source in the sensible things themselves. The same critique will hold proportionally for attempts to base Thomistic philosophy on linguistic analysis or on semiotic and hermeneutic procedures. For the latter the problem would be to reach stable thought and things by means of signifiers that keep endlessly deferring, since in Aquinas the really existent sensible things have to be epistemologically absolute in the grounding of human cognition.

There can, however, be generic groupings of philosophies on the basis of family resemblances. Realism, Idealisms, Linguistic Philosophies, are readily observable instances. Nevertheless the generic resemblance is no guarantee that two philosophies will agree in assessing a particular topic. Radical diversities, obscuring under the generic surface, soon come to light. Even though common formulae may be used, the dialogue and discussion continue to bring out further virtualities in the thought of each, the philosophic pluralism remains radical and authentic. Unlike mathematics and experimental science, where the starting points at any particular time appear the same for all participants, philosophy stems from a deeper stratum in which the individual differences render the generic resemblances finally inoperative in the discussion of particular problems.

Does this make philosophy more of the nature of poetry or of fiction than of scientific knowledge? If philosophy ultimately varies with each individual thinker, is it not a construction comparable to a poem or a novel?

As already noted, philosophy is basically not construction but knowledge. It is the ultimate understanding of reality and thought through the strength of the unaided human intellect. If these objects are ultimately individual, though with generic and specific commonness, the ultimate understanding of them will have to allow for their radical conditioning as individual. They are not like sciences that can be content with common traits. If the objects are that way, the possibilities of different approach on the ultimate level seem unlimited. They offer, then, the possibility of being understood on this level in radically pluralistic ways. This will be understanding, and not construction like poetry or fiction.

But will not this condition leave vague and merely tentative the results of philosophy as a whole? Will it not endorse the rather widespread notion that philosophy is merely an immature stage in the handling of particular areas of investigation, acceptable in lieu of anything better till science catches up and provides the definitive treatment? Just as mathematical and natural science were once included under philosophy, but emerged from its shell as soon as they reached independent development, so may not logic be regarded as now free from philosophy, and similarly may not the treatment of any other subject be looked upon as separated from philosophy once it attains maturity? As in the course of English history the various administrative departments went "out of court" as their development became too complicated and systematized to function within the easy-going, intimate atmosphere of the king's court, so may not the various disciplines be viewed as going out of philosophy once they have really grown up?

This pejorative conception would deprive philosophy of any field exclusively its own. Even spiritual being would remain within its scope only till at some future time an independent positive science develops in the area. Moral questions would await definite solution in sociobiological study. Natural philosophy would be regarded as superseded by experimental science. The overall considerations of objects of thought could be left to a scientific logic. In a word, any of the tasks now undertaken in philosophy is pursued in merely a tentative and haphazard way. These areas, the objection urges, will be explored in a mature and satisfactory manner only when each becomes the object of a non-philosophical science.

In the traditional Aristotelian framework of the sciences, the answer to the question is obvious enough. Each of the philosophical sciences has an object that the mathematical or experimental sciences can never hope to touch. The object in each case is beyond the grasp of any of the latter sciences. Being for metaphysics, corporeal substance for natural philosophy, morality for ethics, present objects that require distinct philosophical disciplines. Other types of philosophical thinking will have their own ways of justifying the existence of philosophy of science, philosophy of history, philosophy of religion, esthetics, and so on. Still other types, such as logical positivism, have on their own principles concluded that philosophy is meant to give way to the mathematical and experimental sciences. Philosophy's estimate of its own status is accordingly one of the problems whose solution varies radically with the radical diversities of the principles used by each different type of philosophical procedure.

The attitude that prompts this question is somewhat similar to the stance that philosophy's sole task is to elucidate or clarify the concepts used by the other disciplines, and then modestly bow itself out of the picture. The notion of a merely ancillary role, once attributed to philosophy by some theologians in respect of their own higher discipline, has in recent years been made to bear especially upon experimental and political science insofar as philosophy is considered able to clarify the concepts used in research and government. Here the solution of the problem is the same as above. Where each philosophical science is shown to have its own distinct object, there is in each case a science in its own right, regardless of subsequent ancillary functions. Where a type of philosophical thinking cannot establish distinct objects for philosophical sciences, it obviously has to look for a different kind of engagement for philosophy itself. It has no distinct area for philosophy to cover, so it seeks to justify philosophic work on the ground of the utility for other disciplines.

Finally, the alleged vagueness of philosophical study may lead to the question whether philosophy is an armchair pursuit, in contrast to the hard work of field research, controlled experiment, and exact mathematical reasoning. A bit of experience may be enough to show that philosophy is not done by reclining on a rocker, but rather in sitting upright on the edge of a stiff-backed chair, pounding at a typewriter, carefully checking and rechecking each step of the reasoning, correcting, deleting, expanding where necessary, providing for all foreseeable objections. It is hard work, it is trying work. There is no reason to suspect that it requires less concentration or less expenditure of energy than the work in any other discipline. The basic seriousness of the great philosophers in the course of western history is beyond question. Even where different philosophies and different disciplines are regarded as different "language games," the seriousness that goes with observing the rules of a game is emphasized. But where the notion of a game is contrasted with the notion of an examined life, the function of philosophy falls clearly within the latter orbit. It is not a pursuit meant for relaxation or amusement. It faces the realities of life and existence on the deepest level accessible to human reason on its own resources. It is work.

In assessing the role and functioning of philosophy, epistemology rounds itself out by assessing its own status, since it is generically a philosophical discipline. It shows why philosophies can be so different from each other, and still be philosophies. It makes manifest the reasons in reality and in human thought why intellection at its deepest level is so highly individualistic, why every man's philosophy is so personally his own.[29] It does not dominate or unify philosophy. But it does explain philosophy's pluralistic nature, and shows how reciprocal understanding and ongoing philosophical enterprise is possible.

Résumé. An all-pervasive pluralism manifests itself in the philosophic panorama, since each philosophy seems notably different from the others. Close scrutiny shows that these differences are radical. They profoundly influence the whole course of each distinct philosophy. They rest broadly on the possibilities of basing one's philosophical thinking either on what is immediately known in really existing things, or in what is immediately known in things as they exist cognitionally in human thought, or on things and thought as they are expressed in the inter-personal medium of language. Inside each of these three broad divisions lie seemingly indefinite possibilities of further diversity. The diversity is accordingly authentic, and explains the pluralistic condition of philosophy. But family resemblances allow classification in various groupings, even though the radical diversity will prevail in the treatment of a particular topic. This permits translation from one philosophy into another, with possibility of dialogue and discussion. The proviso remains, however, that each is assessing the other in radically different terms, namely the principles from which the assessing philosophy itself started. Philosophies have no common measure on their own intellectual level. They are authentically a pluralism.

In explaining in this way its own philosophical status, epistemology completes its inquiry into human cognition. It shows why it itself is so pluralistic in character, even though dealing with an ostensively single topic. Generically it itself comes under philosophy, and for that very reason it will be different in every person who is engaged in genuinely philosophical thinking.

Notes to Chapter 12

1. See supra, c. 11, nn. 7-9.

2. On McLuhan's view that the content of the message is identical with the user of the medium, and thereby identical with the cognitive agent in the Thomistic sense, see Philip Marchand, *Marshall McLuhan: The Medium and the Messenger* (Toronto, 1990), 255

3. For the interpretation of this Aristotelian and Thomistic technique in the extreme sense that "'linguistic' analysis is not radically different from what in the past has been known as 'metaphysical' analysis,' see Frederick Charles Copleston, *Contemporary Philosophy* (Westminster, MD, 1956), 59.

4. See supra, c. 1, nn. 11-20.

5. On this estimate of linguistic philosophy, see W. Weitz, "Oxford Philosophy," *The Philosophical Review*, 62 (1953), 188.

6. Aristotle, *On Interpretation*, 1.16a3-8; Oxford trans.

7. See Parmenides, *Frs.* 8.51-61; 16 (DK). Likewise, according to the interpretation by Aristotle, *Metaphysics*, 9.3.1047a4-7, Protagoras' (*Fr.* 1, DK) well-known doctrine of man as the measure of all things will result from the view that nothing is perceptible unless it is being perceived.

8. *Meno*, 86AB; *Phaedo*, 72E-76E; *Phaedrus*, 249B-250B.

9. "For a human being must understand a general conception formed by collecting into a unity by means of reason the many perceptions of the senses; and this is a recollection of those things which our soul once beheld, . . ." *Phaedrus*, 249BC; trans. Fowler. Aristotle (*Metaphysics*, 1.9.990b1-8) in consequence regards the Platonists as proceeding from the things in the world around us to the Ideas.

10. *Posterior Analytics*, 2.19.100a3-b5.

11. See supra, c. 2, nn. 6-7.

12. Aristotle, *De an.*, 3.5.430a19-20; 7.431a1-2; b16-17.

13. See supra, n. 6

14. Scotus, *Ordinatio*, 2.3.1.1.31-32; in *Opera Omnia* (Vatican City, 1973), VII, 402.17-403.14.

15. See Suarez, *Disputationes metaphysicae*, 31.4.4-6; ed. *Vivès*, XXVI, 235b-236a. A discussion of the topic may be found in my paper "Aquinas on Being and Thing," *Thomistic Papers III*, ed. Leonard A. Kennedy (Houston, 1987), 14-17.

16. On the general modern view of Realism as meaning "that material objects exist externally to us and independently of our sense experience," see R. J. Hirst's article in Paul Edwards' *Encyclopedia of Philosophy*, VII, 77a, s.v. "Realism." A survey of the different types of Realism may be found ibid., 78a-83b. In an epistemological context this definition of Realism is hardly satisfactory. It would bring Plotinus, Augustine, Berkeley and many others under its notion, as well as Aristotle, Aquinas and the Scholastics. To be epistemologically meaningful, the definition of realism has to include the aspect of demonstration of external reality from the starting points of thought or language.

17. See above, c. 4, n. 19, and c. 5, n. 17. As an expressed species, the concept is the means by which knower and thing known are identical in the actuality of the cognition. From the viewpoint of content, the expressed species is identical with the really existent thing taken in the relevant abstraction. It thereby allows conclusions to be drawn about the thing itself, but only as taken in that abstraction.

18. The argument that one's immediately attained sensations require external things as their cause may be seen developed in Descartes, *Principia philosophiae*, 2.1; A-T, VIII, 40.11-41.13; IX^2, 61-62. In this argument Descartes expressly *concludes* to the existence of the external world. See also Désiré Mercier, *A Manual of Modern*

Scholastic Philosophy, trans. T. L. and S. A. Parker (London, 1916), I, 394 (no. 60), for the same argument. The argument seems to presume a "principle of causality" to account for the required action of the external things upon the senses. On the topic, see Walter Russell Brain, *Mind, Perception and Science* (Oxford, 1951), 7-8.

19. Supra, c. l, nn. 12-14.

20.   See Arthur Campbell Garnett, *The Perceptual Process* (Madison, 1965), 12. Accordingly "all philosophy is 'critique of Language'"--Wittgenstein, *Tractatus Logico-Philosophicus* (London, 1922), no. 4.0031. In this new procedure philosophy is thought to reach its genuinely philosophical status, just as "chemistry was developed out of alchemy"--Wittgenstein, reported by G. E. Moore, "Wittgenstein's Lectures in 1930-33," *Mind*, N. S. 64 (1955), 26. The older procedures were "the subject which used to be called 'philosophy'"--Wittgenstein, *The Blue and Brown Books* (Oxford, 1958), 28. The attitude was that philosophy is concerned merely with the approach to the real: "Philosophy, for analysts, is a discipline that does not tell us about the real, but tells us instead about those disciplines that deal with reality"--James I. Campbell, *The Language of Religion* (New York, 1971), 163. See also George Edward Moore, "The Refutation of Idealism," *Mind*, N.S. 12 (1903), 433-453, republished in Moore's *Philosophical Studies* (London, 1922), 1-30. Cf. Moore's *Principia Ethica* (Cambridge, 1903) especially vii-viii.

21. G. Ryle, "Categories," in *Logic and Language*, 2nd series, ed. Antony Flew (Oxford, 1955), 81.

22. On this deconstructionist topic, see John Caputo, "Radical Hermeneutics and the Human Condition," *Proceedings of the American Catholic Philosophical Association*, 62 (1988), 8-10. Cf. "An absolute end to history is as unthinkable as is an absolute being of it"--Gary Brent Madison, "Hermeneutics and (the) Tradition," ibid., 171.

23. A coverage of this debate may be found in my book *Towards a Christian Philosophy* (Washington, DC, 1990), 1-50.

24. Plato, *Laws*, 6,753E. Cf. *Cratylus*, 436D.

25. Aristotle, *Nicomachean Ethics*, 1.7.1098b6-7.

26. On this dialectic as the path to principles, see Aristotle, *Topics*, 1.2.101a36-b4.

27. ". . . in what is now done in the matter of science there is only a whirling about, and perpetual agitation, ending where it began"-- Bacon, *The Great Instauration*, Proemium, in *Works*, ed. James Spedding (London, 1857-1874), IV, 7-8. "I will say nothing about philosophy, except that I saw it had been cultivated by the most outstanding minds who have lived for a number of centuries past. Nevertheless, no single thing is as yet found in it which is not disputed"--Descartes, *Discours de la Méthode*, 1; A-T, VI, 8.18-22. Cf.: ". . . the fact that no two philosophers ever understand one another"-- Bertrand Russell, *Our Knowledge of the External World*, 2nd ed. (London, 1926), 29.

28. An overview of transcendental Thomism may be found in J. Donceel, "Transcendental Thomism," *The Monist*, 58 (1974), 67-85. The trend attained definite shape in Joseph Maréchal, *Le point de départ de la métaphysique*, 5 vols. (Paris, 1926-1949). Maréchal himself merely wished to show that for those who accept Kantian principles a way to the Thomistic starting points lies open. In regard to that tactic Donceel (70) notes: "He warns his readers that he considers this framework artificial, contrived, affected by an implicit contradiction." But positive use of the method as a "strategy for bringing Thomism into the mainstream of modern thought has obviously failed," Robert J. Henle, "Transcendental Thomism: A Critical Assessment," in *One Hundred Years of Thomism*, ed. Victor B. Brezik (Houston, 1981), 110. Henle (ibid., n. 1) lists followers of the method, and concludes that the methodology of Aquinas "is different from and incompatible with any reasonably authentic version of the Transcendental Method." The structured Kantian intellect may well provide the category of reality, but only in direct contradiction to the *tabula rasa* that is required by Thomistic procedure.

29. This in no way implies that all philosophies are of equal

worth. Cf.: "All this does not mean, however, that all metaphysical schemes of speaking are on a level, and that there aren't some most decisively superior to others"--John Niemayer Findlay, *Language, Mind and Value* (New York, 1963), 127. One reason for wishing to put all on a single level may be seen in the use of a model taken from logic: "All philosophy has been bedevilled by the methods and ideals of formal logic--which may be summed up as the attempt to draw sharp lines round all concepts and to make all inferences rigorously deductive"--Findlay, *Values and Intentions* (London, 1961) 15. A philosophy based upon external sensible things immediately known allows each sensible existent to function as a starting point, with each nature known in universal function. With these starting points it can maintain that philosophies based on ideas or on language are absolutely wrong, even while it recognizes the worth of those types of philosophical reasoning. Epistemologically, each is to be judged by the one common standard of the real world. Historically, each is relative to its own author.

EPILOGUE

Epilogue

Manageable focus on the problems of epistemology is not easy to achieve today. In ordinary life the objects seen and touched and heard are unhesitatingly looked upon as external things. They are regarded as existent in themselves and as really different from the percipient who is aware of them. This entirely normal assessment of perceived objects, however, can be blatantly caricatured when it is viewed from the standpoint of a cameraman's activity. The percipient is conceived as adjusting a lens on an alleged external object and somehow producing a photographic replica of it in the act of cognition. Intellectual penetration into the replica or into independent products of the mind is then achieved through understanding and knowledge. All proceeds on the model of material communication. On this model what is immediately present to the mind is the replica or the idea, and not the external object itself. The presence is envisaged in the way one material object becomes present to another through adjacency. Only the internally produced replica or idea would be thereby immediately attained.

Yet that is the way cognition has been regarded since the time of Descartes. Perhaps the most horrendous hoax ever foisted on western philosophy has been the Cartesian tenet that nothing can be more present to one's mind than the mind itself and its ideas. Direct cognition of external things was made too ridiculous and naïve to merit serious consideration. With delightful ease Malebranche (see supra, Chapter 2, n. 9) could remark that to view the sun and the stars the soul does not take a walk around the skies. Today spaceship travel as far as Neptune is a fact. The euphoria following the first landing on the moon had people reserving passage in advance for week-end flights as soon as available. Anyone willing to wait for another favorable conjunction and devote twenty-four years of life for a trip to Neptune might think of making plans. The notion of a journey around the skies is no longer absurd. But that is not the point. You still face the problem how the planet gets inside your cognition. No explanation modeled on material happenings can account for the epistemological priority spontaneously accorded by people to the things they see and feel and know.

Even the infinitesimally short trip from retina to internal nerve centers would not be exempt from this difficulty. In any material change or event there is always the agent, the material, and a third and new thing that results from the loss of one form and the acquisition of another form. But in cognition there is no third thing. What is perceived or known is the object that confronts the cognitive agent. It is not a third thing produced by the encounter of the two. It cannot be explained by material transformation. The form has to be received as form into form, making the cognitive agent be the thing perceived or known. The cognitive agent and the thing perceived or known are one and the same in the actuality of the cognition. The model is not that of material change.

All this can be accounted for by insights and tenets that have been developed in the long course of western philosophy. These have been discussed in the preceding chapters. In retrospect they may be roughly enumerated in a way that may help to set them off against the neglect into which they have fallen since the more or less general acceptance of the notion that nothing can be more present to cognition than the cognition itself. Taken together they allow the priority to the object, quite as one's spontaneous notion of perception requires.

✷✷✷✷✷✷✷✷✷✷✷✷

The first of these tenets appropriate for mention is Aristotle's insight that percipient and thing perceived, or knower and thing known, are one and the same in the actuality of the cognition. But while their identity in the cognitional existence is thoroughgoing, it leaves open the question which of the two is epistemologically prior. For the Stagirite the evidence was that human cognition is always of something else, and of itself only concomitantly. In separate substances, on the contrary, his conclusion was that the cognition is of itself, and of itself only.

A second basic tenet in this regard is the distinction

developed by Islamic philosophers between essence and existence in creatures, and given its most penetrating expression by Aquinas. Only in God do essence and existence coincide. In all other things they are different. As a result one can explain how the same individual thing can have one existence in itself, and another existence in the cognitive agent that perceives or knows it. The thing remains the same thing under both types of existence. In this way the thing that has real being in the outside world is the same thing that has cognitional being in the percipient or knower. Differently from the situation in Aristotle, however, finite supersensible substances are other than their own real existence and thereby are open to becoming in cognitional existence things distinct from themselves.

A third crucial insight is Aristotle's conclusion that form is the cause of being. A form makes a thing be, and be what it is. What is required to make matter be something else, is a new and different form. In parallel fashion, what is required to make a cognitional potentiality be something cognitionally is the form of the thing perceived or known. This may be bolstered by noting with Aquinas (*Summa theologiae*, 1.104.1.ad 1m) how the influx of an efficient cause enables the form to exercise its formal causality. The form of an external sensible thing, say of a tree, is what makes the percipient be that individual tree in cognitional existence. But the external tree in its real existence has to be acting upon the percipient in order that the tree's form be present in the percipient cognitionally. That action of the external thing is efficient causality. This consideration is important and enlightening in regard to any alleged passage of the thing from the real world into cognition, or to any caricature of the thing traveling millions of miles or even a few inches to reach the percipient. There is no astonishment today at signals traveling from the vicinity of Neptune to earth, signals that cause the forms of surfaces and the shadings and colorings to come into being on the television screen. The one difference is that the material reception of the forms on the television screen gives merely a replica, while the immateriality received form in cognition makes the percipient be the individual real thing and not just a replica of it. The same consideration holds in reply to any charge of a time lag in which the thing could have changed in the passage from retina to cerebral nerve centers. The form of the galaxy as really existent at the time of the emission of the rays is the form impressed immaterially upon the percipient, regardless of the external or internal distance through which the signals that efficiently cause the new impression have to travel.

A fourth important notion is Aristotle's account of predication as the identifying of each individual one by one, that is, severally, with its specific or generic nature. This explanation can likewise be bolstered by the insights of Aquinas on intellectual abstraction. The common nature that is predicated of its inferiors abstracts from all being, both real and cognitional. In itself it has no existence at all, for any existence whatsoever would tie it inexorably to either the particular or the universal and would render impossible the thoroughgoing identity of predicate with subject that is required for saying the one is the other. Nothing in the nature of the predicated object is prescinded. As so abstracted it contains all else in the essence implicitly and indistinctly. This allows complete identity with each inferior in turn, but only as one by one or severally. It enables each specific or generic grade to remain intact in itself while allowing the identity to be complete. Only abstraction from every kind of existence could permit this.

A fifth significant insight is Aristotle's tenet that to speak of an accident or to ask anything about it is to represent it as a substance. Size, color, circularity, relationship and so on are made the subjects of predication, as you inquire what they are and how they function. Again the philosophy of Aquinas (see supra, Chapter 5, n. 14) provides the explanation of the way this is to be understood. The nature of the accident is abstracted non-precisively and predicated of its real subject, as when you say that the golf ball is round and white. But roundness and whiteness can also be abstracted precisively. In that case they are cut off or prescinded from their real subject, and golf ball, and are represented as standing in themselves. In a word, they are given the status of substances in your cognition. You can no longer predicate them of their real subject, because they now lack thoroughgoing identity with it. You do not say that the golf ball is roundness or that it is whiteness. A new subject for predication has been precisively abstracted, parallel to the way humanity and animality and corporeality are precisively abstracted within the category of substance.

Finally, one might mention the Aristotelian doctrine of the *sensus communis*, or "the common sense." It is the faculty or power that makes possible the focus on the real and cognitional together in their actual conjunction before the gaze of the percipient. Its object was therefore described as "sensations and things sensed" (supra, Chapter 4, n. 8). It bears on both at once, and can thereby distinguish and compare the different specific sensations from and with one another, and the sensations from and with the things sensed. This of course presumes that the percipient and the objects perceived are already one in the unity of cognitional existence. But since no created agent is immediately active, according to the conclusion drawn by Aquinas (see *Summa theologiae*, 1.77.1c), a faculty is needed to view these sensations and things sensed as distinct and actually conjoined.

The foregoing tenets are surely of prime importance for an epistemological enquiry. They have all received development in past epochs of western philosophy. Yet they have been forgotten in the dominant philosophical trends after Descartes, and have been reduced to near invisibility or been sadly misunderstood in Neoscholastic circles. To bring them back into current view may pardonably be offered as justification for the present journey into the epistemological world.

★★★★★★★★★★★

In the above insights the manageable focus required for epistemological problems should emerge clearly enough. It lies in the strong notional dependence of cognition on existence. To get a correct notion of cognition, a grasp of the decisive role played by existence in bringing it about is imperative. The difference between the cognitive and the non-cognitive is open to no other basic explanation. Unless the object exists in one's cognition, one is not aware of it. But further, unless object and cognitive agent are actuated by the same existence, awareness is not accounted for. Cognitive agent and object perceived or known have each to remain what it is in its own nature. Yet the two have to coalesce in the one cognitional existence. Epistemology is in consequence required to base its explanation on the existential factor if it is to give an acceptable account of what cognition in general is.

In this way the vexed problem of epistemological status for the external world receives explanation in terms of existence. Upon close philosophical examination the objects originally attained are vindicated as sensible things existing in themselves, just as they are spontaneously judged to be. Their cognitional existence at the time they are being perceived does not enter into the direct object of the awareness, and therefore does not being about any change at all in what the object is. The perceived object remains something existentially synthesized in itself without anything from the cognitive activity entering into its constitution. Here the real existence of the thing in itself is no less primitive than anything in the object's nature. This real existence completes its own synthesizing, thereby excluding from the object any basic contamination by the cognitive agent. It accounts for an object definitely and primitively other in being than the agent's awareness of it. The nature of cognition itself allows this epistemological priority for the object, and immediate awareness gives the fact.

Further, the real existence grasped immediately in the sensible thing by judgment does not lie open to the dissatisfaction understandably caused by locating one's original awareness of existence in a concept. The concept of existence is an item of a secondary nature. It presupposes other concepts in terms of which it is formed, such as those of perfection and of actuality. It is unable just in itself to show that anything exists or does not exist, as the historic bouts with the ontological argument for the existence of God have made manifest. Accordingly in any framework based on concepts only, as contrasted with judgments, an immediate grasp of sensible things existent in themselves is branded as naïve. Likewise the charge of "zeroing in" on real existence assumes that one has another starting point from which a hopeless attempt is made to reach external existence. Yet in point of fact the blast-off into epistemological space is just as emphatically from external sensible things as was that of the ill-fated Challenger of 1986. The real existence of those sensible things was perceived and known from the start. Any notion of "zeroing in" or "homing in" on real existence obviously takes for granted that the epistemological starting point is the human awareness and not the sensible existent itself. That approach would regard existence not as an actuality primitively apprehended, but as sort of local habitation added to objects already present to one's awareness. Forms float out in all their vagueness, and then by a superadded existence are given definite contours and location in space:

> And as imagination bodies forth
> The forms of things unknown, the poets pen
> Turns them to shapes, and gives to airy nothing
> A local habitation and a name.[1]

By the same token, the real existence of the percipient and the cognitive activities is apprehended concomitantly as a really different existence from that of the object perceived. In this way it precludes all danger of an egocentric predicament. It is grasped as synthesizing the nature and operation of the cognitive agent only, and not that of anything in the object. It leaves unchanged the things perceived in their own real existence, existence independent of the percipient's activity. Only in cognitional existence do percept and percipient have identical being. In cognition the one is the other. In real existence they can be separate things.

Similarly, existence serves as the measure of truth. Problems concerning truth, whether of correspondence or coherence or emphasis or whatever else, find their basic solution in the grounding of the truth judgment on the thing's existential actuality. No matter what conceptual framework is used, and no matter how different or remotely analogous the concepts involved may be, as long as the actuality represented by the copula is referring to an actuality apprehended by the *act* of judgment, the judgment as *representation* is true.

Likewise, existence is the criterion of certainty. Where upon careful re-examination the necessitating character of the existence definitely excludes its opposite, certainty is present. Not precisely evidence, nor confidence in one's faculties, but the existence encountered in the object is what grounds certainty. The existence may have to be carefully scrutinized and re-scrutinized for the certainty judgment, but it itself is what necessitates the certainty. In face of the certainty judgment the existence in fact is evident, and the faculties are in fact trustworthy. But these considerations do not enter into the precise criterion of certitude. One can be just as certain if one does not know anything about faculties or denies them real status, or if one is not paying any attention to what evidence means. It is the existence, and the existence alone, that makes one certain or prompts one to give some other kind of assent.

With regard to erroneous judgments, too, existence is the factor that accounts for the possibility of the mistake. It allows the mind to synthesize in an originally apprehended existence further predicates that the existence did not at first synthesize. This explains the possibility of substitution and error. Error does not follow from the nature of things. Nothing just in the nature of things can account for it. But the existence of things is beyond their natures. The existence synthesizes the natures, and in the cognitional order can do so wrongly when impelled by the will and not just by the object.

On all the really important epistemological issues, then, the basic explanatory factor turns out to be existence. A genuinely existential epistemology is required to meet the problems. Yet because existence is attained everywhere through judgment and not originally through conceptualization, it can easily elude philosophical acceptance. The existence, closest for one's ordinary vision, fades out as do the objects nearest to the radar apparatus when one undertakes to examine them solely on a conceptual screen. When the problems of cognition are approached through a neutralistic sense datum or through the conceptual content of the phenomena, they become insoluble. The reason is the failure to grasp the fundamental factor involved.

Accordingly the three initial problems faced at the threshold of the present epistemological inquiry[2] are likewise to be viewed in the existential perspective. Why was epistemology so late in appearing as a distinct discipline on the philosophical scene? As long as philosophical procedure remained based on really existent things, it could follow the natural functioning of human cognition in treating of them as they are synthesized by their own existence. It had no need to consider them in any alleged addition through their concomitantly apprehended cognitional being. It could deal with problems of cognition under the general consideration of problems of existence. It could examine them in metaphysics. It had no occasion to group them together in a special philosophical science. Cognition was regarded as fully observable, but only in terms of the new existence the object received in the cognitive agent. There was no addition to the object in the order of nature, for in real existence it was independent and public. Only after the spontaneous procedure of philosophy had been changed by the Cartesian asceticism did the starting point become cognition, and the need for a special and preliminary study of cognition appear. The change in starting point, however, is not at all required, in the light of the close scrutiny of human cognition that has just been undertaken.

The answer to the second question emerges from these same considerations. If things in their cognitional existence are the basic object of human awareness, they will require that the primary philosophical consideration be given to the cognitional order. Cognition can accordingly be set up as the basic topic for philosophical study. Where on the other hand the sensible things in their real existence are the basic object, and their cognitional existence only concomitantly grasped, the way for a direct study of them lies open.   No prior scientific investigation of cognition is required.   The constitution of human cognition shows that no preliminary study of cognition itself is naturally antecedent to the scientific or philosophic inquiry into its direct objects. Epistemology cannot be the most fundamental of philosophic disciplines.

Finally, in answer to the third question, the precise role of epistemology becomes apparent.   As one philosophical discipline alongside others, epistemology has its own designated object.   It has to deal with the problems that do in fact arise when human cognition is set apart as a distinct area of study.   It does not arise from the spontaneous confrontation with the direct objects of cognition.   It does not add anything to one's knowledge of those objects.   The mathematician, the scientist, the logician, or the moralist, can proceed just as surely in his own path without knowledge of epistemology.[3]   The uneducated man can swear just as firmly to a witnessed occurrence as can the one who has studied this new science.   The ground of certainty is the same for both, namely the real existence that confronted both those persons.   Yet when the problems of cognition are raised, they demand solution.   When they are made the area of a special study, they require investigation against the background of their own problematic.   Even though a thorough study of them may turn out to have made no positive contribution to the rest of knowledge, a special and illuminating understanding of human cognition is brought about by concentration on their content.   Further, the defensive role in showing why epistemological doubts need not hinder progress in any other discipline has pertinent value.   These reasons seem to have justified the attention given to a separate inquiry into the topic.

In Aristotle's succinct statement "The soul is in a way all existing things"[4] the introduction to an epistemology adequate for present-day needs may be found.   It can be developed through Augustine's dynamic understanding of cognition as engendered through the double activity of cognitive subject and of the thing of which the subject is aware, with knowledge born of both knower and the thing known.[5] Cognition takes place in an activity of the percipient or knower, but in an activity that has been impregnated by an object acting upon it. The development can continue through the clearcut explanation of being by Aquinas in existential terms, where the one nature is shown to remain the same when actuated by two different kinds of existence, real and cognitional. This explanation spells out what is meant by the Aristotelian dictum that the soul is "in a way" all things. The way is cognitional being, as opposed to real being. But this becomes clear only when one understands that finite natures are of themselves devoid of being but open to both real and cognitional existence. It is the existential understanding of being as contrasted with nature that enables one to explain cognition in accord with the Aristotelian formula. Further, though the real existence of the soul is prior insofar as agent produces act, the epistemological priority against the Aristotelian background of sensible things as the starting point of cognition remains located in the thing of which one is aware:

> . . . to understand something is prior to understanding that one understands. And therefore the soul arrives at perceiving that it itself exists, through that which it understands or senses.[6]

✶✶✶✶✶✶✶✶✶✶✶✶

The variegated garden in which the many different western philosophies continue to blossom has a common soil. This is the real public world in which people live, plus the common culture that shapes their minds before they begin to do philosophy. The common bond is there. It should be strong enough to make people seek the best in each other's thought. In the traditional interest in being that comes from Parmenides through Aristotle and Aquinas down to the present time, there are profound implications that can be brought to bear with profit on the problematic of epistemology. Should these implications be neglected on the ground that they belong to a previous age, or be bypassed because the thinkers responsible for them did not themselves draw them out?   Rather, does not genuine philosophical development suggest that they continue to bring forth new fruit in the contemporary areas of interest?   Is it not foolish to let a sophomoric blindness to the achievements of past ages, merely on the ground that they are of the past, keep one from making use of their intellectual treasures?   Is it not a peculiar type of hubris to look upon them as belonging to a time before the human race had come of age?   Surely chronolatry should have no place in a philosophic study.

Where valuable insights from the past can aid in the understanding of present-day problems, then, they should be welcomed regardless of their source.   Where they give a philosophical explanation of human cognition in terms of efficient, formal and material causes, they live up to what is expected from theoretical philosophy.   They show how the reception of forms, though first known to us in the way of material reception, can be understood in a higher way that for want of a better term may be called immaterial reception. With cognitional existence recognized as an authentic type of being together with existence in the real world, the way is open to a satisfactory philosophical explanation of human cognition.

Against this background of traditional western wisdom, an epistemology today can show how the whole universe can come to exist cognitionally in a single knower. All things can in one way or another enter into the domain of one's awareness.   The reliability of human cognition, yet with possibility of frequent errors and their corrections, can be accounted for, and the presence of genuine pluralism in the world of philosophical thought can be given a satisfactory and welcome explanation.   In this regard the study of thinkers such as Plato, Aristotle, Augustine and Aquinas is far from a cultural necrophilia.   Their thought is still very much alive, and speaks in the present tense.   It is not to be judged by later contaminations.   A story from past centuries has been told of a ship that had entered fresh drinkable waters in the Amazon's broad estuary.   Yet its crew continued to perish from thirst. On calling desperately for water from a passing vessel, the sailors were told to take what was around them. The water was safe and assimilable. This possibility had not even occurred to the seamen who for months had been seeing nothing but ocean brine. Is there not something of that attitude today towards the philosophy of the past? Even though it becomes brackish and distasteful when studied further out and away from its source, that philosophy can still be assimilated if one gets close enough to its origins.

Modern discussions, however, have taken place rather exclusively on the salty oceans over which western thought has voyaged since the time of Descartes. Knowledge in other fields has expanded tremendously. Yet philosophical understanding of what knowledge itself is has threatened to become as unassimilable as brine, even though knowledge has been the instrument for all this expansion. Though obvious to internal reflexion, knowledge has been regarded as defying philosophical explanation. To anyone broaching it as a special object of intellectual thirst, the troublesome question has been posed: "What has this man seen which nobody saw before?" Put that bluntly, the question invites a decidedly negative answer. But it still leaves unapproached the prospect of a much closer look at what others have in fact already seen, yet which unfortunately has been neglected in the course that has been pursued by epistemology in recent decades. In this respect, one's looking back to the ancient and medieval thinkers is by no means indulgence in necrophilia. It is a search for living guidance in doing today's work. In it there is no attempt to revive old cultures. Rather, it is an openminded endeavor to make use of whatever help philosophies of the past may have to offer for our own original thinking. It is a present use of what has stood the invaluable test of time.

Today postmodern hermeneutics may claim, consistently with its own starting points, that it has done away with all epistemology. It accepts unhesitatingly the decisive syndrome of ancient, medieval, Renaissance, Enlightenment and postmodern as the epochs of philosophic development. From this standpoint, epistemology is but an outmoded and useless appendage that emerged from Enlightenment difficulties. The Enlightenment's need to justify its own absolutely and universally valid principles called for the vindication of knowledge as stable whole, with an all-pervading objectivity that permitted the identically same norms to hold everywhere and at all times. The postmodern approach claims, on the contrary, that human thought in all its workings is conditioned fundamentally by particular historical and linguistic circumstances. These allow, it maintains, no room for absolutes or universals. Gone, then, is the requirement that all sciences, including the human sciences, be modeled on the mathematical. In this setting not only the need but also the possibility of an epistemology disappeared.

Interesting though the postmodern hermeneutical approach may be in examining how philosophies differ so widely from one another, and how genuine philosophy can be as individual as fingerprints, it nevertheless misses the basic epistemological consideration at issue here. One may readily agree that thought is handed down through language. But surely a closer look at how this transmission takes place is imperative. There is no question whatever of finished objects bequeathed materially like houses or heirlooms. The new and different philosophical thought was not already existent and able to be transmitted in that way. Words were indeed handed down already formed. But how could speech originate in any actual manner the diversities of thought that come into being in the philosophies themselves? How could linguistic intricacies account for the new trends? A language is passed on to each succeeding generation by the mention of words and the pointing to the things signified by the sounds. A toddler learning to speak comes to associate a word with a thing that has already been indicated to him. At the mention of "nose" he will point to his facial organ. If at that very early age he is being brought up bilingually, he will point to exactly the same organ at the mention of the word nez when the question is posed in French. The word does not induce any difference in the object. It is the thing itself that shapes and differentiates the learner's thought, the thing having been recalled by the word.

One may legitimately ask, then, if the way language itself occasions a new philosophy consists merely in calling explicit attention to differences already present in things or present in human thoughts about the things? Augustine had maintained that a person learns not by the words heard but by the things themselves presented to human gaze in the divine creative Word, somewhat as in the Cartesian setting all things were for Malebranche seen in God. For Augustine the spoken words merely admonished the learner to look at the things themselves so known. Aristotle had explained how speech was dependent upon human thoughts, and human thoughts were in turn dependent for their content upon external sensible things. This background in the history of western philosophy may at least prompt one to question whether the immediate historical and linguistic circumstances are really the determining factor. Does the newly emerging philosophical thought actually arise, as far as deepest origins are concerned, from a particular and distinctive way of talking?

The all-pervasive formative role of the immediate cultural and linguistic circumstances may be readily granted, even with regard to speculative philosophy. But what is the manner in which these highly particularized circumstances and linguistic combinations exercise a formative influence? Could it not be that the new way of thinking gets its direction rather from differences already present in thought and things but now for the first time brought to the explicit attention of reader or listener through words? May not the peculiarities in novel combinations of words, or idiosyncrasies in the new historical circumstances, merely be drawing attention to previously unnoticed aspects in the thought or in the things?

Is it not difficult to see how words or combinations of words could just by themselves exercise the required influence? Whether "horse" or *cheval* or *Pferd* is the word used, no change follows in the thing referred to or in the mental representation by which it is known. Rather, the thing so known is the basis for discussion about its own nature and activities, and about its differences from other things. The differences in the words do not make the differences in the things. On the contrary, aspects in the things and the thought are what ultimately direct the formation of the new philosophies in each particular case. The existence grasped in each new judgment is an absolute, as in the apprehensions that the chair exists or that the table is spatially extended. When these apprehensions are thoroughly examined, the facts can be known with truth and certitude. There is no question here of facing an endless chain of signifiers without hope of ever reaching the real world. Reality, rather, is present as an absolute in external sensible things from the very first moment of the perception. Absolutely known in the most primitive judgments is the fact that the objects exist and are something.

What is at stake here is the formation of a real *habitus* in the learner. A *habitus* is caused efficiently by the learner's repeated acts. Reference by language to attractive or repellent things will bring about the shaping of the *habitus*, quite as pleasure and pain function in Aristotelian ethics. The transmitting influence is by way of things desired or things disliked. That is why postmodern hermeneutics has been able to claim that it is a successor of Aristotle's practical philosophy, insofar as current hermeneutics sees all philosophy as dependent upon the historical circumstances of personal upbringing and training. For Aristotle what is handed down through environment and education does indeed consist in the formation in the learner of real habituation of thought about things. In this respect, quite as external sensible things act efficiently upon the percipient in impressing their own forms immaterially upon the sentient activity, so the words of the teacher act upon the learner. But the perception itself and the formation of the *habitus* result from efficient causality on the part of percipient and learner respectively. The new philosophy is produced through the efficient causality of the person doing the philosophizing. It is not handed down as a completed object in the way a house or pieces of jewelry are bequeathed to someone's heirs.

This shaping of a real *habitus* by language may, if one so wishes, be called transmission by speech. But just as the efficient causality of the new thinker is what produces the new philosophy. Likewise just as the content of the sensation is based upon real external things, so the intelligible content conveyed by the language is based upon thought about things. There is no room for the notion of an independent object handed down upon a platter. We are not heirs of the past in that way. The influence of parents and educators has been exercised upon child and student in fixing the association of words with things and thoughts. But the way a person thinks is shaped by the content of the object brought to the person's attention by the words, coupled with her or his reaction as a free agent to those objects. In this fashion epistemological study explains what has been going on.

Postmodern thought, then, does not by any means do away with the need for epistemology.[8] A philosophical science is still required to explain the respective order of things, thought and language in the transmission of human knowledge and in the genesis of new philosophies. Even for understanding the procedure of current hermeneutics, and for assessing what is being done in it, epistemology proves itself a necessary tool. Contrary to the hermeneutic approach, however, the epistemology developed in the preceding chapters vindicates the absolute and universal character of the required philosophical starting points. It shows how all immediate judgments are absolute, insofar as they immediately grasp existence. It shows how one's judgments are universal insofar as they express the natures of things. In a word, it makes the one real world the standard by which all philosophical thinking is to be assessed. From that viewpoint, it may well appear to many to be an extreme dogmatism.

On the other hand, this epistemology may be regarded by many as giving rise to an extreme relativism, since it maintains that every genuine philosophy proceeds from distinctive starting points and is thereby unable to be either refuted or directly helped in its own procedure by the procedures of any other philosophy. It persists in recognizing philosophy as a profoundly human undertaking, open to choice of starting points either in things or in thought or in language, and with the choice conditioned by individual personality and upbringing.[9]　In this way it respects the inherent dignity of human thinking.　Yet from its own standpoint it requires that all philosophies be judged by the one permanent standard, namely the one real world in which the philosophers live and work and communicate.　It brands as absolutely wrong the location of the starting points in thought or in language.　It shows how those who accept such starting points have to abide by the consequences of their own procedures, and can avoid these consequences only by basic revision of their thinking.　Yet because the same content that exists in things is expressed in thought and communicated in language, possibilities of fruitful dialogue and exchange of ideas lie open to all.

Philosophy is a fact.　It is something that exists in the thinking of countless individuals.　In probing its nature *qua* knowledge, epistemology shows how impregnation by existing things makes philosophy capable of attaining truth, even though it is rendered deeply pluralistic by the human minds that give it birth.

Notes to Epilogue

1. Shakespeare, *A Midsummer Night's Dream*, 5.1.14-17.

2. Supra, c. 1, third section.

3. From this viewpoint it may be said: "We add nothing to the knowledge we have by a theory of knowledge"--Arthur Coleman Danto, *Analytical Philosophy of Knowledge* (Cambridge, 1968), 264. Yet this failure to add knowledge of the kind given by other sciences does not interfere with the type given by epistemology, as was discussed at considerable length in the third section of c. 1, supra.

4. Aristotle, *De anima*, 3.8.431b21; Oxford trans.

5. Augustine, *De trinitate*, 9.12.18; ed. W. J. Mountain (Turnhout,. 1968), 309.30-31. See McKenna translation, supra, c. 2, n. 16.

6. ". . . prius est intelligere aliquid quam intelligere se intelligere; et ideo anima pervenit ad actualiter percipiendum se esse per illud quod intelligit vel sentit." Aquinas, *De veritate*, 10.8.231-234; ed. Leonine, XXII, 321.

7. Kenneth T. Gallagher, "Recent Anglo-American Views on Perception," *International Philosophical Quarterly*, 4 (1964), 122. Gallagher's comment, however, was that "past experience hardly warrants any great expectations in respect to the answer" (ibid.). Yet if the experience is extended back to medieval and Greek times, the response is much more encouraging.

8. For a survey, see Susan Haack, "Recent Obituaries of Epistemology," *American Philosophical Quarterly*, 27 (1990), 179-209. Cf. "The partisans of hermeneutics, specifically including Gadamer, often present it as a new, unprecedented approach, even as a way to overcome the problem of epistemology." T. Rockmore, "Epistemology as Hermeneutics," *The Monist*, 73 (1990), 115.

9. In this respect, postmodern hermeneutics has been regarded as the heir of Aristotle's ethical procedure: "Gadamer not only argues

that phronesis provides a model for hermeneutics, but that hermeneutics itself is the heir to the tradition of Aristotle's practical philosophy." Richard Bernstein, "Hermeneutics and its Anxieties," *Proceedings of the American Catholic Philosophical Association*, 62 (1988), 65. Aristotle himself (*Metaph.*, 2.1.993b14) notes that we are indebted to our predecessors for our philosophical habituation, an habituation that they exercised before us. He made this remark in a context concerned especially with theoretical philosophy. It would seem to imply that not only the fact that we philosophize but also the way we philosophize in general can be traced broadly to the habituation handed down by our predecessors. With him of course this leaves intact the absolute grounding of theoretical truth in real things. Grounding all truth on the model of practical truth remains an innovation with hermeneuticists: "The originality of Gadamer's conception lies in his insistence that both practical reason and scientific reason need to be understood in terms of *phronesis*." John D. Caputo, *Radical Hermeneutics* (Bloomington and Indianapolis: Indiana University Press, 1987), 210. The overall difference between the Aristotelian and the postmodern hermeneutical procedures lies in the respective relations of signifier and thing signified, in our basic cognition of the external world. In the Aristotelian conception the external things are epistemologically prior to the sensations and concepts that signify them. Hence theoretical knowledge and truth are grounded absolutely on things. For the hermeneuticists the signifier must come first, with the resultant indefinite regress in signifiers. Each requires a preceding signifier for its explanation or philosophical interpretation.

Index